Kensington

Portal To A Family, Place & Time

David Gottfred

CLEAR VOICE PUBLISHING LLC
SAINT PETERSBURG, FLORIDA

.

For Mom and Dad and Rita

Preface

I'd never heard of the Kensington or the Singleton family until the fall of 2010. My wife Rita and I accepted an invitation to visit our friends, Colonel and Mrs. Rett Summerville,USAF, at their home, The Ruins, in Stateburg, South Carolina.

Their home had once been the plantation home of a member of the Singleton family, Videau Marion Singleton. The Summervilles told us stories about the history of their home and the Singleton family.

Rett and Pat took us to visit the Kensington Mansion, a completely restored antebellum home, built by Videau Marion Singleton's brother, Matthew Richard Singleton. The approach to the Kensington was up a driveway two-thirds of a mile long lined with magnolias. The mansion is a 12,000 square foot home with twenty-nine rooms, built in a unique European style.

The site manager, Carl DuBose, took us on a tour of the Kensington, regaling us with stories about the Singleton family and the history of the Kensington mansion and plantation.

When the tour was over, I asked Carl if there was a written history of the Kensington and the Singleton family. He said there was not, but he wished there was.

After returning to Florida, I began to think about writing that history. Beginning in May of 2011, with Carl's and other's invaluable assistance, I began to research the history of the Kensington and the Singleton family. This book is a distillation of what I found interesting, ironic, funny, and poignant.

I apologize in advance for my sins of commission and omission. Enjoy the journey. I know I did.

"The outcome of any serious research can only be to make two questions grow where only one grew before." Thorstein Veblen

Acknowledgements

All those who worked to preserve Kensington.

Carl DuBose, for his encouragement, his willingness to help, his tireless, relentless pursuit of everything I asked of him, his generosity, and determination to see the story written. This would not have been possible without you.

Rett and Pat Summerville, for their hospitality, friendship, and interest.

Ralph Boyd, Kensington restoration manager for Union Camp, who shared his knowledge and perspective with good humor and grace.

John Califf, architect in charge of the Architectural and Historical Survey of Kensington prior to restoration, for his professional work, storytelling, and willingness to share with me what he knew.

Charles Broadwell, for taking me around to Singleton family sites in Sumter County, and sharing his knowledge as a local historian, author, and researcher.

Graham Duncan in the Manuscripts Division at South Caroliniana Library, University of South Carolina, for his willing help.

Marty Matthews, Robert Buckley, Tim Bradshaw, A. Paul Weissenstein, for their research.

John and Cyndi Carter: fearless editors, supporters, and still friends. Thank you.

Amy Dilday, my lawyer friend, for going over legal documents and answering that one more question, I had so often.

Friends and family who listened to me talk about this project for four and a half years, expressed their desire to see the completed work, and kept asking me how it was going.

Suncoast Writer's Group members for their interest and critiques: Will Kollock, Robert Davis, Bill Moore, John & Cyndi Carter, Noelle Rutland, Adam and Lauren Gray.

My Maplewood High School students who loved my stories.

Thanks to all the family descendants who generously shared their time, memories, stories, heirlooms, photographs, letters, typescripts, and encouragement. In no particular order, and forgive me if I forgot anyone: Lynn Landreth , Mary Singleton Clement Porcher, Harriet Dwight Travers Yarbrough, Mrs. Jeanie Clay Currie, Eliza Singleton Macaulay Carney, Robert Hamer Peery, Beth Peery, Bill Hamer, Joel A. Smith, Daisy Barron Leland, Melvin Lanham, Luke Lanham.

Those no longer with us who recorded what they knew about their families: Eliza Green Singleton, Mary Carter Singleton Dwight, Eliza Barron Macaulay, Mrs. Leroy Halsey nee Decca Coles Singleton,

Jacob Stroyer, for writing a book about his experiences at Kensington.

My wife Rita, my soul mate, for everything.

Contents

PART ONE

SETTING THE STAGE

Chapter 1-Introduction

The Kensington Mansion is the remnant. It's what remains, providing a portal to the past. This book is about what I discovered as I researched the Kensington and the Singleton family that built it. It includes the people, places and things that I found of interest along the way.

The Kensington Mansion was erected as a symbol of Singleton family wealth, power, influence, and special place in the world in which they lived. Their antebellum empire was built on a bedrock of land and slavery.

The antebellum Singletons owned nineteen plantations in the Midlands of South Carolina, comprising at least 35,000 acres. They were one of the largest slaveholding families in South Carolina, if not the largest. By some standards, their family wealth was equivalent to billions of dollars, most of it in slaves. The family's reach was far flung, touching the highest seats of power and influence in the United States, England, and France. They were on the top rung of Southern planter society.

The Kensington Mansion was built by Matthew Richard Singleton, youngest son of Colonel Richard Singleton, who stood at the apex of Singleton family wealth. At its zenith, the Headquarters/Kensington Plantation with 6,600 acres and 465 slaves was the crown jewel of the Singleton family.

Much of the Singleton fortune would be gone within twenty years of the completion of the Kensington Mansion in 1854. The empire was brought down by debt and the results of the Civil War, which ended slavery. Repeated internecine family law suits further eroded their wealth. Settlement of these lawsuits required cash and some of the Singleton family property had to be sold to meet that need, further depleting their wealth.

The Kensington mansion is beautiful and unusual, a showplace off the beaten path. The mansion of twenty-nine rooms encompasses 12,000 square feet. It is not the typical Greek Revival style fronted by large white pillars that is associated with Southern plantation mansions. It is a one-of-a-kind, French Renaissance or Second Empire or Renaissance Revival or Italian Revival style plantation house, depending on who you believe. Like so much about the Singletons and the Kensington story there are disagreements. When it was completed the mansion sat in a landscaped park of fifty acres, amidst thousands of plantation acres.

Today, the Kensington is a largely undiscovered treasure in lower Richland County, South Carolina, set atop a bluff with a once-commanding view, one and a half miles from the west bank of the Wateree River. Then as now, it is an out-of-the way place in the rural backcountry, located twenty-five miles southeast of Columbia, the state capital. Even though isolated, it was sought out by the rich and powerful in its day and continued to be a hub of family and social activity from its completion until its sale to the federal government in 1941.

After the Kensington property was sold to the government, the mansion was left unoccupied for the next forty years and gradually fell into ruin, a victim of time and neglect. As part of the effort to preserve the Kensington, it was placed on the list of National Register of Historic Places in 1971. Finally, in 1981, The Kensington property was purchased by International Paper Company, formerly known as Union Camp Corporation. As part of the purchase agreement they committed to fully restoring the mansion to its former glory.

For thirty years after, the public was able to experience this antebellum historical treasure. A citizens group, the Scarborough-Hamer Foundation, furnished the Mansion with period furniture and conducted tours to tell the storied history of the Kensington and the people associated with it.

Today the future of the Mansion is uncertain. The Mansion was closed to the public for 2014 and 2015 due to interior water damage from a leaky roof. In February of 2015, International Paper

Company asked the Scarborough-Hamer Foundation to remove its collection and to vacate the Mansion. What all this means for the future of the Mansion and public access to it remains to be seen.

Chapter 2-Singleton Settlement Area

It is claimed that in 1540 the Spanish explorer Hernando DeSoto and his party journeyed up from Florida, becoming the first European visitors to the Midlands of South Carolina. DeSoto, it is said, was received by a female Indian chief named Cofitachequi, near present day Camden, South Carolina, thirty miles north of what would be the first Singleton family settlement.

John Lawson is the earliest confirmed white visitor to the area. At the request of the Colonial Governor, he led a party of ten, exploring and surveying the Carolinas on a 600 mile, fifty-seven day trip in 1701. He wrote a book about his explorations.[1] Lawson found remnants of the Wateree Indian tribe living in villages along the Congaree and Wateree Rivers, future locations of Singleton plantations. He found the Indians were rapidly dying off, having been decimated by exposure to the diseases of white explorers and settlers.

PART TWO

MATTHEW SINGLETON'S TIME (1752-1787)

Chapter 3-Early Settlement

The earliest white settlers were primarily from Virginia and began filtering into the area during the mid-1700's. Among these settlers was Matthew Singleton (1730-1787), progenitor of the Singleton family branch that is a primary focus of this book. Matthew Singleton was the great grandfather of Matthew Richard Singleton (1817-1854), the builder of the Kensington.

(Generation after generation, given names are repeated. It can be very confusing. As an aid to the reader, birth and death dates are often included with the names. Referring to the genealogy below and in the Appendix can also be helpful. Family and place names also received a variety of spellings even within the family.)

Select Genealogy of the builder of the Kensington
Matthew Richard Singleton (1817-1854)

His Great Grandfather-Matthew Singleton (1730-1787)
His Great Grandmother-Mary James Singleton (1735-1784)

His Grandfather-John Singleton (1754-1820)
His Grandmother-Rebecca Singleton (1752-1834)
His Father-Richard Singleton (1776-1852)
His Mother-Rebecca Travis Coles Singleton (1784-1849)
  -His Brothers and Sisters-those who lived past infancy
    -John Coles Singleton   (1813-1852)
    -Videau Marion Singleton   (1815-1867)
    -Sarah Angelica Singleton   (1816-1877)
    -Richard Singleton   (1817-1833)

-**Matthew Richard Singleton (1817-1854)**
(BUILDER OF KENSINGTON)
His Wife-Martha Rutledge Kinloch Singleton (1818-1892)
   His Children
   -Cleland Kinloch Singleton (1844-1920) (Unmarried)
   -Helen Coles Singleton (1846-1924)
      Her Husband-Allen Jones Green (1848-1910)
      His Grandchildren (Helen and Allen)
      - Cleland Singleton Green (1872-1951)
      - Walter Taylor Green (1874-1927)
      - Helen Singleton Green (Brown) (1881-1957)
   -**Richard** Singleton (1851-1921)
      His Wife- "Eliza" Taylor Green (1852-1933)
      His Seven Grandchildren (Richard and Eliza)
      -Mary Lowndes "May" Singleton (King) (1875-1962**)**
      -Matthew Richard Singleton (1877-1910)
            His Wife-Charlotte Cantey Johnson (1879-1963)
            Great Grandchildren (Matthew & Charlotte)
            -Richard Singleton Jr. (1901 -1978)
            -Robert Johnson Singleton (1904-1906)
            -Martha "Dolly" Singleton (1907-1977)
      -Virginia Taylor Singleton (1879-1924)
      -Lillian Singleton (Coker) (1880-1937)
      -Lucy Pride Singleton (1883-1919)
      -Elizabeth "Daisy" Singleton (Barron) (1886-1968)
      -Martha Rutledge Singleton (1887-1889)

Chapter 4-Matthew Singleton (1730-1787)

Matthew Singleton was born on the Isle of Wight in England in 1730. He emigrated to Virginia in 1745 with his father Christopher and several of his brothers. There he met and married Mary Nancy James in 1750. He was nineteen and she was fifteen. Two years later, they moved to South Carolina with members of the James family, several of Matthew Singleton's brothers and members of the Moore family, close friends of the Singletons. Matthew's father chose to stay in Virginia. Two slaves also accompanied the party to South Carolina.

Matthew Singleton is thought to have been a man of large stature, the gene of which seems to have passed down. Contemporaries noted that his grandson Richard Singleton (1776-1852) and great grandson John Coles Singleton (1813-1852), were big men. Matthew Richard Singleton (1817-1854), builder of the Kensington and brother of John Coles, apparently was a smaller man. Being a twin may account for this.

Mary (James) Singleton, Matthew's wife, gave birth to eight children. Two died in infancy. There are reports that Matthew disowned a son or sons, because of moral indiscretions involving drinking and gambling. It is thought that they moved to Mississippi, where they married twin sisters and lived the rest of their lives.

Matthew Singleton settled on the east side of the Wateree River in what is now Sumter County. It is in the Sand Hills region, just south of present day Wedgefield and across the river from the future location of the Kensington.[1.5] He rapidly acquired land through royal land grants, leases and purchases. By 1762 he had acquired 1,250 acres. He may also have inherited some land from his father-in-law, Sherwood James, as well. By 1773 he had a total of 2,300 acres. By the time of his death, he increased these landholdings to over 3,000 acres.[2]

Among his land purchases were properties on Shanks Creek and Beech Creek, with ready access to the Wateree River. These would be instrumental in his creation of a highly profitable river shipping business. This enterprise would be expanded by his son John (1754-1820) and grandson Richard (1776-1852).

Matthew Singleton raised crops of rice and indigo in the Wateree River bottomlands. Both crops were labor intensive and required large numbers of slave laborers. Indigo was a highly profitable, naturally occurring plant, which was used to create a blue dye. (Today's blue jeans use a synthetic indigo dye to create that distinctive blue color.) Because of its high value during the "Indigo

Bonanza" of the late 1700's, it was referred to as Blue Gold. During the Revolutionary War, Continental forces used indigo to dye their uniforms blue, in contrast to the British Redcoats. As Continental paper money lost its value during the Revolution, cubes of indigo were used instead as currency because they were of real value. The indigo boom continued until after the Revolutionary War when England, the primary market, found other better-quality sources to supply their needs. It was a bonanza while it lasted and the Singletons seized the opportunity.

Chapter 5-Melrose

On some of his land, near the Wateree River, Matthew Singleton built his first house, a farmhouse. He named it Melrose. (A marker has been placed by the National Society of the Colonial Dames of America designating this location as the site of Melrose. It is near the Singleton Family Graveyard, established in the 1790s.)

Several years later, he built a second house also known as Melrose, several miles away, higher up from the Wateree River in the Sand Hills. A motivating factor may have been the early infant deaths of two of his children. People knew it was unhealthy to live close to the river although they didn't know why. Malaria and lung diseases were a constant threat in swampy lowlands like those near the Wateree River. These diseases would claim the lives of many Singletons over the years.

The second Melrose utilized frame building construction.[3] Previously, most dwellings in the area were crude log cabins. The second Melrose began a Singleton family pattern of erecting distinctive homes. It was a story and a half with a piazza (veranda) running the length of the house.

Chapter 6-The Frontier

The interior of South Carolina where Matthew Singleton settled still had elements of the frontier. In 1760, during the Cherokee War, 120 miles west of Matthew's home, Cherokee Indians killed twenty-three white settlers in what was called the Long Cane Massacre. (The grandmother of nineteenth century South Carolina Senator John C. Calhoun was among the slain. Several children were killed and scalped. Some were taken prisoner.)

Outlaws and wild behavior were a problem in the newly settled backcountry. It was a sort of early wild-west, without much official law and order. In the latter 1760's, Matthew Singleton and others in the community formed themselves into a vigilante group known as the regulators. The more serious offenders were sent to Charleston for trial. The lesser offenders were dealt with immediately by the regulators, who meted out summary punishment and justice. It seems to have had the desired effect in curtailing some of the lawlessness. Their actions also prompted the colonial authorities in Charleston to establish a county court system in 1769, creating official channels for administering law and order rather than leaving it to vigilantes.

Chapter 7-Community Leader

The following year, Matthew was commissioned Captain of a militia Foot Regiment in Craven County (later Sumter County) by the Royal Lt. Governor, William Bull. Matthew was placed under the command of Colonel Richard Richardson, a friend of Matthew's, and future in-law and Revolutionary War comrade.

Matthew Singleton was a prominent, wealthy, successful man and community leader. In the early 1770's, he pledged £50, toward the establishment of a new chapel and parsonage for St. Mark's Parish. This was almost double the amount of any other donor. He also held public offices as Justice of the Peace, tax collector and served on provincial Congresses and assemblies as well as Grand Juries.

Chapter 8-Lifestyle

We don't know much about the lifestyle of these early settlers except for one account from a newspaper article published in 1916. In it, the early settlers from Virginia were characterized by an early observer as being, "addicted to sports and social gaiety, commonly assembling at each other's houses and closing the labors of the week with dancing." An active social lifestyle was a Singleton hallmark for generations. The article also mentions that the settlers were fond of literature and literary societies formed early on.[4]

Chapter 9-John and Rebecca Singleton Marriage

John Singleton (1754-1820), eldest son of Matthew Singleton, married Rebecca Richardson Cooper in 1774. Her father was Richard Richardson, Matthew's close friend and one of the leading landowners and citizens in the area. It was a second marriage for Rebecca Richardson Cooper. Her first marriage at 16 was to a man named Thomas Cooper.

In family story handed down for generations, it is said that Rebecca's father heartily disapproved of her marriage to Mr. Cooper, a man twenty-four years her senior and that he disowned her when she married against his wishes. Some time later, Rebecca's father was riding though the countryside and stopped at a house along the road to get a drink of water. He was greeted by his daughter, Rebecca, who invited him in and made him dinner. It is said that he was deeply disturbed that Rebecca had to prepare the meal herself, instead of having servants to prepare and serve the meal. He is said to have restored her fortunes and amply provided for her from then on. Mr. Cooper is also said to have been killed by a house slave who put poison in his gourd of drinking water. Ever after, Rebecca mistrusted the house slaves.[5]

John Singleton (1754-1820) married Rebecca (Richardson) Cooper (1752-1834) on August 3, 1774. Their first son, John Peter (1775-1800) was born on March 5, 1775, seven months later. The Singletons had four more children—Richard (1776-1852), Harriet

Richardson (1779-1817), Matthew Richardson (1783-1793) and finally, Mary Martha (1785-1863).[6] Richard Singleton and Mary Martha Singleton figure prominently in this story; to a much lesser extent, so does Harriet Richardson Singleton.

Chapter 10-Revolutionary War

Both Matthew and John Singleton played an active role in the Revolutionary War on the Patriot side. They, along with other South Carolinians in the area, declared their position in the following document. It was composed shortly after the clash between the Massachusetts Patriot Militia (the Minutemen) and the British Army at Lexington and Concord in 1775. The clash became known as "the shot heard round the world".

Revolutionary Association for Public Defence

South Carolina Association

The actual commencement of hostilities against this Continent by the British troops in the bloody scenes on the 19th of April last, was Boston, the increase of arbitrary impositions from a wicked and despotic ministry and the dread of instigated insurrections in the colonies, are causes sufficient to drive an oppressed people to the use of arms: We, therefore , the subscribers, inhabitants of South Carolina, holding ourselves bound by that most sacred of all obligations, the duty of good citizens towards an injured country, and thoroughly convinced, that, under our present distressed circumstances we shall be justified before God and man, in resisting force by force, do unite ourselves under every tie of religion and of honor and associate as a band in her defense, against every foe: Hereby solemnly engaging that, whenever our continental or provincial councils shall decree it necessary, we will go forth and be ready to sacrifice our lives and fortunes to secure her freedom and safety. This obligation to continue in full force until a reconciliation shall take place between Great Britain and America, upon constitutional principles, an event which we most ardently desire, and we will hold all those persons inimical to the liberty of the colonies, who shall refuse to subscribe this association.

The last sentence of the declaration clearly draws the line between those who support the Crown and those who support the Patriot cause and the implicit threat that awaits those who oppose the signers.

Of the signatories, five are Singletons, including Matthew and his 20 year old son, John, as well as Robert, John, Joseph, presumably Matthew's brothers, or close relatives. John James (probably Matthew's brother-in-law), and Isham Moore, Matthew's son-in-law, also signed. There are 107 signatures including twelve who made their marks (X).[7]

In South Carolina, the Revolutionary War was fought not just between the American and the British Armies in set piece battles, but between Tories (Loyalists) and Patriots who were often friends and neighbors. Seventy-five percent of the engagements fought in South Carolina during the Revolution involved South Carolinians fighting on both sides.[8]   The area east of the Wateree River, including Singleton property, was bitterly contested during this conflict.

In October of 1775, a few months after the declaration of intent, Matthew Singleton was commissioned a Captain in a voluntary horse troop and his son, John, was appointed a second Lieutenant. They both served under the command of Colonel, later General, Richard Richardson.[9]

In November of 1775, Matthew and John Singleton were both part of the force of some 3,000 Patriot militia under the command of Colonel Richardson. He conducted what was known as the Snow Campaign against Loyalist forces in the uplands of South Carolina. It effectively eliminated Loyalist military actions for a number of years by killing or capturing most of the leadership. The name Snow Campaign came from the huge snowfall that fell on the Patriot forces as they made their way back to the Midlands of South Carolina. Some two feet fell, a record snowfall to this day, for which the soldiers were woefully unprepared.

Matthew Singleton was later promoted to the rank of Lieutenant Colonel and his son, John, to Captain. John Singleton was called Captain John by his family and friends for the rest of his life. Both men would also serve as officers under the command of General Francis Marion, the legendary Swamp Fox, whose guerilla tactics were used against loyalist forces as well as British regular army units. (The Revolutionary War as fought in South Carolina, by Matthew and John Singleton, was presented in the movie, *The Patriot*, filmed on location in South Carolina. (Francis Marion often rode into battle with a tin pot on his head rather than the more common tri-cornered hat.)

Chapter 11-War Stories

A family story says that during John Singleton's Revolutionary War service, he had a narrow escape. There had been a fight with the British at Singleton's Mill on Matthew Singleton's property near the Melrose House. The infamous British officer, Colonel Banastre Tarleton, (the villain portrayed in the movie, *The Patriot*) was involved in this fight. John Singleton, stricken with small pox, was hiding out on an island in the Wateree Swamp, a few miles from Melrose, in order to avoid capture. A slave of John Singleton's named Jimmy would come every night to the Singleton house, tap on the window and receive food and other necessaries from Mrs. Singleton to take back to John Singleton. He avoided capture and recovered.[10]

Another report says that John Singleton, as part of General Sumter's Patriot force, was singled out for recognition for his role in commanding a partisan militia force that decimated a small Tory unit. They killed ten of the eleven Tories in a battle that took place ten miles from Sumter. A few miles away, near the site of General Sumter's house that had been burned down by Colonel Tarleton, a Tory was hung. This was not a *clean* war.[11]

Chapter 12-The Spoils of War

As the war wound down and in its aftermath, there was a settling up of old scores, as Tories left the area voluntarily or had their lands confiscated. For example, in 1782, the South Carolina General Assembly confiscated 400 slaves and lands from Tories and distributed them among General Sumter's troops. In 1784, as a reward for his service during the Revolutionary War, Matthew Singleton received from the State of South Carolina the 4,000 acre Cane Savannah plantation near Sumter. Matthew's wife, Mary (James) Singleton, died the same year. Matthew Singleton moved to Cane Savannah, dying there in 1787, at the age of fifty-seven.[12]

Chapter 13-Matthew Singleton's Estate

The will of Matthew Singleton was destroyed in a fire in the Sumter District Clerk of Courts office in 1805, but accepting the figure of approximately 3,100 acres that he acquired during his lifetime and the 4,000 acres of Cane Savannah, his estate was a large one of at least 7,100 acres. There is no record of slave numbers, but to produce crops of indigo and rice and other crops on even a portion of that land, it must have been substantial. Matthew's eldest daughter, Nancy Anne (Singleton) Moore inherited Cane Savannah Plantation. Her husband, Isham Moore, according to the Federal Census of 1790, had 145 slaves and was the largest slaveholder in Claremont District (present day Sumter County), South Carolina. It stands to reason that all or a great portion were from the Cane Savannah Plantation.

PART THREE

THE JOHN SINGLETON ERA (1787-1820)

Chapter 14-John Singleton (1754-1820) Takes Over

With the death of Matthew Singleton in 1787, a large part of the Singleton family fortunes fell into the capable hands of Matthew's eldest son, John. He continued in his father's footsteps as a successful landholder, slaveholder and businessman. His business interests were diverse: planting, shipping, warehousing, shipbuilding, even investing in a tailor shop in Charleston.

John Singleton also explored landholding opportunities in other locations, making a trip to New Orleans in 1807 looking for land. [1] Unlike many of their planter friends including the Hamptons, the Singletons did not invest in the newly opened lands of Louisiana, Mississippi and Alabama that increasingly yielded fabulous wealth raising cotton. A John Singleton grandson, John Peter Broün, however, did buy land in Alabama and established a plantation there. The Singletons preferred to increase their landholdings locally, by buying acreage from their neighbors as it became available.

Chapter 15-The Cotton Business

The raising of cotton would provide the largest part of nineteenth century Singleton family wealth. The cotton boom began in the early 1800's, thanks to the invention of the cotton gin by Eli Whitney and Europe's demand for cotton for its textile mills. It also made slave labor very cost effective. This lead to huge increases in the slave population. More cotton gins were needed as the demand expanded. The gins also received hard use and the teeth that separated the seed from the cotton boll also needed to be replaced or the blades sharpened.

For these services, generations of the Singletons turned to William Ellison of Stateburg. He was a free black entrepreneur who made high quality cotton gins and repaired them. He was also a substantial landholder, slave owner and fellow church member of the Singletons. (For more on William Ellison, see Appendix.)

Chapter 16-The Shipping Business

Although cotton was the biggest moneymaker for the Singletons, the shipping and warehouse business begun by Matthew Singleton and expanded by John Singleton was highly profitable well into the 1840's, when railroads began became the preferred commercial shipping method.

The Singletons' property at Warehouse Lake, near Manchester, was ideally situated to take advantage of the shipping business opportunity. Located close to the Wateree River and navigable feeder streams, their property was one of the only high landing areas on the northeast side of the Santee and Wateree Rivers south of Camden. It provided an ideal shipping location to the Charleston market. Indigo, rice, groundnuts (peanuts) and cotton were brought to the Singleton-owned warehouses and stored prior to shipping them south to the port at Charleston. They were then transported to other markets.

When the twenty-two miles long Cooper River canal was completed in 1800, it made for a much more direct and faster river route to Charleston from upriver. A Singleton boat made the trip from Manchester to Charleston in thirteen days in 1821, bringing forty-one bales of cotton and three hundred bushels of peas.[2]

Goods were often shipped downriver in an ingenuously designed type of pole boat, called a match boat. They were capable of transporting one hundred twenty-five bales of cotton on the downriver leg and twenty-five tons of freight on the upriver return trip.[3] Match boats were made to nest into each other, as many as eight at a time. This was done to avoid toll charges that were assessed per boat drawing water as they passed through the river locks. Once a boat's cargo had been unloaded at the destination downriver and was empty, the boats were reloaded with goods and began the journey back upriver. Any of the match boats that were not loaded could be seated into another match boat to save the toll charges. The boats were propelled along by the boatmen using long poles fitted with hooks to grab on to overhanging tree limbs to pull themselves or push against the river bottom to move the boats along.[4]

The upriver cargo was then stored in the very same Singleton warehouses where the products going downriver had been stored before shipment. The finished goods remained there until they could transported by wagon to waiting markets in the interior of the Carolinas, utilizing the Great Charleston Road and other roadways.

Along with shipping and warehousing, John Singleton was also involved in river boat building with his brother-in-law, Isham Moore. In 1796, they had a boat built that was fifty-eight feet long and over fifteen feet wide. Four boat hands manned it.[5]

John Singleton also shipped his crops of indigo, cotton, peas, and groundnuts (peanuts) to his agents in Liverpool, England. Reputedly, John Singleton also owned sailing ships to ship his crops to England.

Chapter 17-River Pirates

There are stories of river pirates preying on the Wateree traffic shortly after the Revolutionary War. Jack Moore, reputedly a mulatto (a person of African-American and Caucasian ancestry), lived on an island in the Wateree River, an island that still bears his name, and raided river traffic. His piracy led some of the local citizenry, led by Dr. Willis Ramsay, one of the founders of the town of Manchester and friend of Matthew and John Singleton, to take action. Dr. Ramsay led a group that caught and killed Jack Moore, cut off his head and put it on a pole and posted it on Jack Moore Island as a warning to others who might choose to follow his path.[6] Another version tells that the head of Jack Moore was paraded through the streets of Manchester before it was posted on the island. Both versions may be correct.

Chapter 18-Midway Plantation

When John Singleton married in 1774, his father Matthew is thought to have given him 1,479 acres as a wedding gift. This became Midway plantation. The property was located just south of present day Wedgefield, at Manchester on the King's Highway/Great Charleston Road (present day Highway 261), the main road from the interior to Charleston.[7]

John Singleton built a large house there of two stories with twenty rooms and a large stable and race track to support his horse racing. The home was a showplace, perfect for entertaining and accommodating visitors. There was a banquet room spanning the width of the house at one end and a ballroom at the other end, connected by a long hallway. Since Midway was on the main road from Charleston to the new capital at Columbia, many legislators stopped and stayed there. An oft repeated family story says that during the Christmas Holidays, after a "liberal" dinner (sounds like alcohol may have been involved), the legislators, would leapfrog down the long hallway.[8]

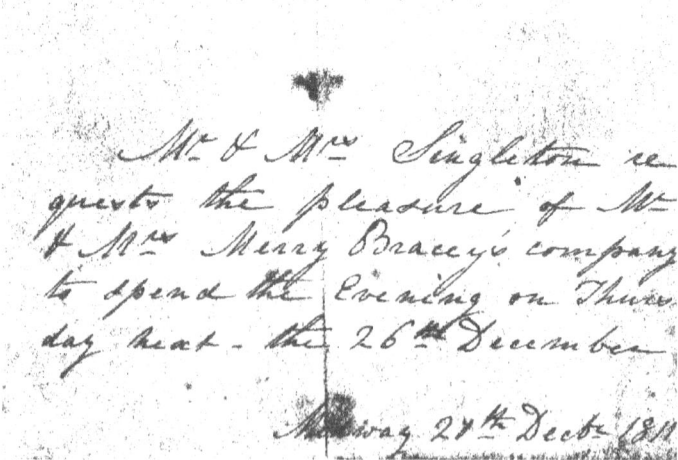

Christmas Holiday Invitation from the Singletons

Captain John's tastes were very English. Furniture, horses, jockeys, trainers and carriages as well as his silver were imported from England. Present day descendants of Captain John have some artifacts from his household.[9]

Two heavy glass tumblers (pictured below) bearing the initials JS, for John Singleton, have an image of a plow, etched into the glass. It is believed that his son Richard had these made for his father. The plow was probably chosen as a symbol because the Singletons were planters. (Some family descendents believe that these tumblers were used at the wedding celebration of Angelica Singleton, granddaughter of Captain John, when she married Abraham Van Buren, son of the President Van Buren in 1838. The symbol of a plow appears to have been also used by Matthew Richard Singleton on the lintel above the entrance door to the Kensington Mansion many years later.)

Glass Tumblers

Chapter 19-Manchester-Wicked and Sinful

Just to the south of Midway plantation was the town of Manchester. It began as a resort, founded by Isham Moore, John Singleton's brother-in-law, on Singleton property. The town developed, before 1799, on the site of an Indian trading post on the Catawba Indian Trail that ran from the coast to the Carolina uplands. This trail grew into what became known as the Great Charleston Road or Kings Highway, running from Charleston north to the Carolinas and beyond. Manchester was a stage coach relay stop on that road and shipping center for Wateree River traffic.

The town grew into a vibrant trade town, with a well-earned reputation for wild living and entertainments—gambling, fist fighting, cockfighting and drinking to excess. It boasted taverns, various businesses, a seldom-used school house that rarely doubled as a church, and a race track. The town was one mile square with streets laid out in a grid pattern and at one time was said to be the tenth largest town in South Carolina.

Robert Mills, famous architect and original designer of the Washington Monument, said of the area, "The amusement of cards and billiard playing is carried to an extreme. The sports of the field occur occasionally; and with great regret, it is added, a practice with some encouragement, cockfighting." [10]

When the name Manchester was spoken, the adjectives "wicked and sinful" usually accompanied it. More genteel entertainments such as lavish parties and balls were also much in evidence on the local plantations. These included Midway and Home Place, owned by Richard Singleton, John's son. Horse racing was the unquestioned king of entertainments, with a variety of accompanying amusements for the wealthy planters and the common folk. This was especially true during the twice annual race week held at Raccoon Savannah, the local racetrack.

Town life was described by Edwin Scott, whose father owned a tavern in Manchester from 1806-1811. In his *Random Recollections of a Long Life*, he recalled how every winter a few Catawba Indians would bring their hand made bows and arrows, moccasins, and earthenware pots and pans to trade for needed commodities like salt, gunpowder and whiskey. Yankee peddlers, travelling the road, were welcome visitors. They came in one-horse covered wagons and brought household goods and various "goo gahs" to sell. [11] (John's son Richard Singleton, owner of Home Place plantation, would find out how good a horse that could be in a story to be related later.)

Following the Great Road/King's Highway, huge wagons, drawn by four horses, full of apples, chestnuts, wheat, corn, potatoes, other produce and whiskey travelled down from the North Carolina and Tennessee highlands through Manchester to their final destination at Charleston. [12] The journey took many long slow weeks and they sold goods along the way. Once the teamsters arrived in Charleston, they would return back up the highway, having sold their wagon and all but one horse to ride home and begin the cycle again the next fall. It is also said that turkeys and hogs in great numbers were also driven down the road through the town to market.

Edwin Scott, observed of Manchester,

> Some of the villagers and neighbors met every day at a store, where the card table was brought out into the piazza soon after breakfast, and gambling went on till night, winding up now and then, with a supper and ball, to which the young ladies were invited and that lasted to a late hour. This, with drinking freely, was the regular habit week after week, varied by quarter races, feats of strength and activity, and an occasional fistfight…For health's sake, my brothers and myself were given a small quantity of whisky before breakfast every morning, and I had learned to play cards before I could read. It would seem that nothing but a special providence or a lucky chance saved me from becoming both a drunkard and a gambler, for certainly no one ever had a fairer start in that direction. [13]

Chapter 20-The Commodore

Captain John Singleton owned a summer place on the Hudson River at Tivoli, New York. [14] He and the family would journey there every summer in a carriage and a wagon loaded with baggage, accompanied by their household slaves. To cross the Hudson River they would take a ferry at New Brunswick, New Jersey. The ferryman would complain loudly and cuss a blue streak because he had to make multiple trips to ferry the party and all its belongings across the river. Meanwhile, the ferryman's wife would prepare and serve meals to the Singleton family.

The ferryman's name was Cornelius Vanderbilt, the "Commodore", early on in his career, on his way to creating one of America's great family fortunes. In future years, John Peter Broün (1806-1895), a grandson of Captain John, would repeat his eyewitness story to his grandchildren, taking a special delight in pointing out Vanderbilt's humble early beginnings and rough manner.[15]

Chapter 21-The Heir Apparent

According to family stories, John Singleton sent his eldest son John Peter to sea as a young man of twenty-five, onboard one of the sailing ships he owned. John Peter was given full responsibility for a cotton shipment to England to test his business acumen. This included getting the best price for the cotton. As the eldest son, he was being groomed to take over the family business.

Several slightly different versions of the following story have been passed down.

One version says that Mrs. Singleton was sleeping and heard a horse ride up the drive at Midway plantation. She got up and saw her son, John Peter, ride around the house and wave to her. Mrs. Singleton roused a house slave to meet him and take his horse. After searching for John Peter, the slave reported back to her that no one was there. Weeks later, after John Peter's ship docked in Charleston, they learned John Peter had drowned on the return trip to Charleston the same night that she had seen him wave to her.[16]

A slightly different version says that at twilight, John Peter's mother was walking on the veranda and saw her son ride into the yard and hitch his horse at the place he always had. Surprised, Mrs. Singleton quickly went inside and inquired of her husband, "Isn't John Peter at sea?" He replied that he was. When she returned to the veranda, no one was to be seen. After the ship docked, it was said that he had drowned at sea at that some hour.[17]

John Peter Singleton died at 25, unmarried. One source says that he was washed overboard. No other details are known as to the circumstances of his death.

Upon the death of John Peter in the year 1800, Richard Singleton, just before his twenty-fourth birthday, became the eldest surviving son. With it would come the rights and responsibilities that position entailed. Full assumption of those responsibilities would wait until his father's death twenty years later.

Chapter 22-Horse Breeder and Racer

Captain John Singleton had a passionate interest in raising and breeding "blooded horses" (horses whose blood or lineage is derived from the purest and most highly prized origin or stock). Fine horses and horse racing were an integral part of planter life in South Carolina. Thoroughbred racehorses were an interest he shared with his father, Matthew; and were a passion that his son, Richard, and grandsons, John Coles and Matthew Richard, also embraced. John Singleton's own one-mile racetrack was located just to the south of his house, and shared with his son Richard, whose Home Place plantation adjoined his own to the south. Captain John's stable is said to have accommodated 100 horses.[18]

John Singleton served as treasurer of the Stateburg Jockey Club and was known far and wide for his race horses. There is disagreement as to how much he raced them. Some Singleton family sources say Captain John did not race horses under his own name, but left that to his son, Richard. Others say he did race them under his own name. South Carolina had an active horse racing circuit and was considered "the Kentucky" of its day.[19] A silver racing cup trophy from the 1842 Pineville Races, one of those horse racing venues, still exists. It was most probably won by John Coles Singleton, grandson of Captain John and brother of Matthew Richard Singleton, builder of the Kensington, as his descendant has the cup in her possession.

Pineville Jockey Club Trophy

Chapter 23-Captain John and Rebecca's Daughters

John and Rebecca Singleton had three daughters. Rebecca (1788-1810) married John Kirkpatrick and moved to Jackson County, Tennessee where she died after giving birth to twins. The other two daughters would marry and live in South Carolina. The eldest daughter, Harriet Richardson Singleton (1779-1817), married Robert Broün in 1804 and gave birth to three sons. Robert Broün would die in 1809 leaving her a widow. She married John Russell

Spann in 1813.[20] Four years later, in 1817 she passed away. The Broün boys then went to live with their grandparents, Captain John and Rebecca Singleton, at Midway.

John and Rebecca Singleton's youngest daughter, Mary Martha Singleton (1785-1863), married Powell McRae Sr. in 1812. He was the son of a Camden merchant and not considered by the family an appropriate choice for a husband. Their marriage produced two children, Powell McRae Jr. (1814-1844) and Arabella (1815-1822).

In 1817, Mary Martha Singleton McRae legally separated from her husband. Divorce was illegal in South Carolina at that time. Mrs. McRae retained custody of the children. Powell McRae Sr., her husband, it is said, lived with his mistress and fathered two other children.[21] Powell McRae Sr. remained a concern to Mary Martha's father, Captain John. He would later put a special provision in his will to try to protect his daughter from Powell McRae Sr.

Mary Martha and her two children began living with her parents at Midway plantation, joining the three orphaned Broün sons already there. With the death of John Singleton in 1820, the three Broün sons and the two McRae children were all left under the care of Mary Martha McRae and her mother, Rebecca Singleton. In 1825, Rebecca Singleton and her daughter Mary Martha purchased a house in Hyde Park, New York, twenty-five miles south of Tivoli, location of Captain John's original summer place. Rebecca would stay close to her daughter, Mary Martha, who grew increasingly erratic in her behavior. Rebecca Singleton would die in Philadelphia in 1833. Mary Martha McRae, suffered from mental illness for much of her adult life and in 1843 was hospitalized in the Pennsylvania Asylum for the Insane, where she received the best care available at the time. She would live out the rest of her life there, dying in 1863.

Chapter 24-The Passing of John Singleton

John Singleton died in 1820 and was buried in the Singleton Family Cemetery. A marker was placed there by his wife, giving the date of his birth and death with the inscription- "erected by his affectionate consort". (Consort means a wife, husband, or companion, in particular the spouse of a reigning monarch.)

John Singleton left a large estate, almost doubling the property that his father Matthew had accumulated. Captain John's estate included eight different properties totaling some 13,107 acres, slaves as well as $30,000 in cash to be invested in land and slaves.

> One dollar in 1820 would be worth $20.80 today in buying power, however, the actual economic power of that dollar in the much-smaller America of the time would be far greater: $24,400. John Singleton's $30,000 estate cash would be worth $625,000 in buying power and $733,000,000 in economic power. I used www.measuringworth.com to do the conversions in the book.

His estate was all to be dispersed in the provisions of an unusual will. Some property and personal items went directly to the next generation, including generous provisions for his son Richard, as chief heir, but most of the property was put into trust to be managed by Richard. The pattern of inheritance was that the next generation had only a life interest and the property was actually inherited by the grandchildren. Richard Singleton would put similar provisions into his own will. The intent was to provide for future generations. These attempts at control would lead to family squabbles and lawsuits down the road.

Captain John also made provisions in his will that the Singleton family name would continue. He specified that the male heirs of his son, Richard, and daughter, Harriet Richardson Spann, by age twenty-one, had to have Singleton in their Surnames or they would be cut out of their inheritance.

Captain John left his widow Rebecca amply provided for. He also made special provisions for his three Broün grandsons as well as his daughter, Mary Martha McRae and her children, Powell and Arabella McRae. None of the five grandchildren were under their father's care-the McRaes being separated and both Broün parents deceased. John Singleton gave each of the Broün grandsons plantations or tracts of land, slaves, as well as personal items such as individual horses, a double-barreled silver mounted shotgun and his library of books.

Well aware of Mary Martha McRae's mental condition, John Singleton expressed special concern for her and her children's care in his will. His concerns were well founded as evidenced by her and her son Powell's future commitments to insane asylums. Richard Singleton would provide money in the future for the best care available for his sister and nephew when they were hospitalized, fulfilling the desire of his father.

John Singleton also gave special attention to Powell McRae Sr., Mary Martha McRae's husband, in his will:

> I give and devise after the decease of my beloved wife to my son Richard Singleton and his Heirs all the land plantation called the Midway plantation described above ... that the said Richard and his Heirs will permit my daughter Mary Martha McRae to Occupy, possess, and enjoy the same during her Natural life, ..., not subject in any Manner to the interference or control of her Husband Powell McRae...[2]

PART FOUR

COLONEL SINGLETON REIGNS (1820-1852)

Chapter 25-"The Colonel"-Richard Singleton

Colonel Richard and Rebecca Singleton

With the death of his father in 1820, eldest son Richard, at the age of forty-four, assumed center stage of the Singleton family story. He took over managing the Singleton's family businesses and administering his father's estate and the special provisions of his will.

Richard Singleton was an imposing figure. He stood over six feet tall, had a large head, prominent jaw and large thick hands. He often wore a stiff neckband fastened in the back called a stock. Underneath the stock, he wore a very high collar, and his hair was combed straight up in a pompadour. The high collar and stock pressing into his jowls emphasized his height, formal personality and bearing. He was a fastidious dresser. It was said that he took up to two hours in the morning to get dressed, with his wife combing every strand of his hair so it would be just right, while reading him the newspaper, the Bible and his correspondence. Some say that he never read or wrote a letter himself if he didn't have to. This is a Singleton male trait that was noted by later family descendents.[1] When chided by his friends about the length of time it took him to get ready for the day, he reputedly said, "It did not matter when you started, but what you did after starting." [2]

Richard has been described as man of sober temperament, fastidious in every way with a love of show, but possessed of a "quiet charm that drew other men to him".[3] He was said to be "a good judge of human nature and fortunate in his selection of overseers", some of whom stayed with him for a lifetime.[4] Possessor of vast wealth and high social position, he received and gave favors freely and was said by his friends to be generous, a man of honor, and a true Southern gentleman. He is also said to have loved his family "with an almost desperate love." [5]

He was known as Colonel Singleton. It may have been an honorific title of respect rather than an actual commission. His grandfather, Matthew Singleton had been commissioned a Colonel during the Revolutionary War. Richard Singleton's son, Matthew Richard Singleton (1817-1854), builder of the Kensington, and grandson, Richard Singleton (1851-1921), would both be commissioned Colonels in the South Carolina militia.

Enormously wealthy, fueled by the cotton boom in the first half of the nineteenth century, Colonel Singleton spent extravagantly and lived luxuriously. He also lent and borrowed in the same way, which would later come back to haunt him. It is said that by the end of his life, Colonel Singleton had no idea of how much he owed in general nor had he kept track of all the promissory notes he had signed. From other sources he does not seem to be unique in this regard. Some have said this was just part of the lifestyle of wealthy planters like the Colonel. General Sumter and Governor Richard Richardson seem to have suffered similar fates. *Gentlemen* do not trouble themselves with these matters and do not demand payment for debts incurred. It was part of the code.

A lawyer from Alabama in the 1830s, writing about the process of obtaining payment from planters for goods and services rendered:

> They all run in debt – invariably, … never pay cash, and all always one year behind hand. They wait for the sale of their crops. The roads are bad, the prices low, they cannot pay. They all wait to be sued. A suit is brought – no defense is made – an execution is taken out and is paid with all the costs and they even think it a good bargain. The rate of interest allowed is but 8%. So much is this below the real value that a man will let his debts go unpaid, pay interest and costs and buy Negroes for making cotton or land and think it even then profitable and will be much obliged to his plaintiff if he will wait for the due course of law and not personally fall out with him.[6]

Colonel Richard Singleton was a Southern aristocrat, planter and sportsman, known as a backcountry gentleman by those from the Low Country of South Carolina, in particular, the Charlestonians. It was a description not altogether appreciated by those it was bestowed upon.[7]   He may have been seen as somewhat of an upcountry upstart by some of the haughty Low Country rice planters.

Chapter 26-The Yankee Peddler

In a story repeated for generations:

Colonel Singleton's plantation, Home Place, was on the main road from Charleston to the interior and peddlers often used this roadway. One stopped and asked if Colonel Singleton could provide lodging for the night, a common practice, and he agreed to do so. After dinner the Colonel and his guest were seated in the parlor, lit by candles in silver candlesticks. When it came time to retire for the evening, the candles needed to be snuffed out. Rather than use the silver candle snuffers that were readily available for that purpose, the peddler, not being familiar with them, moistened his thumb and forefinger and snuffed them out. The Colonel then explained to the peddler the *proper* way to extinguish the candles, to the peddler's great embarrassment.

The next morning some of Colonel Singleton's fine racehorses were being exercised on his race track next to the house. The Yankee peddler was preparing to leave and drove up in his wagon drawn by a single horse to say his goodbyes to the Colonel. The horse was an unattractive animal, bony and looked like a nag.

Colonel Singleton began making disparaging comments about the appearance of the horse and jokingly challenged the peddler to race his horse against one of the Colonel's racehorses. The peddler agreed. To the great embarrassment of Colonel Singleton, the peddler's horse won the race. It is said that after hitching his horse to his wagon, the peddler turned to the Colonel, moistened his thumb and forefinger and said, "That's the way I snuffs 'em, Sir," and drove away in triumph and vindication.

Chapter 27-The Colonel's Plantation Empire

Richard Singleton inherited great wealth in land, slaves and businesses from his father and he expanded them all. He was at the pinnacle of wealth, power and influence in antebellum South Carolina when cotton was king. The economic engine that drove Southern cotton wealth were the twin pistons of land and slavery. The Singletons were "flush" with both. The Singleton family, for generations beginning with Matthew, then John, then Richard, expanded their landholding and slaveholding. The family is thought to have been the largest cotton producers and slaveholders in the state of South Carolina in 1850.[8]

Chapter 28-The Cotton Market

Antebellum Singleton family fortunes rose and fell with the cotton market, which fluctuated wildly.

In 1818, the price of cotton temporarily soared to 32.5¢ a pound.

As a result of the Panic of 1819 the price fell to 14¢ a pound, then

12¢ a pound in 1823, and finally about 9¢ a pound from 1826 to 1832.

Prices had risen in early 1837 to 18¢ a pound, but with the Panic of 1837 setting in, the price plummeted to 8¢ a pound by May. By 1840 the price had dipped to 4½¢.

The price rose to around 10¢ a pound through most of the 1840s and into the 1850s, when it finally rose above that level in 1855, reaching 15¢ in 1857. South Carolina had been the number one cotton producing state in 1820, but its pre-eminence declined from 1820 on.

To make up for declining prices, more and more land was brought under cultivation. It was a short term solution however, because cotton production wore out the land. New cotton lands were being opened in Mississippi, Alabama and Louisiana, offering much greater yields per acre. By 1860, South Carolina's position had slipped to seventh among cotton-producing states.

Chapter 29-Other Business Interests

Richard Singleton's business interests were not limited to the businesses begun by his grandfather and father. He also imported livestock from overseas to improve his herds, including the best breeds of cattle from England and Broad-Tailed sheep from Africa. These sheep were crossbred with common sheep to produce a new strain that adapted well to the hot climate of the South. He was given credit for this in a farm journal of the time.[9]

After a rocky start, Colonel Singleton also developed interest in the railroad business. On January 10, 1840, he sent a letter to the Louisville, Cincinnati & Charleston Railroad strenuously objecting to the construction of the railroad across his True Blue plantation property. He labeled it an "oppression and injustice" and sought to be paid damages. Twelve days later, an officer of the railroad responded—inviting Colonel Singleton to the next meeting of the board.[10] The problem was resolved. Colonel Singleton purchased a piece of the railroad; and, it is thought by some, served on the board of directors as well.[11]   A train depot was established on Singleton property at Acton, just south of the Headquarters/Kensington plantation. It provided a convenient and ready shipping point for both goods and people. This is probably not a coincidence.

Chapter 30-Managing His Interests

To conduct his far flung business affairs, Colonel Singleton had factors (business agents) representing him in Charleston, Philadelphia, and Liverpool in Great Britain. His Liverpool and Charleston factors wrote him letters on a regular basis keeping him appraised of market values of various commodities, most importantly, cotton. In Charleston, his factor and longtime friend, Duke Goodman, would write him weekly to keep him up to date on commodity prices as well as handling other purchases for him such as slaves, bank shares, plantation supplies, land, or having a new boat built.

Goodman also wrote to the Colonel regarding searches for runaway slaves and hiring tutors for the Singleton children. Colonel Singleton also managed the business affairs of the trust plantations from John Singleton's estate. Goodman also wrote numerous letters to Colonel Singleton regarding those. After Duke Goodman moved to Alabama in 1832, a number of different firms performed the same functions for Colonel Singleton.

Colonel Singleton traveled frequently, visiting Tennessee; New York; Richmond Virginia; Philadelphia; Albemarle County, Virginia, the family home of his wife; as well as spending every summer season at White Sulphur Springs in what was then Virginia. His horse racing interests took him far afield, not only in South Carolina, but out of state as well. A horse magazine in the 1840's mentions his attendance at a horserace in Nashville, Tennessee with his friend Wade Hampton II. He is thought to have raced his horses as far north as New York.

In addition to the updates from his factors, Colonel Singleton received written reports regarding his plantations from his overseers; his sons, Matthew Richard and John Coles; and his son-in-law, Robert Marion Deveaux. He also relied heavily on his close friends, Wade Hampton II and Benjamin Franklin Taylor, to watch over his business interests when he was away.

Chapter 31-Colonel Singleton's First Marriage

Richard Singleton married twice. His first marriage was to Charlotte Videau (Marion) Ashby (1784-1805) in 1802. She died within two months of the birth of their daughter, Mary Rebecca Singleton in 1805. Most sources indicate that her death was due to complications from the birth. Other sources say it was consumption (tuberculosis). It may have been a little of both. She was buried in the Singleton Family Cemetery. Little Mary Rebecca become her father's constant companion and would later marry a good friend of her father's, George McDuffie.

Chapter 32-Second Marriage

Richard Singleton married again in 1812, this time to Rebecca (Travis) Coles (1782-1849) of Albemarle, Virginia. Albemarle County is the location of Charlottesville; the University of Virginia, and the home of Thomas Jefferson. She came from a prominent Virginia family and brought with her important family connections.

Her father was John Coles (1745-1808), a wealthy plantation owner, and close friend and neighbor of Presidents Jefferson and Madison.

Her sister, Emily (1790-1871), married John Rutherfoord (1792-1866), a future Governor of Virginia.

Another sister, Sarah, known as Sallie (1789-1848), became the second wife of Andrew Stevenson (1784-1857), future

Congressman and Speaker of the House of Representatives. During the administration of President Martin Van Buren, Stevenson would serve as Minister (Ambassador) to Great Britain, the Court of St. James. Andrew Stephenson became a close personal friend of Richard Singleton, his brother-in-law. Stevenson's son, John White Stevenson (1812-1886), would later serve the state of Kentucky as a U.S. Congressman, Senator, Lieutenant Governor and Governor.

Her brother was Edward Coles (1786-1868). Like his father he was a close personal friend of Thomas Jefferson and James Madison. Edward Coles served as secretary to President Madison and later become the 2nd Governor of Illinois. He was instrumental in keeping slavery out of Illinois and an abolitionist. He maintained a long and close relationship with his brother-in-law, Colonel Richard Singleton. (For more on Edward Coles, see Appendix.)

Rebecca Singleton's cousin was Patrick Henry (1736-1799), twice Governor of Virginia and a fiery orator, best remembered for his "liberty or death speech" promoting revolt from England. "Is life so dear, or peace so sweet, as to be purchased at the price of chains and slavery? Forbid it, Almighty God! I know not what course others may take; but as for me, give me liberty or give me death!"

Her 2nd Cousin was Dorothea "Dolley" Payne Madison (1768-1849), wife of President James Madison. Dolley Madison set the standard of what a "First Lady" should be. She was the queen of Washington society and would later be a matchmaker for Angelica Singleton, daughter of Colonel Richard Singleton.

Chapter 33-Richard & Rebecca Singleton's Children

At the time of her marriage to Colonel Richard Singleton in 1812, Rebecca Travis Coles was 29 years old. She gave birth in rapid succession to seven children in seven years, including Matthew (Richard) Singleton, future builder of the Kensington.

-Elizabeth Isaetta Singleton (1812-1812) (lived only 2 weeks)

-John Coles Singleton (1813-1852)

- Videau Marion Singleton (1815-1867)

-Sarah Angelica Singleton (1816-1877)

-Richard Singleton (1817-1833)

-Matthew (Richard) Singleton (1817-1854)

-Tucker Coles Singleton (1819-1820)

The first and the last children died in infancy. Four of their children lived to adulthood. They all left generations of family descendants except Angelica, whose three children, all sons, never married.[12] All the children were named after family members, with the possible exception of Elizabeth Isaetta and Sarah Angelica. Videau Marion was named after her father's first wife, Charlotte Videau (Marion) Singleton.[13] (Videau Marion and Sarah Angelica will usually be referred to simply as Marion and Angelica for the rest of the book.)

The children grew up at Home Place plantation, enjoying a life of wealth and privilege. They were educated by tutors at home, followed by boarding schools. Then the boys were sent to college and the girls to female academies.

Other than his family and businesses, the three passions of Colonel Singleton's life seem to have been Home Place, White Sulphur Springs and Horse Racing.

Chapter 34-"Home"

Colonel Singleton always referred to his home as Home, not as Home Place or Singleton Hall, as others did. It was built circa 1800. The Home Place plantation encompassed 2,050 acres and was situated just to the south of his father's place, Midway, on top of a knoll.

The two plantation houses, Midway and Home, were separated by only a mock-orange hedge, typical of English gardens: a fast growing shrub, growing six to ten feet tall in maturity, fragrant, with white blossoms appearing in the late spring and early summer.

Captain John had built a one mile long oval racecourse located between the properties. He shared it with his equally avid horse racing son, Richard. One straightaway of the racecourse ran parallel with Home Place, so near to the house that orders could be given to the trainers or jockeys from the piazza.[14]

Fronting Midway and Home Place, along the Great Charleston Road, was a four mile long trimmed hawthorn hedge, planted by Captain John Singleton to provide privacy. The hawthorn, of the rose family, has abundant white or pink fragrant blossoms. According to Captain John's great great granddaughter, the hedge was kept trimmed until just before "the Confederate War".[15]

The Home Place mansion was a large, square, solidly built home of approximately 4,000 square feet, perched above a raised (English) basement. Nineteen white marble steps, guarded on each side by crouching stone lion statues, provided a grand entrance to the front piazza with its tall white pillars.[16]

The first floor consisted of four rooms, twenty-two feet square each, with ceilings eighteen feet high. A huge central hall divided the rooms with a library and drawing room at the front and a breakfast and dining room at the back. At the back end of the hall, a mahogany staircase, as wide as the hall, gave access to the second floor, which consisted of four large bedrooms and two dressing rooms. During balls held in the main floor hall, the second floor stair way landing provided a place for the musicians. At the foot of the staircase was a newel post. Inside was a box of chalk which the dancers rubbed on the bottoms of their leather soled shoes to avoid slipping on the smooth waxed ballroom floor.[17]

Furnishings

Richard Singleton lavishly furnished Home Place mansion, mostly in the English style, like his father before him. "In the drawing room there was a pedal harp [also known as a concert harp, typically 6' tall] that cost $450 and a Viennese pianoforte [piano is a foreshortened word of the Italian] of equal value." [18]

The furnishings were chosen from the best Europe had to offer. Carpets were Belgian, hangings and draperies were French, and most of the china, cut glass and silver was English. The Colonel introduced forks into the family. His nephews and nieces called them Uncle Singleton's "split spoons". A double dinner set of twenty-four stoneware pieces was made in the pottery patronized by the Prince of Wales, afterwards King George IV.[19]   In the dining room was a maple dining table and chairs imported from England to seat twenty-four. It was used at Angelica Singleton's wedding to Abraham Van Buren in 1838.

Out Back

A wide piazza extended across the back of the house and its steps were guarded by crouching greyhounds. There was no cellar, the stone basement…had tiled floors, a laundry and dumb waiter. The kitchen was a separate building some distance to one side of the house, and corresponding to it on the other side was the 'office', where all the business of the plantation was transacted. Beyond the kitchen was the smoke house, the gardener's home and the gardens and hothouses; to the right of the 'Big House' stood the school building. Opposite to the gardener's house was the dairy – a square room, the upper part of which was latticed. Inside, a dry well some sixteen feet deep contained a square wire safe with shelves. This safe could be raised and lowered by a rope and pulley and meat and milk were kept fresh in this storage place. When winters were cold enough a supply of ice was cut from a small pond and stored. Behind the hot houses and vegetable gardens were immense stables, and the carriage house, while to the right and left ran the row of servants' quarters known as 'The Street'. [20]

Lifestyle

Home Place was a hub of social activity: lavish entertainments, weddings, barbecues and receptions for visiting dignitaries.[21]

A food and spirits bill from the Christmas season in the year 1825 give hints of the lifestyle: Can of Gunpowder tea (Chinese green tea), fifty-three seven oz. loaf sugars, ten boxes of currants, twelve dozen almonds, nutmegs, cinnamon, an eight oz. isinglass gift box, a dozen raspberry cordials, lemon syrup, lime juice, capers, olives, raisins, cheese, cranberries, keg of barley, a case of gin, ten gallons of brandy, one keg of brandy, ten gallons of rum, brown sugar, limes and pineapples.[22]

A Christmas Present

R.R. [Richard Richardson] Singleton [eldest son of John Coles Singleton] was visiting his grandfather, Mr. [Colonel] Richard Singleton, in the Christmas time when he was four years old [1844], and at breakfast his grandfather said: 'Your Christmas present is behind that chair, Richard.' He looked around and there stood a little Negro boy, Tucker George, who was but a few years older than himself. From that time they never separated, and when a mere lad in his teens, Richard entered the army in that terrible war between the North and South, his faithful body servant was Tucker George, who watched over him and his belongings, often preventing the appropriating of blankets and other things, by boys in the company, who were not over scrupulous in supplying themselves from Richard's effects…many times [my cousin Richard] knew nothing about how he was guarded. [23]

The View

Home Place was surrounded by a fifty acre park with a formal English garden, designed and tended by an English gardener. Trees were planted in rows radiating out from the mansion to the Charleston Road, running through the race course and forming a pattern like spokes of a wheel. The editor of the *American Turf Register Magazine*, seeing Home Place as he approached along the Charleston Road, commented on the beautiful effect the partial views of the mansion revealed. The final approach to the house was up a broad avenue, shaded on either side by oaks. Its "picturesque beauty" could not be surpassed, he said.[24]

Mrs. Anne Royall, travelling by stagecoach in 1831, observed that the area

…contains many very handsome farms, one in particular, the property of a Mr. Singleton, is a great curiosity—being at once, the largest, neatest and the most beautiful I ever beheld. The man, and the land must have been well matched—for more taste, more industry, or more beautiful fields are not to be found in America—high, rich and level. One field lay on the road, it was paled [fenced] for about two miles on the road, and must have been laid off with the compass. The field was swarming with active, stout negroes, with white clothes on, some ploughing [period spelling] and some hoeing. But the house, the gardens, the avenues, and the hedges of roses: It yields to none…It was said this field contains 1000 acres.[25]

(Mrs. Royall was rarely so generous in her opinion. She was famously acerbic, critical and intrusive, an infamous muckraker, one of the first female journalists, and the only person ever convicted of being a public scold. For more on Mrs. Anne Royall, see Appendix.)

Chapter 35-The Springs of Virginia

Many Southern planters trekked north to escape the summer heat and this included the Singletons. They chose the area known as the "Virginia Springs" in northern Virginia and today's West Virginia. The entire area boasted mineral springs. Many resorts grew up around these springs.

Taking the waters (the various mineral spring waters) was considered by some to be a health cure as it had been for thousands of years. The Singleton's first foray to the Springs of Virginia was by Richard's father, John, to Sweet Springs in 1818. He sought a cure for his various ailments, thought to include malaria. Drinking the waters made him worse and he nearly died.

Aside from whatever health benefits the waters themselves might bring, the location of the Springs at higher elevations *was* a health benefit. The heat, humidity and fertility of the Southern bottomlands grew cotton and rice bountifully, but were unhealthy in the summertime. Mosquito-borne diseases like malaria, yellow fever and lung ailments were endemic. The summer was often referred to as the "sick season". (For more on the "sick season", see Appendix.)

If John Singleton's father's generation had gone to the Springs of Virginia for health reasons, Colonel Singleton's generation would make it the "go to" social place for the summer season for a whole generation of Southerners with means. The Virginia Springs and, preeminently, the White Sulphur Springs resort, would attract famous people and prominent politicians, a few Northerners and members of European royalty, but its ethos remained Southern.

Chapter 36-White Sulphur Springs

White Sulphur Springs became a second home to Colonel Richard Singleton for over thirty years. He first visited there in 1818 and he began to bring his family annually to spend the summer season there. The season was July, August and September, often stretching into October. There was no public transportation available at that time. Colonel Singleton's family of seven, any additional guests and three household slaves travelled in their own carriages and wagons in a mini wagon train.

They made the roundabout trip (some say 750 miles) by way of Charleston, Staunton, Richmond and Fayetteville; some of it along rock strewn mountain roads and bone jarring corduroy roads through the swamps.

It made the three week long journey a misery, especially if you were sick.[26] (Corduroy roads were made of logs laid side by side perpendicular to the direction of travel, usually used in low or swampy places.)

See a picture of the Corduroy Road on the next page.

Corduroy Road

By 1825, the family began using a more direct route through the mountains via Asheville and Abingdon on improved roads, shortening the journey and getting the party into the cool of the mountains a week sooner.[27]

Early on in his visitations, Colonel Singleton became an investor in the resort. It is said that initially he took over a debt of $1,200 to help the owner of the inn, By 1825 he assumed responsibility for the first mortgage on the Springs to the tune of $22,000. At that time cotton was bringing 16-17 3/4 cents a pound and Colonel Singleton was selling thousands of bales of cotton at that price. A thousand bales at three hundred pounds a bale would bring $50,000. By then, he owned a private cottage at the Springs, "a neat little cabin at the foot of an old oak…" A visitor to the Springs described it as "the prettiest cottage at the place." He also purchased a new carriage for $425 and almost new Chariette for $450.[28]

By 1830 after having granted other additional loans, it is thought that he had an investment of $30,000 in White Sulfur Springs, from which he received very little in return. Without his financial support in the 1820's and 1830's it's not at all likely the place would have survived.

The McDuffies

In the summer of 1828, according to a family story, George McDuffie, a South Carolina Congressman, (later governor), accompanied the Singletons on their annual family journey north for the season. He was a close friend of Colonel Singleton's. During the trip, Mr. McDuffie, riding in a carriage with Colonel Singleton's daughter, Mary Rebecca, proposed marriage to her.[29] She accepted and they were married in 1829. A year later, Mary McDuffie gave birth to a daughter who they named Mary. Mrs. McDuffie died within two months of her daughter's birth, as had her own mother, who died shortly after Mary Rebecca's own birth.[30] Mary Rebecca Singleton McDuffie was laid to rest in the Singleton Family Cemetery. Her daughter, Mary Singleton McDuffie, would lead a star-crossed life, weaving in and out of this story of the Singleton family and eventually marrying Wade Hampton III, a South Carolina icon. (For more on George McDuffie, see Appendix.)

Colonel Singleton Pre-eminent

By his financial backing of the resort, an eager willingness to loan money to friends who sought his help and by the force of his personality and gracious manner, Colonel Singleton put his imprint on the social standards, hospitality and entertainment at White Sulphur Springs. He was acknowledged as the pre-eminent personage there for thirty years.

Politicians galore were attracted to the Springs, but there was no talk of politics. To have done so was to breach an unspoken protocol of the Springs: No political wrangling. The entire tone of the resort was Southern and all that meant in terms of ethic, style and activities.

Colonel Singleton was also a man on vacation. It was a place where he sought relaxation. J. L. Petigu, a Charleston lawyer and friend, commented that, "Mr. Singleton is here a different man entirely from what he is at home. There he is an indefatigable planter and inveterate turf man. Here he is the politest man of the age, scrupulously attentive to his dress and marked in his civility to the ladies." [31]

The Social Scene

The draw of being the "in place" set it apart from the other area resorts. Richard Singleton and his close friend, Wade Hampton II, one of the richest men in the South, were instrumental in its popularization among the Southern gentry.

The centerpiece of the resort was the spring itself which was enshrined in a spring house in the shape of a Greek temple with twelve columns with a small statue of Hygeia, the goddess of health in Greek mythology, on top. It exists to this day.

The grounds of White Sulphur Springs were laid out in a hollow square that elongated into an oblong. Different areas along the edge of the hollow were referred to as Virginia Row, Baltimore Row, Carolina Row, etc. In each area there were cottages available for accommodation.

Certain guests like the Singletons had their own cottages, but many stayed at an inn on the grounds. People clamored to be part of the social scene that was the summer season there. Guests arrived in huge carriages brought from a landing on the Ohio River or from other directions and vied noisily for a place at the main lodge. During August of 1838 as many as fifty people a day were turned away.[32] Early on, the hotel could accommodate a hundred guests. It was expanded and by 1840, close to one thousand total guests could be accommodated at the Springs.[33]

Daily activities abounded. Fencing took place on the lawn as well as quoits (a game similar to horseshoes or ring toss). A lawn bowling alley existed near the kennels. People rode and raced their horses on the grounds or ambled about the grounds in their carriages. Great barbecues, picnics with orchestras, dress balls every night and deer hunts were all part of the scene, as well as indoor activities like billiards and the newly socially acceptable card game of whist.

A dinner (noon meal) was described in one account. The fare was sheep, beef and fried chicken served on twelve tables, each sitting fifty people. Desserts were abundant. After dinner, the ladies retired to the drawing room for conversation and music. Many took a one to two hour siesta. At 5 p.m. many of the guests took a carriage ride around the grounds and would visit the springhouse as they had before dinner in the early morning to promenade and socialize. After twilight the ballroom was open for dancing every weekday with a fine orchestra to provide music.[34]

Famous Visitors

During the Colonel Singleton years, White Sulphur Springs attracted a raft of famous visitors, including many sitting and future Presidents: Adams, Jefferson, Madison, Monroe, Jackson, Van Buren, Tyler, Fillmore, Pierce and Buchanan. (During his Presidency, John Tyler married Miss Julia Gardner, known as the Belle of White Sulphur Springs. They spent their honeymoon at the President's Cottage, formerly Henderson's cottage, now known as the President's Cottage Museum.)

Other prominent political figures like Henry Clay, Daniel Webster, John C. Calhoun and Davy Crockett also visited. Luminaries like Stephen Decatur (War of 1812 naval hero) and Dolley Madison visited as well.

During the Van Buren season of 1838, the sisters of Mary, Lady Wellesley, sister-in-law to the Duke of Wellington, (vanquisher of the Napoleonic menace at the battle of Waterloo) visited. Jerome Napoleon Bonaparte, the nephew of Napoleon Bonaparte, also owned a cottage at the Springs and was a frequent summer visitor and friend of the Singletons.[35] John James Audubon, the famous ornithologist, naturalist, and painter also visited.

Not everyone, however, was enamored with the Springs. There were complaints of flea infestation, too much noise, dirt, and pigs running wild all over the grounds. One such complainant was Francis Scott Key who wrote a poem to a friend discouraging him from visiting White Sulphur Springs.

A word of advice about matters and things
May be useful to people who come to these springs:
First, there's a bell in the morning that rings
To awaken the people who come to the springs,
And the folks fix their ribbons and tie up their strings,
And look very beautiful here at the springs.

There's an insect or two, called a flea, that here stings
The skins of the people who stay at the springs;
There's a broom and a half here, for nobody brings
Such implements here, to sweep out the springs;
There's a maid and a half, too, for one of them swings
Rather much to one side; for she's lame at the springs.

There's a bawling all day – but the ball at night clings
The most to my fancy of all the springs –
To conclude, though some things here might do e'en for kings,
If you wish to fare well, say farewell to the springs.[36]

Colonel Singleton would continue to visit White Sulphur Springs for the rest of his life. (The Springs would later evolve into the Greenbrier, still one of America's premier resorts. For more about White Sulphur Springs and the Greenbrier, see Appendix.

Chapter 37-Horse Racing

When Richard Singleton wasn't at White Sulphur Springs or attending to other business, he was involved in another of his passions—a consuming interest in blooded horses. He raced them, bought and sold them and bred them. In 1827 his horses—Ariel, Red Gauntlet and Nondescript—won every race at the Washington Race Course in Charleston during Race Week. It was the annual high point of South Carolina horse racing—like the Triple Crown all rolled into one week. He was one of only three men to ever earn the distinction of winning every race. The others were Wade Hampton I, father of his close friend, Wade Hampton II, and Governor James B. Richardson, a cousin by marriage.

Colonel Singleton was referred to by some as the Napoleon of the

South for his racing feats. He was an active member of the South Carolina Jockey Club for fifty years. In 1850, he was singled out for honorary membership, the highest honor the club could bestow. He was one of only five men to ever receive that distinction.

Colonel Singleton's horse racing interests took him all over the South, including Louisiana, Kentucky, Virginia and New York. He also raced the extensive horse racing circuit in South Carolina and along with Wade Hampton II, he founded the Columbia Jockey Club in 1828.[37] (For more on Horse Racing, see Appendix.)

Chapter 38-The Horse Business

Colonel Singleton sent many of his mares to be bred by the famous stallion Sir Archie, one of the prime foundation horses of American Thoroughbred racing. Red Gauntlet and Nondescript, two of the three horses that won every race for the Colonel during Race Week of 1827, were from the lineage of Sir Archie. (For more about Sir Archie, see Appendix.)

Colonel Singleton owned famous studs of his own: Godolphin, Crusader, and Kosciusko. Both Crusader and Kosciusko were sired by Sir Archie. Godolphin earned $853.50 in stud fees for Colonel Singleton in 1834.[38]

Col Singleton's horse sales and breeding interests went far beyond South Carolina. Letters from horsemen in Cincinnati, Ohio; Kentucky; Augusta, Georgia; Virginia; Washington, D.C.; New York; North Carolina; Alabama, and Tennessee confirm this. Part of the business of breeding thoroughbreds was the need to furnish pedigrees to that effect. A number of letters indicate that Colonel Singleton was slow in doing so. Frustrated owners of mares bred to the Colonel's studs wrote repeated letters to him in this regard.

Colonel Singleton was so well known and renowned as a breeder of blooded horses that a horseman from Tennessee, the Rev. Hardy M. Cryer, contacted the then-sitting President of the United States, Andrew Jackson, himself an avid horse racer and breeder, to arrange an introduction. The Rev. Cryer wanted to purchase the racehorse and stud "Crusader", from Colonel Singleton, which he did.

Those who raised racehorses usually relied upon their slaves as riders, groomsmen and even trainers. Richard Singleton imported horses and trainers from England, but Cornelius, one of his slaves, trained racehorses for the Colonel for thirty-five years and was singled out for recognition in the *History of the Turf in South Carolina*.[39] His skill was so esteemed that Wade Hampton II wrote a letter to Colonel Singleton asking to borrow Cornelius to help with training his own race horses.

Colonel Singleton not only purchased horses in the U.S., but also imported English blooded racing stock from the Prince of Wales yearling sales and the King of England's stud. The South Carolina Jockey Club history noted that, "In 1836 Col. Singleton bought, at a sale of yearlings at the King of England's stud, a brown filly…rather small for her age, but neatly formed, with very fine shoulder..." [40]

The Jockey Club history mentioned another of the Colonel's horse buys,

> …in 1834, Col. Singleton imported, in the ship Dalhousie Castle from Liverpool, bound direct to Charleston, a bay horse named Non Plus…He kept him for a while, but not meeting his expectations in the stud, he offered him for sale at the Columbia Race.

Col. Butler, another horse racer and breeder, commented at the time, "As far as Non Plus had proved of any use to Col. Singleton, his proper name should be Sur-Plus!" [41]

The editor of the *American Turf Register and Sporting Magazine* declared that the Singleton stud had bred "more High Mettled [ardent, full of fire, spirited] Racers than almost any other in the Union." [42]

History of the Turf in South Carolina stated that, "At one time the produce of Col. Singleton's stud were accustomed to bring the best prices and were sought after with avidity by all, who are either engaged upon the turf, or were anxious to make their debut with some credit on it". [43] The author went on to say that, "As a breeder Col. Singleton was, at one point of his career, unequaled." From his old stock were descended some of the best horses of their day. However, "from some cause or another, adhering too long, perhaps, to one particular strain, he was rendered almost 'hors de combat' [out of the fight] for many campaigns" after his great success in 1827.[44]

In later years *American Turf Register and Sporting Magazine* also noted a decline in the quality of Colonel Singleton's stud, ascribing it to "the cares and constant attention incident to the management of an immense estate." [45]

By the mid 1830's, Colonel Singleton raced less and less. For several years he did not enter a horse during Race Week. His eldest son, John Coles Singleton, entered a race in 1836 and Matthew Richard Singleton, his youngest son and builder of the Kensington, began racing there in 1843, but Colonel Singleton never regained the racing success that he had enjoyed in the 1820's, although he did return to racing on a more regular basis during the last decade of his life.

The *History of the Turf in South Carolina* noted that, "In point of judgment and tact in managing a race, Col. Singleton was undoubtedly equal to any man in the world", but it was "often lamented" that he was "so characteristically cautious in entering and making engagements for his horses." [46]

Chapter 39-The South Carolina Jockey Club

Horse racing in South Carolina was synonymous with the South Carolina Jockey Club. The Club officially began in 1758 in Charleston, although there are claims that it began meeting as early as 1734, and if so, it is the earliest jockey club on record in the United States. The year 1792 also marked the movement of the Charleston racing site from New Market to the new track, the

Washington Race Course. It featured the finest horse racing in the South, and by most standards of the time, was considered the best in the country.

During its antebellum heyday, the Jockey Club was an exclusive gentlemen's club. It consisted mostly of rich lowland rice planters and upland cotton planters, the Singletons and the Hamptons being among the best known and most prominent members of that group. The club oversaw racing in South Carolina until the Civil War, when racing was suspended.

Washington Race Course Grandstand

In the 1830's and 1840's, improvements were made to the Washington Race Course. In 1836 a new grandstand, designed by the noted architect Charles F. Reichardt, was erected along with other buildings with special provisions for the ladies. The club also provided a citizens' viewing stand gratis.[47]

During this time, a seven foot high fence was built around the entire race course to restrict the view to those who had paid admission.[48] However, The Jockey Club history noted that,

> Respectable strangers from abroad or from other states are never allowed to pay admission...On their arrival they are immediately considered guests, and provided with tickets and a ribbon, which frank them everywhere, entitling them to the hospitalities of the Club during this whole meeting.[49]

In 1845, the South Carolina Jockey Club instituted racing colors.

> Every person entering a horse for any race over the Washington course, shall have previously registered on the books of the Secretary, the colors his jockey is to wear. When once recorded the right to that color to be perpetual, and no other person is to use the same. The following gentlemen have designated and claimed the colors which are attached to their names below: [partial list follows]
>
> Richard Singleton – red jacket, black sleeves, black cap.
>
> Wade Hampton – blue jacket, red sleeves, blue cap.
>
> John Coles Singleton – fancy dress. [black and white ?][50]

(Richard Singleton had his bed sheets monogrammed in his racing colors-red and black.) [51]

Chapter 40-Race Week

Race Week was the annual series of horse races conducted by the South Carolina Jockey Club, held every February at the Washington Race Course. It was the highlight of the racing and social season in South Carolina from 1792 until the Civil War began. It was not just for the planter elite, but for all classes of society. Tyrone Power, great grandfather of the actor Tyrone Power, commented in his book, *Impressions of America*, that "...the race – meeting draws the whole State together; and, for a period of four or five weeks, few places, as I learned, can be more lively or more sociable." [52] During Race Week, the South Carolina Jockey Club hosted a dinner on Wednesday night and a ball on Friday nights for members and guests with the proper social connections. [53] Other social events were held in private homes and by the ultra exclusive St. Cecilia Society.

The races themselves generated tremendous excitement among the populace. A carnival-like atmosphere, like a State Fair, prevailed with a wide variety of amusements available for all tastes and interests. The entire area was caught up in the preparation and excitement of Race Week. Entrepreneurs rented nearby houses to convert to temporary use as hotels, restaurants and bars. Booths were set up adjacent to the course where liquor, gambling and other amusements were available.

According to the South Carolina Jockey Club history:

> The arrangements on the Course are such as to ensure good order and etiquette; refinement and high breeding characterizing those who prefer lingering about the Grand Stand, whilst those who wish to diversify the scene, and witness life in other phases, can seek it in other parts of the Course, at the booths, where ample preparations are always made, by the different proprietors of these restaurants, to minister, in every conceivable way, to the tastes and votaries of fun and frolic, and to those also who require, in a long day, to have their inner man regaled from time to time.[54]

Like any carnival there were oddity attractions like the "Learned Pig", who demonstrated his abilities, much to the wonder and amusement of the crowds. ("The learned pig was a pig taught to respond to commands in such a way that it appeared to be able to answer questions by picking up cards in its mouth. By choosing cards it answered arithmetical problems and spelled out words".[55] These trained pigs created a sensation in England and later in America. Some pigs like Toby (pictured next page) were claimed to have even greater powers.)

Another highlight was the militia demonstrations that took place for forty years during Race Week until the advent of the Civil War. On occasion, real estate was sold in public auction, as were slaves and horses. During most of the year the Race Course and nearby grounds were rarely used. Due to its isolated location, it provided a ready dueling ground and was utilized for that purpose many times over the years.

TOBY

SAPIENT PIG,

Greatest Curiosity of the present Day

THIS MOST EXTRAORDINARY CREATURE

Will Spell and Read, Cast Accounts,

PLAY AT CARDS;

Tell any Person what o'Clock it is to a Minute

BY THEIR OWN WATCH

ALSO

TELL THE AGE OF ANY ONE IN COMPANY;

And what is more Astonishing he will

Discover a Person's Thoughts,

A Thing never heard of before

To be exhibited by an Account of the SWINE RACE.

The Performance of this truly SURPRISING CREATURE

must be seen to be believed.

He is now Exhibiting EVERY DAY, at the

Royal Promenade Rooms, Spring Gardens,

Where he may be seen precisely at the Hours of 1, 2, 3, & 4

ADMITTANCE ONE SHILLING.

Toby, a famous English Learned Pig

The Horse Races

Horse Racing is what brought everyone together. The official racing card was conducted on Wednesday, Thursday, and Friday. Other races in addition to the regular race calendar (usually match races between two competitors going head to head) took place during the week on Monday, Tuesday and Saturday or separately on the regular racing days.

Unlike modern track racing where one race determines the winner, antebellum racing was run in a series of heats of two, three or four miles in length, with the number of heats varying according to the specifications of each race. Heats were run by the same horse and

70

jockey, in an arduous test of both horse and rider. Horses sometimes broke down after running a heat and could not continue, leading to a forfeit. A strict time limit, usually of twenty to thirty minutes between heats, added to the tension. It might take as many as four heats until the clear winner could be established. Besides pride, purse money was at stake and side betting was always present. The races were run on the Washington Race Course's one mile oval track with thousands of spectators trackside.

Chapter 41-The Singleton Children

The Colonel's five children, John Coles, Videau Marion, Sarah Angelica, Richard and Matthew, grew up living a life of wealth, privilege and ease. The children all received educations to prepare them for their futures.

Eldest son, John Coles, after being privately tutored at Home Place, was sent to a boarding school in Hyde Park, New York.[56] His grandmother Mrs. (Captain) John Singleton and his aunt, Mary Martha McRae, had bought a home there in 1825, so nearby family support was available. Another source says that John Coles and Matthew Richard were sent off to school in New Jersey.[57]

Sending the boys to boarding schools up North was common practice in the area. Not everyone thought this Northern education was a good idea. A Singleton cousin, Mrs. William Campbell Preston, wife of Senator Preston, wrote in her diary,

> Young Mr. Singleton [probably refers to Matthew] is here on his way to Princeton, preparatory, he says, to going to the Virginia University. I doubt though, if he ever gets to the South College. Most of our Stateburg and Camden gentry have a proclivity to the North. Perhaps Mr. McDuffie [Matthew's Uncle] may right him, however.[58]

The sisters, Videau Marion (1815-1867) and Sarah Angelica (1816-1877), were born a year apart, almost to the day. Marion and Angelica were given similar educations and advantages, but their lives would be very different. After receiving instruction from private tutors, they both attended the Columbia Female Academy. Following in the footsteps of their half-sister, Mary Rebecca Singleton, both attended Madame Grelaud's Seminary for Young Ladies, a boarding school in Philadelphia.

Madame Grelaud's operated from circa 1808-1849. It was a fashionable, exclusive and expensive boarding school for young ladies of the elite. Noteworthy attendees in the year 1836 were Varina Banks Howell, known to history as Mrs. Jefferson Davis, and three great-granddaughters of Martha Custis Washington, wife of George Washington.

The cost for one year at Madame Grelaud's boarding school was $500. The young ladies studied science, grammar, literature, history, French, art, music and deportment; and were also offered multiple opportunities to attend dances and social activities in the community.

After a hint of scandal at the school in 1830, involving one of the students, the local community in South Carolina was aghast, but Marion was able to convince her parents to allow the sisters to continue to attend the school. In doing so, Marion demonstrated a quality of strong determination and self will, even at the age of sixteen. Those qualities would be sorely tested in future years. After agreeing to allow the girls to return to the school, their mother warned the sisters in a letter that Madame Grelaud would be instructed "to trust you as little as possible from under her eye." Also, however, their mother sent each daughter $30 for jewelry and $20 for "pocket money".[59]

(At this time the average unskilled farm worker or production worker in the U.S. earnied about $65 a year.)

The school year at Madame Grelaud's began October 1 and went through August 31. The girls had the month of September for vacation. When Madame Grelaud's school year was over, Marion and Angelica spent the remaining summer season with the rest of the family at White Sulphur Springs.

Chapter 42-Marion's Romance

Robert Deveaux (1812-1843), a college student from Thomas Jefferson's University (The University of Virginia), was a descendant of Francis Marion, the "Swamp Fox", and a distant cousin of Marion Singleton's. They renewed their acquaintance in the summer season of 1831 at White Sulphur Springs. Robert and Marion saw a lot of each other as Robert "attached" himself to the Singleton family for the rest of the summer season. At the end of the season both Marion and Robert expressed a desire to see each other the following spring in Charleston, presumably for Race Week. Smitten Robert wrote in his diary, on Marion's departure from White Sulphur Springs, "Farewell, M--, may heaven prosper you wherever you roam, and may your voyage through life be as fortunate and favorable as your own estimable qualities entitle you to deserve." [60]

Videau Marion Singleton Deveaux

Upon meeting the following spring in Charleston, they found that their attraction continued. However, Marion wrote to Angelica a year later: "So far we have had a houseful of agreeable company— and at one time I could muster nine beaux all staying in the house at the same time." [61]

Whatever the other flirtations may have been, Robert and Marion moved quickly to receive the blessing of Marion's parents for marriage. Colonel and Mrs. Singleton expressed misgivings about her marrying Robert and living so far (sixty miles) from family among people she did not know at the Belle Isle plantation, Robert's ancestral home. Her parents relented upon Marion's insistence. (General Francis Marion is buried on what was the grounds of Belle Isle Plantation, in Pineville, South Carolina.)

Marion and Robert were married in the spring of 1835 at Home Place by the Reverend Augustus Converse, rector of what would become the Church of the Holy Cross in Stateburg. He would later officiate at the marriage of Angelica and later still would become Marion's second husband.

Robert Deveaux's family was well to do and from the same social stratum as Marion. The marriage appears to have been a happy one, producing five children: two daughters and three sons. Sadly, none of their sons lived past twelve years of age. Both daughters married well.[62]

During the early years of their marriage, it is said, the Deveauxs traveled extensively during the summers, as far as Quebec, Canada. Marion and the children spent much of the winter at Home Place with her parents, while Robert stayed at Belle Isle, in Pineville, overseeing its operation. It was a painful separation and one that Marion's parents had warned her about before the marriage.

Chapter 43-The Ruins

In 1837 or 1838, Colonel Richard Singleton purchased a small plantation of 400 acres for his daughter, Marion and her husband, Robert Deveaux. (Others believe that it was Robert Deveaux who made the purchase.) The plantation, later to be named The Ruins, was located in Stateburg about seven miles north of Home Place.

It is believed The Ruins property was first acquired by General Thomas Sumter in 1783. He was a hero of the Revolutionary War and said to be the owner of more than 300,000 acres at one time. The Ruins property passed to the Mayrant family. John Mayrant had been midshipman to John Paul Jones, (of "I have not yet begun to fight" fame). He was on board the United States warship, the Bon Homme Richard, in the Revolutionary War, in the famous naval battle with the British warship, Serapis. John Mayrant was said to be the first over the side to board the Serapis during the engagement. He was immediately promoted to lieutenant for his gallantry and leadership.

The Ruins property passed through several more owner's hands and various uses until the Deveauxs took possession. It was said to be in a fairly dilapidated state by that time. Marion and Robert began to refer to it as The Ruins and so it has remained until the present day. It is thought that the couple stayed at Home Place and frequently journeyed to their new home while it was being renovated. Once finished the young couple summered at The Ruins.

A heart-shaped drive led up to the house of 9,000 square feet. The grounds of the home were adorned with magnificent flower gardens as well as abundant fruits: grapes, peaches and figs. A neighbor, Natalie Delage Sumter, the widow of Thomas Sumter, son of General Thomas Sumter, was renowned for her beautiful garden. She recorded in her diary bringing a "load of rose cuttings" to Marion for her garden.(Natalie Delage Sumter was born in the Palace of Versailles, a member of French nobility, the godchild of King Louis XVI and Marie Antoinette. She lived her life on three continents and ended up in Stateburg, South Carolina.)

The Ruins

The Ruins became a showplace and boasted a lively social life. Elizabeth Allen (Sinkler) Coxe wrote about the lifestyle that existed at The Ruins at the time of the Civil War:

> We always enjoy our visits to the Deveaux in Stateburgh (sic) on the 'High Hills of the Santee,' as it was picturesquely called. Their place was one of the most beautiful and luxurious that I knew in the South, and during the war they had a good many of their Virginia relations, the Coles, etc., staying with them for months at a time.
>
> Not only house and garden and grounds were so lovely, but the mode of life was, it seemed to me, quite like a great French château. Trays of coffee and fruit were brought up to the rooms in the morning by deft, well-trained servants and for those who wandered downstairs early there were in the broad overshadowed back piazza, large fanners of splendid peaches and beautiful figs.
>
> One morning I remember a maid bringing to the room where I slept with two other girls, such a large bunch of hothouse grapes that she hung it on a hook behind the door for us to

eat at intervals. Breakfast was at twelve o'clock and a delightful *mean* [meal) with many varieties of Virginia hot breads. So many people stayed at the 'Ruins' at the summer house parties that I have a confused remembrance of thrilling flirtations, bitter jealousies, intrigues, a duel and sudden girlish friendships that were almost as warm as the love affairs. One never forgets the scent of certain flowers on certain moonlit nights.[63]

Chapter 44-John Coles (1813-1852)

Eldest son John Coles graduated from the University of Virginia in 1832 at the same time as older sister Marion was being courted. The *Genealogy of the Singletons* describes him as a man of powerful build with a quick and impulsive temper, but with a gentle, tender nature, full of hospitality.

A family story says that shortly after John Coles returned home from college, his father found him sitting and reading. Richard Singleton wanted to know why he wasn't working. His answer was that he had nothing to do. His father told him that if he didn't have anything else to do, he should direct the slaves at work. John Coles took offense and declared that that was the work of overseers. One word led to another and John Coles picked up his hat, walked to Columbia a distance of forty miles, found a plantation about twelve miles southeast of Columbia and with the signatory backing of two of his father's closest friends, Wade Hampton II and B.F. Taylor, purchased it. On seeing his son's determination, Colonel Singleton paid for the property.[64]

Chapter 45-The Marriage of John Coles

Like his father before him, John Coles went to Albemarle, Virginia to find a wife. This was also the location of the University of Virginia, where he had graduated. He married Mary "Bonnie" Lewis Carter (1817-1899) in 1836. Her family tree and connections were impressive. She was related to George

Washington, Thomas Jefferson, Meriwether Lewis of "Lewis and Clark" fame, Light Horse Harry Lee, Robert E. Lee, and present day Queen Elizabeth II of England.[65]

John Coles brought a great deal to the marriage as well. He was the eldest son and in first position of inheritance of one of the richest men in South Carolina. He owned Raiford's Creek plantation, which he had acquired after the argument with his father. He also bought a 4,000 acre plantation near Columbia, adjacent to Wade Hampton II's Millwood plantation. It was named Albemarle, perhaps in honor of Bonnie's home county, or John Coles's mother, or a little bit of both. John Coles and Bonnie would make their home at Albemarle and have eight children: three sons and five daughters.[66]

Bonnie was a powerful force, like so many of the Singleton women. Blue laws were being enforced in Columbia by the middle of the nineteenth century, although they had been on the books much longer. In May of 1860, a new German brewery had just opened and Bonnie and her two daughters, Decca and Mary, drove up in a carriage and purchased six bottles of beer, flying in the face of convention. Oscar Lieber (geologist, metallurgist, translator and author) observed, "I think that shows a most praiseworthy boldness, for I scarcely know another lady in Columbia who would have done the same". [67]

Bonnie was a close friend of Mary Boykin Chesnut, famed Civil War diarist, who would later write movingly in her *Diary From Dixie* about family tragedies that would befall Bonnie.

Chapter 46-The Twins

In 1833, according to another family story, part of the Singleton family, including the twin boys, Richard and Matthew, both fifteen years old at the time, were journeying north to White Sulphur Springs. The family stopped for the night at the home of a Mr. Thayler. Matthew was sent on ahead to arrange for the next night's lodging. Both boys were taken ill. Richard died of what was described in the language of the times as a congestive chill (probably malaria). Matthew recovered. Richard was buried in a coffin made by the home carpenter, in the garden at the Thayler's place the next day.

Colonel Singleton planned on having his son's body returned to South Carolina to a final resting place the following winter. In order to insure that the body would not be tampered with and that no mistake would be made that this was the body of his son, Colonel Singleton placed his gold watch in the casket with his son. That way, when Richard's remains were returned to South Carolina and the coffin opened, the family would know for certain that it was Richard and that his remains had not been disturbed or substituted.

After the family returned home to South Carolina in the fall, a wagon was sent to bring Richard's body back to Home Place. When the casket was opened, the gold watch was still there, but what was most surprising was that Richard's body did not appear to have deteriorated. It was well preserved, almost lifelike. Colonel Singleton had his son's body placed in one of the front rooms, the drawing room, the normal place to receive visitors, and he refused to bury him. It became a local scandal. This went on for some time, despite the increasingly desperate pleas of his wife to proceed with the burial.

Finally, she contacted Wade Hampton II and Benjamin Franklin Taylor to convince their friend that it must be done. He finally agreed. Richard was laid to rest in the Singleton Family Cemetery.[68] Afterwards, Matthew adopted his twin's Christian name for his middle name and was from then on was known as Matthew Richard. For the rest of his life he signed his name M.R. Singleton.

Chapter 47-Keeping Up with the Hendersons

The mid-1830's were prosperous times for Southern planters of sugar and cotton with prices booming. Stephen Henderson, a proud possessor of Louisiana sugar money, built a two-story cottage, the present day "President's Cottage Museum," in 1835. It offered a grand view overlooking the entire White Sulphur Springs resort including the Singleton cottage.[69] Up until that time dwellings were modest. It was the opening salvo of "keeping up with the Joneses," in this case, the Hendersons.

President's Cottage Museum

South Carolinians and close friends, Colonel Wade Hampton II and Colonel Richard Singleton, answered the challenge, in 1837. They erected three adjacent *cottages* on a high hill with a commanding view overlooking the resort, including Henderson's cottage. There was one for each family and the third one was designated as a guest house. The new style of architecture, Greek revival, which today we recognize as the classic Southern plantation style house, was used. All three cottages, side by side, two stories high, each with six soaring columns with eighteen pillars in all in one long row produced an effect, capturing "some of the grandeur that was Greece, some of the splendor that was Rome" gushed twenty-one year old Angelica, Colonel Singleton's daughter. "We are to have our kitchens and stables there and live like princes." [70] The complex became known as the Colonnade.

With private kitchens and their own cooks brought from their home plantations, the Singletons and Hamptons entertained in a grand manner. (One of the three Colonnade cottages, Colonel Singleton's, survives to this day at the Greenbrier resort. It is now known as the Colonnade Estate House, and is available for use and able to accommodate up to 100 people.)

Colonnade Cottage

Chapter 48-Angelica meets Abraham Van Buren

In the spring of 1838, Angelica was in Washington, D.C. for the social season, staying with Senator and Mrs. William Campbell Preston, distant cousins, who chaperoned her social activities. It appears that her sister, Marion, accompanied her, although she was married by this time.[71]

Angelica was introduced into the Washington social scene by her mother's second cousin, Dolley Madison. She was the recently widowed wife of President James Madison and had served as hostess of the White House for her husband. (The term First Lady was not used at that time. It was introduced during the Buchanan administration in 1857, when Harriet Lane, niece of the President served in that capacity or was applied to Mary Lincoln, by an Englishman, depending on which source one believes.)

At one time Dolley Madison had been the grand dame of the Washington social scene and was still such a force that President Van Buren had tried to convince her to be the hostess in his bachelor White House. She had recently returned to the social scene and was ensconced in a house across the street from the White House

Angelica Singleton

Angelica's gracious manners, beautiful corkscrew curls, framing a perfect oval face, made her an instant hit on the Washington social scene. She was described as having "a long and lovely neck."

Angelica and Marion were introduced to President Martin Van Buren and two of his sons, Abraham and Martin Jr., at a White House dinner that was arranged by Dolley Madison. The two young men were described by Marion in a letter to her mother as "pleasant, unpretentious, unpretending, civil, amiable young men."[72] At the time, however, Angelica was enamored with a young Englishman by the name of Vivian who served on the staff of Lord Gosford, an English diplomat. Angelica described him as "the most charming, fascinating, courteous young man I have ever met." [73]

Chapter 49-The Van Buren Summer

President Van Buren and his family spent the summer of 1838 at White Sulphur Springs. They stayed in the newly completed guest cottage in the Colonnades, with the Singletons on one side and the Hamptons on the other. That summer season at the Springs was known thereafter as the "The Van Buren Summer." The Singletons had brought five slaves and six of their best horses with them from South Carolina. They entertained lavishly in their cottage, utilizing new furniture bought from the finest Philadelphia furniture makers. The dining room table seated twenty-four. Endless teas, luncheons, dinners and other entertainments were administered by the Singletons in the most gracious Southern manner of hospitality. Angelica's wardrobe included the latest and finest. By the end of the summer season, Vivian was forgotten and Angelica was engaged to Abraham, President Martin Van Buren's eldest son.

When Angelica met the sandy haired Abraham Van Buren, ten years her senior, he was his father's private secretary. Prior to that, he had been a career military man and West Point graduate. He had served as a Captain of the Dragoons and was a veteran Indian fighter on the frontier and in the Seminole War. Entering West Point at fifteen, his classmates had included Jefferson Davis and future Confederate Generals Albert Sydney Johnston, Leonidas Polk, Joseph E. Johnston and Robert E. Lee. (Several years after his father left office, Abraham Van Buren returned to the military and served with distinction in the Mexican War where he was brevetted a lieutenant Colonel for his gallant and meritorious conduct. He retired from the army in 1854 and spent his remaining years editing and publishing his father's presidential papers.)

Chapter 50-Trouble During the Van Buren Summer

The Van Buren Summer was also the scene of another event that would impact the Singletons and their future. Gamblers always had their place at the Springs. They rented cottages where Faro could be played. (Faro is a card game, with fast action, simple to learn rules and better odds on winning than in many games of chance.)

The games ran far into the night after the rest of the resort was in bed asleep.

Percy Reniers, in his book, *The Springs of Virginia*, described the scene:

> The rooms were low-ceilinged and hot, thick with segar smoke and the smell of horsey men and oil lamps and the strong cutting odor of whiskey and cognac brandy. At one side of the room with the table with the drinks, a Negro in attendance filling the gentlemen's glasses. A large table in the center would be the 'bank' with the faro layout spread over it and the keeper moving about it, making change, selling counters to the players, standing watch over the game. The dealer, always a man of resplendent though not notably clean garments, sat in the middle of the table's long side, in front of the layout, sliding the cards from Capt. Bailey's patent box and calling the play.

> ... the gentlemen of the South wagered everything from hard crop money to the horses and Negro servants they had brought with them to the Springs. Others might cry out against Calwell [the owner of the Springs] for permitting this 'blot on the fair face' of the establishment, but they, never. This is what they came for.

> ...One Midsummer night in the Van Buren season there were two men in that low, odorous gaming room who were to make some trouble for themselves, for their friends and for two gentlemen of consequence in the Colonnades.

One young man was J W (John White) Stevenson. He was the son of Andrew Stevenson, the well-liked Minister to England, and nephew of Mrs. Richard Singleton. His antigambling resolution melted away this night and he was losing. The older man involved was Powell McRae, nephew of Colonel Richard Singleton, who had a reputation as a drinker and gambler and was seen as erratic as was his mother Mary Martha (Singleton) McRae, Colonel Singleton's sister. Powell McRae was not playing but was observing the play.

The next morning word spread rapidly that on the previous night that JW Stevenson had been accused of cheating by Powell

McRae, although he said he had not witnessed it but he was speaking for a friend. Stevenson left on an early-morning stage for Lexington, Kentucky, decrying the slander. News of the incident was quickly carried to Colonels Hampton and Singleton, who were the unquestioned leaders and arbiters in such matters.

Stevenson wrote to Colonel Singleton pleading his innocence, declaring he had not cheated and demanding to know who his accuser really was. For Colonel Singleton, this was an extremely delicate manner pitting his own nephew against his wife's nephew, to say nothing of the potential lethality involved. Duels were fought over much less.

Colonel Singleton finally resolved to write a letter to Powell McRae in New York. He wrote that Stevenson had been publicly proclaimed to be innocent by his friends and if sustained, he said, "you [Powell] will stand charged with an unfounded slander..." He told Powell to come to the Springs and "...fight or admit your error." This was a debt of honor. However, the letter was never sent and the duel was never fought. Powell McRae Jr, is said to have been banned for life from the resort by Colonel Singleton for falsely accusing a guest of cheating.

Several years later, Colonel Singleton was called to an insane asylum in Massachusetts to see his nephew, Powell McRae, who was being held in solitary confinement there. This went a long way in explaining Powell McRae's previous behavior.[74] The accused, John White Stevenson, was absolved of any wrong doing in the court of public opinion and later went on to become a Congressman, Senator, Lieutenant Governor and Governor of Kentucky. Powell McRae Jr. spent the rest of his life in an insane asylum, dying in 1844.

Revenge

Years later, the daughter of Powell McRae Jr., Mary Singleton McRae Livingston, married to one of the richest men in New York, brought suit against the estate of Colonel Richard Singleton concerning a debt incurred years before. Settlement of this lawsuit caused Colonel Singleton's grandson and heir to sell Home Place to cover that debt.

Chapter 51-Matthew (1817-1854) Graduates

During the Van Buren summer of 1838, Matthew Richard Singleton, builder of the Kensington, graduated from South Carolina College (now the University of South Carolina). It is believed Matthew Richard spent his first two years at the University of Virginia and transferred to South Carolina College to finish his degree. Because of a housing shortage he stayed with his brother, John Coles, and his newlywed wife, Bonnie, at their home near Columbia.[75] While at the College, Matthew studied Greek and Latin, as well as mathematics and algebra.[76] He is generally acknowledged as the most intellectual of his siblings.

Upon graduation, Matthew served on the staff of his cousin, Governor John Peter Richardson, and was commissioned a lieutenant-colonel in the South Carolina militia. The following spring in 1839, Matthew was also appointed military attaché to the American mission or legation in London. Andrew Stephenson, his uncle by marriage, was minister (ambassador) to England at that time. For Matthew's trip to England, his father, had smoothed the way with letters of introduction as well as having his business agent in Liverpool put one hundred bales of cotton on Matthew's account for any financial needs that might arise.[77] (The value of 100 bales of cotton at that time was $1,800)

PART FIVE

ANGELICA TAKES CENTER STAGE

Chapter 52-The Van Buren Wedding

After a whirlwind courtship during the Van Buren Summer, Angelica married Abraham Van Buren, November 27, 1838, in a lavish wedding at Home Place. President Van Buren, was pleased to have a delightful female presence to grace what had been a widower's all male household. Angelica would bring her beauty and charm to her role as hostess of the White House. Angelica displayed an even, sweet tempered disposition that the President also found appealing. Colonel Singleton saw his daughter married to the son of the President of the United States, ensconced in the White House to a husband who seemed to have bright prospects. It must have been a moment of great satisfaction for them both. Officiating at the wedding was the Reverend Augustus Converse, rector of the Episcopal Church of Claremont. He had also officiated at the wedding of her sister, Marion. The Reverend Converse would also play a major future role in the Singleton family story.

There are contradictory stories as to who attended the wedding. A family source says that the President attended and served as best man to his son.[1] Other sources say that the entire cabinet attended, along with Senators, Congressmen and other notables and that the President stayed on for weeks. Other versions say the President did not attend. Given the social position and power of the individuals involved, it stands to reason, that all who could attend would have done so.

Chapter 53-Angelica's New Year's Eve Triumph

Soon after the wedding the couple returned to the White House where Angelica quickly assumed the duties of hostess. Given her background, as a daughter of a wealthy Southern aristocrat, skilled in the social graces, refined and used to interacting with high society and the wealthy elite, Angelica seemed ideally suited for the job.

Angelica's first appearance as White House hostess was at the New Years reception, barely six weeks after her marriage. It was an auspicious beginning. After encountering Angelica in the receiving line, a reporter for the Boston Post commented on her performance,

> A lady of rare accomplishments, very modest, yet perfectly easy and graceful in her manners, and free and vivacious in her conversation. She was universally admired and is said to have borne the fatigue of a three-hour levee [reception] with the patience and pleasantry which must be inexhaustible to last one through so severe a trial.[2]

Another account described Angelica as regal as a queen. Angelica was the toast of Washington—a beautiful, charming young woman full of grace and manners, at the peak of her popularity in the social scene. She was stunningly beautiful and elegant, bringing the "magnolia scent of Southern hospitality "to the White House.[3]

A few months later, in March of 1839, still a young woman of twenty-two, Angelica turned to her cousin, Dolley Madison, the quintessential White House hostess, for advice. She dashed off a note to her saying, "I am very anxious to consult with you for a few minutes on a very important matter." At that time Angelica was following the model and protocols of her cousin Dolley. That would change.

Chapter 54-Angelica's European Honeymoon

Angelica and Abraham Van Buren did not linger long at the White House, both being eager for a European honeymoon. It is said that Colonel Singleton had given Abraham Van Buren a wedding gift of $3,000 for that purpose. After completing her spring appearances at the White House, including a White House reception for 3,000, Angelica and Abraham sailed for Europe. (A trip to Europe at that time, either by sail or steam power, was a daunting three to six weeks journey, crossing an often storm tossed North Atlantic. Ships were often lost at sea, but they made the crossing successfully and relatively trouble-free. Angelica thus became the first "first lady" to travel abroad.)

Chapter 55-Almost Royalty

Angelica's younger brother, Matthew Richard, twenty-one years old at the time, was already in England serving as a military attaché to his uncle, Andrew Stevenson. Aunt Sallie, Andrew Stevenson's wife, was Angelica's mother's sister. Sallie Stevenson wrote many letters to her sisters and brother in the States during this time. In the letters she commented extensively about Angelica, as well as Matthew. She also gave her opinions of President Van Buren and several of his sons.

Andrew Stevenson   **Sallie Stevenson**

(The following letter excerpts provide the most extensive personal observations that I encountered about Angelica and Matthew Richard. How many of them were seen by Angelica's mother is unknown. The letters have not been altered. They are rendered here in Sallie Stevenson's distinctive grammar, capitalization and punctuation.)

Regarding Angelica's arrival—An entry from May 15, 1839:

> Well, my precious sisters, my beloved A [Angelica] has arrived, I seen her, embraced her, & shed tears of joy over her. But ah ! how different is her feeling from mine. She just from the bosom of her family the pet of all, comes here to bestow upon me a calm kiss of kindred kindness. It is very natural it should be so and I ought to have known that she could not feel as I do, who have been pining in absence from all I have most loved for three years besides, my heart has always been my torment...[4]

Regarding the Van Burens—In another letter from May of 1839 to her sisters, she gives her opinions of Angelica's new husband, Abraham, his brother and father.:

> The Major [Abraham] seems very amiable and we like him very much—he is very different from Prince John [Abraham's brother], who resembles his Father [President Van Buren] in using his fellow men as a ladder upon which to mount & when he is up, kicks it down, & without any scruples of conscience denies he has had any aid.[5]

Regarding Matthew Richard—From the same letter:

> ...& now a word of Mat—It was I fear in an evil hour when his parents thought of sending him to Europe, & he is like a wild-man he dined with us with his sister, but when we asked him again on the Saturday after he neither came nor sent an apology & yesterday he was invited to dine at the Bates with his sister &c [company], but no Mat nor no apology.[6]

While in England, Matthew Richard visited Oxford University's Bodleian Library and was impressed by its massive collection of volumes and many works of art.[7] Matthew did other sight-seeing in England and it is believed he also travelled to the European continent during this time. He was quite taken with French culture, style and architecture. When it came time to build his dream home, the Kensington, he would incorporate many of the architectural features that he had seen in France.

The Royal Courts

Sallie Stevenson devoted much time, energy and money in preparing Angelica for her introduction into London society that included the English Royals and the future Czar of all the Russias, Crown Prince Alexander. The Crown Prince was visiting in England at the time and was referred to as the Grand Duke.

Aunt Sallie wrote:

> Angelica's dress will be blue watered silk trimmed with blond & silver, the under dress white satin & blond over it trimmed to correspond—mine green velvet train—with satin & lace dress a present from manufacturers of Nottingham with a trimming of gold & green leaves for which I have to pay some 3 or 4 pounds. Heigho! Well it cant be helped - & must be endured. I have tried to do it as economically as possible but there are no short cuts here, the 'Ambassador's lady must be well dressed' everybody says—but then I say, I am a poor ministers wife—still all the others are so gorgeously dressed, especially at the Birthday D Room. Angelica & myself get on very well since our talk on the etiquette of England & America. She has too much good sense, and right feeling not to feel and act as she ought upon the subject.[8]

The Stevensons arranged to have the Van Burens formally presented to Queen Victoria.

Sallie Stevenson writes:

> On Thursday, we attended the drawing-room. Angelica looked very well—sweet, pretty, and lady-like. The Queen received her very graciously, asked her the usual questions—How long she meant to stay? and inquired after the President. The drawing-room, being the first day was crowded, at least 2000 persons, & no one presented but Mrs. Van Buren & a lady attached to the corps diplomatique. Angelica was delighted, and dazzled by the blaze of diamonds.[9]

Queen Victoria was reported as being noticeably pleased with Angelica. The Van Burens were treated as a kind of American royalty.

It is said that Angelica observed that Queen Victoria was seated on a elevated platform (dais), surrounded by ladies in waiting to receive her guests. Each one was announced by a footman. The Queen and her royal retinue did not mingle and shake hands with their guests in the style Dolley Madison had made popular in the White House. The queen maintained the strict decorum dictated by social hierarchy and merely nodded at the guests as they were presented.

From accounts by Mrs. Stevenson, it appears that Angelica was much impressed by her proximity to the Queen, and the glamour that surrounded the English court. At the time of the visit, Queen Victoria was twenty years old, one season past her coronation and a contemporary of Angelica's, who was only twenty-three.

Young Queen Victoria

Mrs. Stevenson writes about accompanying Angelica to a grand party on the same Thursday as the drawing room presentation. "[I] took her on my arm through the splendid suite of rooms and presented her to everyone I knew that I thought it would profit her to know…"

She continued…

On Friday night, the Queens ball, which perfectly enchanted

Angelica. Mr. Stevenson left us before 11, & I should have been glad to have gone, too, but I stayed to introduce Angelica, until after supper, and got her, by a little management, into the court circle at the supper-table, where she saw the Queen take her strawberries, &c.[company], and the Grand Duke his champagne, & all the royal circle make their bows of recognition & courtesy to those who ventured to approach, or had the right to do so.[10]

Matthew Singleton was also part of this social scene and attended the Queen's State ball with the Stevensons, the Major, Angelica and Daniel Webster who was in England at the time.[11]

In another letter to her sisters and brother, Edward Coles, Mrs. Stevenson commented further on Matthew—her changing opinion of him, his health, and his relationship with Angelica.

Mat is still here acting as attaché and I hope it will be of service to him…I take special care that he shall not get his head turned as a certain young gentleman of our acquaintance [I believe she is referring to Prince John, Abraham Van Buren's brother]. Mr. Mat is I assure you a much more prudent and sensible youth than I had thought him, but for his bad health [my underline] which has prevented his making the best use of his time he would have been a very remarkable person with his present advantages. I treat him exactly as I would a son, and altho' his Mother has given me no authority—I exercise it as far as I think is for his good. I do not think he quite likes my adherence to the republican Princess [my underline] as he calls her [Angelica], & thinks me a very gullible person-but I had rather be deceived than not to trust, & to tell you the truth this is what I like least in my nephew—however—Time will show who is right—To me there is something so tender & so holy in the tie which binds brother and sister that I must confess I would wish to see them more blind to each others faults—to say the least of it—It is painful to me even to think of, therefore I feel unwilling to say more on paper.[12]

In a final comment on Matthew, three weeks later, in another letter to her brother, Edward Coles, Sallie Stevenson writes:

I have been persuading Mat to take a master on several branches of education, above all—a writing master to teach him a good and bold hand writing & secondly, to make him a good accountant for his Fathers sake —I give him books— religious & of a lighter character, that he may have light topics for the girls.[13] (This Letter was written on August 18, 1839 fifteen years to the day, before Matthew's death.)

After leaving England the Van Burens proceeded to the Continent stopping in The Hague, Netherlands and Brussels, Belgium for sightseeing, and then on to France. After their arrival in Paris, the Van Buren party was presented to King Louis Philippe and his wife. They were again being treated with great deference. While in Paris, the Van Burens were given a personal tour of the palace at St. Cloud by King Louis Phillippe himself.

In further comments on Angelica, Sallie Stevenson wrote to her brother Edward, referring to a previous letter from their sister, Betsy. She had written that Angelica had come to England "with the most extravagant expectations."

Mrs. Stevenson wrote:

I hope she [Angelica] became sensible of the unreasonableness of her expectations before she went away, but it is very difficult to awaken one from such a dream as hers, and woe unto the unfortunate being whose duty or necessity it may be to give the rousing shake…[14]

Sallie Stevenson was very concerned that her niece had her head turned by what she had experienced in the European royal courts.

Chapter 56-Back to America

Matthew and the Van Burens returned to America in the fall of 1839. Angelica resumed her duties as hostess of the White House. When Matthew returned to South Carolina, he was given direction of the Headquarters/Kensington Plantation by his father.

It appears that Angelica and her husband told President Van Buren that the Stevensons were living an extravagant lifestyle and criticized Andrew Stevenson's ambassadorship. Sallie Stevenson's sister, Betsy, wrote Sallie informing her of this. The Stevensons were deeply offended and hurt, especially after all their efforts to present Angelica to London society "with feelings almost of parental fondness."

Sallie Stevenson wrote a letter to her sisters, on Christmas Day, 1839, pouring out her feelings about what she saw as Angelica's betrayal.

> As to what you tell me of Angelica it does not surprise....Let us endeavor to remember always she is our Sister's daughter. I assure you I had to keep it in mind when she was here & often has it restrained me when I was about to offer a retort.

She goes on to say that in past letters to the family she had used great restraint in making Angelica "quite presentable to the whole family"...

> I endeavored to give you some light upon the subject altho there is so much I shall never communicate except verbally. I must, however, in justice to myself, say, I suffered with Job-like patience, injury for benefits insults for kindness annoyances of every kind & sort which could have been inflicted by ones greatest enemy...[15]

Chapter 57-Style and Controversy at the White House

Prior to Angelica's arrival at the bachelor-only White House, small gatherings with Senators and Congressmen were the preferred method of entertaining. The first formal open house at the White House in the Spring of 1838 before the arrival of Angelica had attracted a crowd of 5,000, but that was the exception. The small gatherings had been frugal affairs with little wine and liquor served.

Angelica was accustomed to a more lavish entertaining style as was President Martin Van Buren before he assumed the Presidency. Overseeing twenty or more servants, Angelica began planning and hosting elaborate state dinners and large receptions as well as the more-intimate smaller groupings that Van Buren enjoyed. Sumptuous European style dinners served with fine wines and liquors were in vogue at the White House.

Angelica is given credit for introducing the State Dinner into the White House where foreign dignitaries are feted. This is a model that she had observed in Europe, and remains a White House staple to this day.

After he became president, Van Buren became convinced that the White House needed refurbishment after eight hard years of use by the Jackson administration. This was probably warranted, given the already-legendary rough crowd of Westerners that Jackson's presidency had brought to Washington. Reputedly, 20,000 people had rampaged through the White House at an open house on Jackson's first inauguration day. President Jackson had to be lowered out through a window to escape the press of the crowd at three o'clock in the morning.

President Van Buren went to Congress for $27,000 for redecoration and furniture replacement He also repainted the White House. The funds were granted, but his timing was not the best. The country was in the throes of the Panic (economic recession or depression) of 1837. This would come back to haunt him in his reelection bid of 1840. In 1841, after Van Buren's defeat for re-election, during the new administration, Congress would pass an appropriation for the upkeep and refurbishing of the White House in the amount of $20,000, but that was too late to save Martin Van Buren from criticism for doing the same.

Angelica, much impressed with what she had seen in the courts of England and France, began to emulate the receiving and entertaining techniques she had witnessed and admired there. At the 1840 New Year's reception, Angelica positioned herself on a dais (a raised platform), set apart from the crowds and seated herself on a low bench, surrounded with female attendants dressed in white flowing gowns. This was done to form a tableau, a living picture grouping to create a striking scene. It did. To acknowledge her guests, Angelica nodded instead of shaking hands. She wore a headdress composed of white peacock feathers, of a style believed to be reserved for the royal family in England. Her headdress may have been meant to emulate the white turbans made famous by her cousin, Dolley Madison, but Angelica's entire presentation and manner was seen by many to be foreign, royal, undemocratic and pretentious. Criticism rained down on her.

It is believed that she did not continue the practice for long. Her style and comportment, full of charm and elegance were now seen by some as more like European royalty, an especially sharp contrast with the previous Andrew Jackson administration which conducted itself in a "rough and ready" frontier style, like Old Hickory himself. All of this in the midst of a time of economic hardship didn't help.

On the other hand, she did have her admirers. The French minister (ambassador), Adolphe Fourier de Bacourt, typically critical of Americans, remarked that Angelica would "pass for an amiable woman of graceful and distinguished manners and appearance" anywhere in the world.

Angelica brought gaiety to the White House with her youthful, feminine presence. Children's parties were held on the lawn of the White House. It is said that President Van Buren would flap his arms and strut like a turkey to the amusement of children and adults alike. Dinners and picnics were the order of the day. For many of the Washington ladies, the gracious female presence of Angelica was very welcome. Much to their delight, she hosted afternoon teas and fancy dress balls. They were curtailed after Angelica became pregnant with her first child and entered into seclusion as was the custom.

Chapter 58-Rebecca's Birth

Angelica's daughter, Rebecca, was born in March of 1840 and both mother and child were ill after the birth. Matthew travelled with his mother to visit Angelica at the White House in April. He commented that he found her to be "unusually cheerful" and much delighted by the arrival of her mother. A final note in the letter to his father about the trip says that the President expresses his regrets that Colonel Singleton should not have "honored him with his appearance." [16] Rebecca died in the fall of 1840. Angelica's sister, Marion Deveaux, also gave birth to a child, a son, Robert Marion, in March of 1840. He also died in infancy. The following year Marion would give birth to another son and also name him Robert Marion. He died tragically just days before his eleventh birthday.

Chapter 59-Angelica & the 1840 Presidential Campaign

The style that Angelica brought to the White House became not just a matter of gossip and criticism, but part of the politics of the times. Around the time of Matthews' visit to the White House, an opposition Whig Congressman, Charles Ogle, delivered a three day avalanche of personal invective and accusation in what became known as the "Gold Spoon" speech. In it, he lambasted Martin Van Buren for being a spendthrift, renovating the White House in a time of economic scarcity, living a monarchical lifestyle and being out of touch with the economic hardships of the time.

When he entered the White House, Van Buren had brought with him his own flatware, glass and china to maintain the style of living to which he was accustomed. He did use his personally owned gold spoons on his dinner table, providing ready ammunition for his political opponents. The speech clearly resonated with a populace eager for a way out of a economic depression and looking for a scapegoat.

From the Gold Spoon speech:

> Your [Abraham Van Buren's] house glitters with all imaginable luxuries and gaudy ornaments. Will they [the people] longer feel inclined to support their chief servant in a Palace as splendid as that of the Caesars, and as richly adorned as the proudest Asiatic mansion?

And:

Harrison [Van Buren's Presidential 1840 election opponent]

would scorn to charge the people of the United States with foreign cut wine coolers, liquor stands and golden chains to hang golden labels around necks of barrel-shaped flute decanters...[17]

Although not named specifically in Ogle's speech, Angelica was the perfect symbol of wealth and aristocracy. Ogle also accused her, by insinuation, of trying to get Congress to approve money for re-landscaping the White House grounds to rival those she had seen in the royal courts of Europe.

It is probably fair to say to that Angelica was a political liability in her father-in-law's 1840 re-election bid. To be seen as royal, elitist, and out of touch with the common man in hard times is not usually a good formula for election in a representative democracy.

The bitter Presidential Election Campaign of 1840 between William Henry Harrison and Martin Van Buren is seen by some historians as the first modern election campaign in its use of image making, campaign slogans, sound bites, and class warfare. Martin Van Buren was soundly defeated in his re-election bid. Some contemporaries, including John Quincy Adams, former President of the United States, were deeply concerned about what the tenor of the 1840 Presidential Campaign bode for the future of American democracy.

(For more on the 1840 Election Campaign, see Appendix.)

Chapter 60-After the White House

In *The Ladies of the White House*, Laura Holloway summed up her view of Angelica's time in the White House, "She was a cultivated, elegant-mannered person, considerate of others, sweet in disposition, and gracious in speech." [18] She was one of the youngest—graceful, aristocratic, flamboyant and well educated and arguably the most beautiful "first lady" to ever grace the White House. In 1842, George Inman painted her portrait. (See next page.) It still hangs in the Red Room of the White House. (For more on Angelica's portrait and jewels, see Appendix.)

Angelica Singleton Van Buren

After President Van Buren's reelection defeat, the family took up residence at Lindenwald, the Van Buren estate, in Kinderhook, New York. Angelica and Abraham were given the master bedroom.[19] Angelica and her husband and other members of the Van Buren family visited her family in South Carolina on a regular basis, often wintering there. In 1841, Angelica was again pregnant and her husband described her as looking "prosperous and ponderous." Their son, Singleton, was born at Home Place that year.

It is believed that in the following year, Martin Van Buren visited Colonel Singleton for several weeks at Home Place in order to attend the christening of his grandson, Singleton. He may have also visited The Ruins at this time. It was just up the hill. Two years later, Angelica gave birth to a little girl, Hannah Van Buren, named after President Martin Van Buren's deceased wife, but she died the same day. Angelica had three sons, but none married or lived past 40, maintaining an all-too-often Singleton family tradition of early adult male deaths.

PART SIX
TROUBLING TIMES

Chapter 61-Murder

The same year as Martin Van Buren's visit to Home Place, a murder occurred on one of the Singleton family plantations.

On July 23, 1842, the dead body of Daniel McCaskill, an overseer on the Big Lake plantation, a Singleton trust plantation, was found in the Congaree River. He had bruises on his chest and shoulder and his head was nearly severed. He had gone to Columbia on July 18, 1842 and was planning on returning to Big Lake Plantation, three miles south of Columbia, the next day. After an early breakfast the next day, he was last seen heading for the ferry to take him across the Congaree River to Big Lake. [1]

Suspicion fell almost immediately on the slave population at Big Lake, not unexpectedly. The tension that always existed between master and slave and the implicit threat posed by the overwhelming numbers of slaves vs. whites on plantations was a constant, if not often talked-about fear among the white population. An overseer's job in an absentee landlord situation like Big Lake was to manage the entire plantation. He had greater power and control than in a situation where the planter lived on site. This was the case at Big Lake. The overseer's job was to produce the greatest profit for the owner

The Singletons had a reputation for hiring hard overseers who believed in the practice of "overhauling": systematic violence to produce obedience. Jacob Stroyer, a slave born and raised at the Kensington, later wrote in his memoir, *My Life in the South*, about his personal experience with this practice. He also wrote specifically about the Big Lake plantation and how life there and on other absentee owner plantations was harder for the slaves. He wrote about the murder of an overseer at Big Lake and the summary execution of those thought guilty. He gives the names as Cyrus and Stepney. It may have been a different incident. He also mentions instances of the killing of slaves at Big Lake for disobedience.[2]

The person directly under the overseer in the power hierarchy was the black slave driver. (The phrase "don't be a slave driver" says it all.) He was given responsibility to produce maximum results. He had to walk a fine line while being a member of the underclass. Jacob Stroyer noted in his memoir that in his experience a driver could be as cruel or more so than the overseer.[3]

As word of the murder spread to the outlying community, thirty whites showed up at Big Lake demanding justice and accusing Plenty, the black driver, of McCaskill's murder.[4]

Colonel Richard Singleton, who ran Big Lake plantation as a family trust per his father's will, was at White Sulphur Springs at the time of the murder. As he so often did, the Colonel relied on his closest friends Benjamin Franklin Taylor and Wade Hampton, as well as relatives and overseers, to look after his interests when he was gone. Colonel Singleton did not believe Plenty had committed the murder, but it was not clear to anyone who had.

An investigation was conducted by Hampton and Taylor and several slaves were arrested and subsequently released.

Not having an overseer was a serious problem. A suitable replacement was sought, but not found. The 1842 cotton crop was especially good and harvest was beginning. In late August a flood threatened the crops as well and slave labor had to be used to deal with that situation instead of attending to the harvest. The importance of Plenty's leadership became more and more apparent.

In the midst of all this, new information was brought forth and four slaves: Bacchus, Paul, Daniel and Jacob were accused of the murder. On Tuesday, August 30th, a trial was convened at Big Lake Plantation. An actual judge, the Honorable Judge Earle, was brought in to preside. A key witness was Plenty's brother, Joe, who may have been involved, but was given immunity. He identified Bacchus and Paul as the murderers. He could not or would not identify Daniel and Jacob and they were acquitted. Bacchus and Paul were found guilty and sentenced to be hung in November.

After the trial, Colonel Singleton still had doubts about their guilt. Saying he had new evidence, he tried to get a new trial and even hired a lawyer to pursue it. William C. Preston, well respected former Senator from South Carolina and cousin by marriage, was the Colonel's advocate to argue for a new trial in front of Judge Earle. He argued that Paul and Bacchus had an alibi and that their accuser, Joe, had given falsified testimony.[5] It was to no avail. Judge Earle would not grant a new trial.[6]

Colonel Singleton finally gave up and accepted the inevitable. Bacchus and Paul were finally hung on March 3, 1843 in downtown Columbia at the southwest corner of Lincoln and Gervais, three blocks from the State Capitol Building on the main street, in a vacant lot to accommodate the crowds. An eyewitness, Julian Selby, ten years old at the time, said three were hung. "My first recollection of the terrible was the hanging of three Negroes, belonging to Col. John Singleton, for the murder of the overseer, McCaskill."[7]

Chapter 62-More Bad News

Colonel Singleton's sister, Mary Martha Singleton McRae, was committed to an insane asylum in Philadelphia in 1843. There she would receive the finest care available, but she would live out the rest of her life in that institution. Her son Powell McRae Jr. had been hospitalized in a Massachusetts insane asylum in 1840 and passed away in 1844, leaving a widow and two children. His widow, Julia May McRae, sought financial help from Colonel Singleton and was rebuffed. It's not clear why. (Julia May McRae later married Herman Oelrich, a wealthy and powerful man. In the 1870's Julia May McRae Oelrich, with her husband's backing, and Powell McRae, Jr.'s daughter, Mary Singleton McRae Livingston, would sue the estate and heirs of Colonel Richard Singleton forcing the sale of Home Place plantation to pay off the settlement.)

The Passing of Robert Deveaux

The year 1843 would also claim Robert Marion Deveaux. After eight years of marriage to Marion Singleton Deveaux, Robert died at age thirty. He left his wife a widow at twenty-eight, well provided for financially, but alone to raise four children. Marion and the children returned from Belle Isle to live at The Ruins full time. Rather than sending her children off to boarding schools, she hired a governess and raised them at home. Her friend, Gabriella Huger, wrote to her in 1844 saying, "What a comfort it must be to you to have your children educated under your own eyes, and to have them with you always..." [7]

Marion had family support in close proximity with her father and mother seven miles down the King's Highway and her brother, Matthew Richard, at the Kensington, some fifteen miles away. She was not without resources and support, but she had no husband.

PART SEVEN

MATTHEW AND MARTHA

Chapter 63-Enter Martha Rutledge Kinloch

Meanwhile, Marion's brother, Matthew Richard, builder of the Kensington, found his future wife, Martha Rutledge Kinloch. It appears likely that Matthew met her in Charleston at a St. Cecilia Society ball, South Carolina Jockey Club ball or another social event hosted in private homes held during Race Week. Matthew and Martha were both members of the same wealthy and exclusive social set.

The ultra exclusive St. Cecilia Society began in the mid-1700's as a subscription concert organization, but by the time Matthew and Martha met, it was a private social club for the elite. Though membership was all male, once a gentleman had secured a membership, all members of his household were granted access to all their social events. Martha's grandfather and ten of her relatives were members of the St. Cecilia society. Matthew Singleton was listed as a manager of the society on an 1845 invitation to one of their balls.[1]

From a New York Times article published on February 14, 1896:

> "There is perhaps no social organization in America that is so old or so exclusive as the St. Cecilia of Charleston S.C...The St. Cecilia is run entirely upon a pedigree basis, without regard to wealth or worldly goods, the only essential being that each member must in every sense be a gentleman, and not have his hands soiled by having been in 'trade.' The balls, all characterized by dignity, are informal and very delightful, for everybody knows everybody else. The proceedings are never given for publication." [2]

Martha Rutledge Kinloch was known to her close friends as Mattie and would even be listed as Mattie in the 1860 Census. Mattie was the only girl and eldest child of Frederick and Mary I'on Kinloch.

Mattie's family was well educated. Her paternal grandfather, Francis Kinloch Jr., was educated in Europe as was her father, Frederick Kinloch. Her grandfather served in the Continental Congress and South Carolina House of Representatives. He married Martha Rutledge, daughter of the Governor of South Carolina, and was a friend of George Washington.

On his return to the U.S. from his schooling in Europe, Mattie's father attended and graduated from Harvard. He spoke three foreign languages—French, Italian and Spanish and enjoyed the life of a scholar. However, he suffered severely from mental illness and Mattie and her mother had to take an active part in managing his affairs. This experience of business management at a young age would serve Mattie well in the coming years.

Education did not stop with the male side of the family. Mattie's maternal aunt, Harriet Lowndes Aiken, was well educated and was said to have spoken four languages. Mary I'on Lowndes Kinloch, Mattie's mother, would have most likely received the same type of education as her sister.[3]

Mattie herself was a highly educated woman, especially for her time. She was educated by private tutors and later she most likely attended an exclusive and expensive female academy which prepared members of her social class for a "good" marriage within the elite. She would have likely studied academic subjects such as history, rhetoric, literary classics, science and foreign languages, as well as the more practical arts like needlework. Instruction in the social graces and developing an appreciation of art, music and dancing would all be part of the preparation or *finishing* of a young woman in preparation for assuming her place in society.

Mary Hering Middleton, a friend of Mattie's, commented in a letter to her daughter that Mattie spoke Italian and wrote French very well.[4] Martha and Matthew both had an interest in French culture and the life of the intellect. Matthew has been referred to as the most intellectually inclined of the Singletons and that would have certainly been a match for Martha.

Matthew and Mattie were married February 28, 1844, the week

following Race Week in Charleston. Mattie's family lived mainly in the low country in the Charleston or Georgetown area. Matthew's family lived in the Midlands, in Sumter and Richland districts.

Their marriage was the joining of two powerful and influential families. Matthew was related by either blood or marriage to nine South Carolina governors, two governors of Virginia, an Illinois and a Kentucky governor, a Speaker of the House of Representatives and Ambassador to England, two Congressman, three Senators, a South Carolina Supreme Court Justice, and two "first ladies" of the White House.

Mattie was related by blood or marriage to two signers of the Declaration of Independence, four members of the Continental Congress, a Chief Justice of the United States Supreme Court, three ambassadors-one to Great Britain, one to Spain, one to Russia, four South Carolina governors, and four Congressmen. (Some of these individuals served in multiple offices. For more on Matthew and Mattie's relatives, see Appendix.)

Chapter 64-Life at the Kensington

The newlyweds moved onto the Headquarters Plantation which was under the direction of Matthew. It was a large cotton plantation of thousands of acres worked by hundreds of slaves. The Headquarters/Kensington property was most likely purchased by Colonel Richard Singleton from Edward Croft in the late 1820's.[5]

The date of the original main building on the property is unknown, but slave cabins were probably constructed during the 1830's.[6] The present day St. Phillip AME church, an African-American church, is located just south of the Kensington property. It traces its origins to slave church meetings in an arbor in 1835 on the southern edge of the Kensington property.

This would have been a familiar situation for Mattie. Her grandfather and father owned slaves in substantial numbers. Her father owned sixty slaves in 1820 and her grandfather 137 in 1824. It is said that Mattie did not like the name: Headquarters. The name was changed to the Kensington, being the name of Mattie's fraternal great-grandfather's plantation, located near Georgetown. Mattie's grandfather, Francis Kinloch Jr., had been forced to sell it in 1824 to cover family debts, not of his own making. Mattie was five or six years old at the time. While Matthew was in London as military attaché he had visited Kensington Palace, a royal residence. So, there may have been personal appeal for him in the name, Kensington, as well as pleasing his new wife.

Kensington (Headquarters) Owners		
Owned (O) or Managed (M)		
Edward Croft	1820's?	(O)
Richard Singleton (1776-1852)	1820's?-1852	(O)
Matthew Richard Singleton (1817-1854)	1852-1854	(O)
Martha Kinloch Singleton (1818-1892)	1854-1879	(M)
Richard Singleton (1851-1921) *	1879-1910	(O)
Cleland Kinloch Singleton (1844-1920) *	1879-1920	(O)
Helen Coles Singleton Green (1846-1924)	1920-1924	(O)
Walter T. Green/Cleland Singleton Green	1924-1925	(O)
Robert Pickett Hamer Jr. (1863-1912)	1910-1912	(O)
Robert Cochrane Hamer (1890-1945)	1912-1941	(O)
United States Government	1941-1946	(O)
James Christie Lanham Family	1946-1982	(O)
Union Camp/International Paper Company	1982-Now	(O)

Matthew Richard Singleton had a life interest only in the Kensington. His sister, Helen Coles Singleton Green, had a life interest only ownership in what had been Cleland Singleton's portion of the Kensington. Upon their deaths, ownership went to the party or parties designated in the wills of Colonel Richard Singleton (1776-1852) and later, Cleland Singleton (1844-1920).

*The brothers split the property in 1879. It was re-united under the ownership of the Hamer Family. Robert Pickett Hamer Jr. bought Richard's parcel in 1910. His son Robert Cochrane Hamer, bought Cleland's parcel from Cleland's nephew, Walter T. Green, in 1925.

Kensington Lifestyle

Matthew and Mattie lived a lavish lifestyle, commensurate with other well-to-do planters and exceeding most. They ordered the finest of everything, from clothing to art to necessities, from Charleston, Boston and New York. Two letters from 1844 reveal the lifestyle, the purchases, and the way debt was handled. The year they were married, Matthew ordered for himself a frock coat, a dress coat, six vests, six pairs of pants, twelve dozen kid gloves, six buckskin gloves and books. In the same letter to Wright and Hawks in New York, Matthew writes that he is "astonished" to hear that a previous bill is unpaid and says he told Mr. Rogers and Company to pay it.[7]

In a follow-up letter dated July 19, 1844, Matthew says he received the clothes, but no earlier bill. He then requested one overcoat, a green riding coat, a pair of pants "of stock material for riding," one vest, six handkerchiefs or scarves, matching in color the clothes, 1/2 ream of letter paper monogrammed...[8]

The couple travelled a great deal to Charleston, White Sulphur Springs and Flat Rock, North Carolina. They seem to have socialized primarily with family and friends, but not so much with their local neighbors.

The Kensington had a large and vibrant social life visited by such luminaries as Jerome Napoleon Bonaparte, nephew of Napoleon. He was a friend of the Singletons who they knew from White Sulphur Springs. An inventory done at the Kensington in January of 1855, revealed 100 chairs plus sofas, lounges and rocking chairs, a 200 book library and a wine and spirits supply.[9]

Chapter 65-The Children

Matthew and Mattie had three children, Cleland Kinloch Singleton (1844-1920), Helen Coles Singleton (1846-1924), and Richard Singleton (1851-1921). All three children lived to maturity. Their first born was named Cleland Kinloch, after two of Mattie's family names. Cleland appears to have been Mattie's favorite. On the day before his fourteenth birthday, Mattie sent him a letter saying that the day of his birth was the happiest day of her life. They shared a mutual lifelong interest in books and the life of the intellect.[10]

When Helen Coles was born, Mattie was initially disappointed her daughter was not a boy. However, she got over it quickly and they had a long, warm relationship. Mattie lived the last years of her life with Helen Coles.[11]

Richard, the youngest son, was probably named after his grandfather and/or his deceased Uncle Richard, who died young. As an infant of three months, his cousin, Mary Singleton McDuffie, wrote a letter to Colonel Singleton describing him as strong and large for his age.[12] Richard lived in the Kensington mansion over fifty years, longer than any other person.

The children had an English governess and their early lives were spent much as their father had, in a life of wealth and privilege, members of the elite.[13]

Cleland was educated in Charleston and later at St. Timothy's in Baltimore. In the same letter to Cleland expressing that his birth was the happiest day of her life, his mother, Mattie, sought to encourage him as he prepared to go away to school. She affirms her belief in his character, but expresses concerns about academics.

> I do [her underline] feel anxious and uneasy that you may not exert your mind sufficiently, and lest you should be discouraged by seeing others of your age more advanced. Do Not [her underline] be discouraged. Just do as well as you can and I shall be quite satisfied.[14]

Helen Coles' education began with a governess, continued in a private school in Charleston, and then in Flat Rock, N.C. at Misses de Choiseul's "select school" during the Civil War. Richard was educated initially in Columbia at a private school run by future Governor Hugh Thompson. After the War, Richard attended Virginia Military Institute (VMI), but did not graduate.

Chapter 66-Mattie's Duties

Mattie was trained in the duties of a plantation wife by her mother, Mary I'on Kinloch, in preparation for her marriage. Mrs. Kinloch lived with Matthew and Mattie at the Kensington and played a key role in its survival later on. Mattie's duties as plantation mistress required her to oversee the household food production as well as managing the domestic house slaves. She was also in charge of ministering to the minor medical needs of the slaves. In more serious cases, the Singletons brought in area doctors who attended to their medical needs.[15]

Mattie was also responsible for overseeing the production of clothing for the entire slave population of the plantation. The material favored for these garments by Mattie was osnaburg. It was cheap, coarse, durable, unbleached cotton fabric, left in its natural color of brownish gray and was commonly used for slave garments, grain sacks and upholstery. This task needed to be done each Spring and Fall and was a dreaded, time consuming but necessary task.[16]

Chapter 67-Matthew's Interests

At the Headquarters/Kensington plantation, Matthew pursued his strong interests in farming and horticulture. He devoted himself to a scientific study of agriculture and is regarded as an innovator. In pursuit of his interest in agriculture, Matthew subscribed to many farm magazines.[17] Besides growing cotton and other agricultural products, Matthew, along with his father, is given credit for helping introduce two new breeds of cattle, the Ayreshire and Durham, which were imported from England; and being one of the first to import African Broad Tailed Sheep to America.[18] (On some of the exterior columns at the Kensington mansion there are ram or sheep's head decorative carvings, said to represent this interest.)

Matthew paid great attention to creating beautiful grounds. An English gardener that Matthew shared with his father directed the installation of gardens on the river side of the house.[19]   The gardens were laid out in a spoke pattern, like his father's grounds at Home Place. They contained both native and exotic trees, including water oak, magnolia, cedar, haw and holly. The formal rose garden contained one hundred plants, bordered by boxwood. Other shrubbery included lilacs and syringia.[20]   When Matthew was finished, the landscaped area around the home was fifty acres.

Matthew also had a passionate interest in horse racing, as did his brother, John Coles; his father; grandfather; and great grandfather. It is believed that Matthew raced in Charleston, Columbia, Augusta, GA and New York as well as other tracks. He began racing during Race Week in Charleston, the year before he got married. He continued to do so every year until the his death, with the single exception of the year he got married.

Horse racing was an expensive passion. Some of Matthew Singleton's horses were bested during Race Week of 1851 by a horse named *Inspector*. Matthew's response was to purchase him "at the handsome sum of $2,500—pretty well for a gelding. Regarded…as the best animal of his age in America, it is no wonder he has commanded the best price." His investment could only pay off on the racetrack and not for stud.[21]

Chapter 68-Mattie and Matthew's Relationship

It is difficult to get a personal picture of the daily married life that Matthew and Mattie shared. Neither appeared to have a kept a diary or journal. No personal letters between them are known to exist. (It is rumored that letters and other personal items were thrown down a well at the Kensington.)

There is a glimpse of their lives through the eyes of a cousin, John Peter Broün, on an encounter with Matthew, in a letter he wrote to his wife, Abby,

> At Branchville [a railroad junction seventy-five miles from Charleston] , I met Col. Hampton and Mat Singleton on their way to the city[Charleston]…Mat tells me that his wife has

presented him with a daughter [Helen Coles Singleton] on Wednesday last [April 15,1846] whom, he has not yet seen, she [Mattie] has been in the city ever since the races [February] and he has not seen her since the first of March…[22]

Chapter 69-Flat Rock

In 1847, Matthew bought a property in the mountains of North Carolina, thirty miles from Asheville and 160 miles from the Kensington. Flat Rock had been popularized by Charlestonians as a summer refuge from the heat, humidity and disease rampant in summer coastal, low country South Carolina. It became known as "Little Charleston." Mattie's maternal grandparents had been among the first to build residences there. South Carolinians from the interior also established summer residences there as well.

Matthew and Mattie Singleton chose Flat Rock over White Sulphur Springs as their generation's preferred summer place, although Matthew and Mattie continued to visit White Sulphur Springs on occasion. An active, vibrant social scene went on among the elite who made Flat Rock their summer residence. Matthew's home was called Hemlocks, named for the hemlock forest which surrounded the property. It was a large square dwelling with Tudor chimneys. (The home no longer exists.) Mattie would continue to visit Flat Rock long after Matthew's death.

Matthew also invested in the development of the Farmer Hotel in Flat Rock, along with other notables like William Aiken, Governor of South Carolina, a relative of Mattie's. It was completed in 1852. (The Farmer Hotel was later renamed the Woodfield Inn and is presently known as the Mansouri Mansion. It is listed on the National Register of Historic Places, as is the entire Flat Rock district.)

PART EIGHT

MORE CHANGES

Chapter 70-Angelica Moves to New York City

A year after Matthew bought a summer home in Flat Rock, Angelica and the Van Burens moved to New York City. Angelica and her family continued to visit South Carolina on occasion, but New York City would be Angelica's home for the rest of her life.[1] She kept up an active letter correspondence with Singleton family members and was involved in several Singleton law suits. She spent her time raising her family and being actively involved in charitable work, while her husband worked on his father's Presidential papers.

Chapter 71-Marion Remarries

A half mile away down the hill from The Ruins was the Episcopal Church of Clarmont (later renamed Church of the Holy Cross). Marion, other members of the Deveaux family and her father, Richard, were parishioners. The church rector was the Reverend Augustus Lawrence Converse, who had presided at Robert and Marion's marriage as well as Abraham and Angelica Van Buren's and, previous to that, Rebecca Singleton's McDuffie's wedding in 1829. He also conducted the christening of Singleton Van Buren, Angelica's son. For all intents and purposes he was the family pastor. During Robert Deveaux's illness, the Reverend Converse and his wife had been most helpful and kind to Marion, even offering to take care of her children, so Marion could devote herself entirely to taking care of her seriously ill husband. They continued to be supportive of Marion after she took up full time residence at The Ruins.

The same year that Angelica moved to New York City, the wife of Reverend Augustus Converse, Mary Ann Kellogg Converse, passed away. A year later, Marion chose to re-marry, an exception among many slave-holding widows in the South. This was especially true of those who were as well-connected with family and friends, as was Marion. Nevertheless, she chose to marry the Reverend Converse, much to her family's dismay and disapproval. He came to the marriage with a clergyman's salary, augmented by teaching, and his wife's estate. Over the years, he had demonstrated a disgruntled attitude about his station in life and income. Converse was eighteen years Marion's senior, characterized as a *Northern man* with bald head and a wooden leg that caused him to use a cane that led to an ungainly walk.

A prenuptial agreement was signed by both parties, putting Marion's property into the hands of trustees to be held for her; the land would return to her upon the death of Augustus Converse, or to her children should she die before him. All appeared to be well for awhile, but it wasn't to last. Meanwhile, Rev. Converse laid the cornerstone for the new church, to be known as the Church of the Holy Cross in 1850.

A witness around this time observed that his interest had shifted from his rectorship to managing his plantation. Soon after the marriage, at her husband's insistence, Mrs. Converse signed the deed giving her husband a share of the property, which he would have for life if he survived her.[2] Trouble was on the horizon.

Chapter 72-The Decline of Colonel Singleton

The price of cotton was the roller coaster of Singleton fortunes. Cotton prices had boomed in early 1837 to 18 cents a pound; the bust came later in the year as the Panic of 1837 set in. Cotton prices plummeted. By 1840, cotton was selling for less than nine cents a pound. The effects would be felt for years, with the price of cotton falling below five cents a pound by 1845.

Creditors pursued debt-ridden planters including Colonel Singleton, who had always spent freely, lent freely and borrowed freely. What once had been manageable, now became almost unmanageable.

From Percy Renier's *Springs of Virginia*:

> Col. Singleton,....the man who had once sent his agent to buy thoroughbreds at the King's Sale in England was now so pressed for cash that the carpenter who made the verandah couches had to dun [to make repeated and persistent demands for payment] him for eighty dollars. Once he had maintained a great stud and swept the field at the Charleston Races; now he had to keep small tradesmen waiting for their money. Bashan, the animal molder of New York, clamored loudly to be paid for the concrete lions that crouched so imposingly at the top of the Colonel's steps. Once when his son Matthew bought so many horses in London that his credit ran out, it'd been an easy matter to ship 100 bales to square it. Now his name was on so many notes for himself and others that he could not always meet the interest.

> The Northerners whom marriage had brought into the family were, in his own words, 'harassing him to death.' Julia McRae, Powell's widow, was suing for her share of the Negroes. Nobody sold slaves in a market so suicidally low, but that made no difference to her; she wanted her pounds of flesh. Abram Van Buren [Angelica's husband] was threatening to drag Singleton's dear old friend Calwell [the owner of White Sulphur Springs] into the courts for non-payment of a $12,000 note which the Colonel had given Angelica. He needed it to go into business with, the Major said. These were the acts of mercenary, uncomprehending people. In the South one didn't do such things.

> Another twist on the screw was the case of Matthew [his son, builder of the Kensington], whom Dr. Buckner ordered to the Red Sulfur [Springs] for the summer. That meant consumption; Mary, his firstborn, had died of it. Writing his nephew in Alabama, [John Peter Broün] the Colonel cried, "I have known nothing but sorrow and affliction in the past 12 months. My cares, duties and labours are almost insupportable." [3]

It had only been seven years since the glory days of 1838: the Van Buren summer and Angelica's marriage to the son of the President of the United States. Times had changed.

As Colonel Singleton entered his 70's, his health declined. The South Carolina Jockey Club history mentions his "recent severe illness" that might have kept him from attendance at the 1847 Races, but did not. His wife Rebecca was ill and went to the Sweet Springs for several summers in hopes of healing, but to no avail this time. She died in the spring of 1849. Colonel Singleton was left lonely and distraught. Angelica urged her father not to go back to White Sulphur Springs where everything would remind him of his now-dead wife, but he ignored her advice. His daughter, Angelica, said her father's life was "an utter wreck." [4] For the next three years after his wife's death, Colonel Singleton returned to the place of former triumphs, to old friends that remained, and to where he had once been king of all he surveyed.

Chapter 73-More Bad News

In September of 1852, Colonel Singleton was ill and alone in his cottage in the Colonnades at White Sulphur Springs. His loneliness was relieved only by his servants and daily visits from the few old friends who were still alive. They tried to persuade him to see a doctor, but he refused. He had no faith in doctors, "having seen his loved ones die" and the doctors not able to do anything to save them.[5]

He wrote to his son, Matthew:

> White Sulfur Springs, Va, Sept. 10th /52
> To Col. M.R. Singleton
> Hendersonville No. Carolina
>
> Dear Matt,
> Here am I, quite Sick, not able to Travel or leave my Room, as soon as I am, if ever, which is very problematical, I shall commence my Journey, Homeward, where I hope to be by the middle or 20th of Oct.
> My intention was to have gone on to Philadelphia to see my unfortunate Sister, Mrs. McRae, and to thank Mr.

Edward Coles in Person for his kind Care and attention to her, and for the very many Services he has been pleased to render me, on her account, but I feel that I am not able to [embark on?] the Journey, in addition to the journey from there Home, prostrated as I am. I shall return Home via Danville, Salisbury and Charlotte, having my own Horses and Carriage with me.

The disastrous account given of the Damage done to the Crops, Lands, Horses and Merchandise on all the Southern Water Courses, I presume, you have seen an account of, which hastens my return. I am too Sick to say more and must conclude.

God bless you and yours My Dear Matt

Sincerely yours
       Richard Singleton[6]

(Edward Coles was Colonel Singleton's brother-in-law, the antislavery former Governor of Illinois. He lived in Philadelphia where Mrs. Mary Martha Singleton McRae, Colonel Singleton's sister, was hospitalized in an insane asylum.)

Matthew's brother, John Coles Singleton, was called home from a trip to Virginia to deal with the same outbreak of flooding on his own property.[7]   An unexpected flood on the Congaree River, cresting five feet higher than normal, threatened the crops on his Raiford's Creek plantation. After writing to Matthew, Colonel Singleton set out for home and was met on the road with the news that his eldest son, John Coles, had died.[8]   He is said to have contracted fever and died of "congestive chills" on September 20, 1852.[9]   It was most likely malaria. Another Singleton male was dead before he reached forty.

Chapter 74-Sold South

Besides impacting the friends and family who knew him, the death of John Coles Singleton profoundly affected others in a different way. Many times when a slaveholder died, it meant the sale and relocation of slaves either from specifics in a will or the need to pay a debt. (This happened after the deaths of Colonel Singleton and Matthew Singleton.)

Jacob Stroyer, a slave born and raised on the Kensington plantation, wrote in his memoir, *My Life in the South*, about what happened to some of John Coles Singleton's slaves upon his death.

Matthew Singleton had loaned Jacob's sisters, Violet and Priscilla, to his brother, John Coles, to assist in the cotton harvest on his plantation. This was common practice among the Singleton siblings. While there, the sisters met and married two slaves on John Coles's plantation. They were allowed to remain with their husbands at John Coles' plantation through mutual agreement of the Singleton brothers.

Upon John Coles's death, however, slaves were sold off to pay debts,. These included Jacob Stroyer's sisters and their husbands. A slave trader bought them for resale in Louisiana. Some of the men, including Violet and Priscilla's husbands, were reluctant to go and were temporarily imprisoned in the Sumterville (Sumter) jail awaiting transport. Those who had not expressed any unwillingness to go were allowed to visit their friends and relatives for the last time. This included Jacob Stroyer's sisters who came to the Kensington to visit their family and friends.

Jacob Stroyer's eyewitness account of what happened next:

> When the day came for them to leave, some, who seemed to have been willing to go at first, refused, and were handcuffed together and guarded on their way to the cars by white men. The women and children were driven to the depot in crowds, like so many cattle, and the sight of them caused great excitement among master's [Matthew Singleton's] negroes. Imagine a mass of uneducated people shedding tears and yelling at the tops of their voices in anguish and grief.
>
> The victims were to take the cars from a station called Clarkson turnout, which was about four miles from master's place [Kensington]. The excitement was so great that the overseer and driver could not control the relatives and friends of those that were going away, as a large crowd of

both old and young went down to the depot to see them off. Louisiana was considered by the slaves as a place of slaughter, so those who were going did not expect to see their friends again. While passing along, many of the negroes left their masters' fields and joined us as we marched to the cars; some were yelling and wringing their hands, while others were singing little hymns that they were accustomed to for the consolation of those that were going away, such as

'When we all meet in heaven,
There is no parting there;
When we all meet in heaven,
There is parting no more.'

We arrived at the depot and had to wait for the cars to bring the others from the Sumterville Jail, but they soon came in sight, and when the noise of the cars died away we heard wailing and shrieks from those in the cars. While some were weeping, others were fiddling, picking banjo, and dancing as they used to do in their cabins on the plantations. Those who were so merry had very bad masters, and even though they stood a chance of being sold to one as bad or even worse, yet they were glad to be rid of the one they knew.

While the cars were at the depot a large crowd of white people gathered, laughing and talking about the prospect of negro traffic; but when the cars began to start and the conductor cried out, 'all who are going on this train must get on board without delay,' the colored people cried out with one voice as though the heavens and earth were coming together, and it was so pitiful that those hard-hearted white men, who had been accustomed to driving slaves all their lives, shed tears like children. As the cars moved away we heard the weeping and wailing from the slaves as far as human voice could be heard; and from that time to the present I have neither seen nor heard from my two sisters, nor any of those who left Clarkson depot on that memorable day.[10] (Jacob Stroyer wrote this account about twenty-five years after the event.)

Chapter 75-Colonel Singleton Dies

Several months after the death of his son, Colonel Singleton was returning home by railroad from a visit to his True Blue plantation in present day Orangeburg County, South Carolina. He was accompanied by his ten year old grandson, Robert Marion Deveaux, his daughter Marion's son. They changed cars at the Kingville depot. The last short leg of the trip would take them across the Wateree River to their home station at Middleton, near Home Place.

They never made it.[11] They were killed in a railroad accident on November 26, 1852. It happened just east of Kingville on the Camden branch of the South Carolina Railroad, one mile from the Clarkson turnout, just south of the Kensington. (The accident occurred on the same railroad line to whose construction Colonel Singleton had strenuously objected twelve years earlier.)

There are two family versions of what happened.

In a letter dated two weeks after the deaths, December 9, 1852, Marion Singleton Deveaux Converse, daughter of the Colonel and mother of Robert, wrote:

> Thursday, … it poured in torrents all day, and on Friday, even before it cleared away, they attempted to come home, hearing that the bridge over the Congaree might be washed [away] by the threatened freshet [flood]. They passed that bridge in safety, but within a mile of Clarkson's Turnout [close to the Kensington] in crossing a little ravine, the rain had washed the foundation of the trestle work over it, and though the Engine and tender passed safely over, the first car in which they were, fell in and the other cars on them, and life was taken, and limbs were broken in an instant.[12]

A slightly different family version is in the *Genealogy of the Singletons* :

> After changing cars at Kingville, ….he [Colonel Singleton] found the passenger coach crowded and he with his grandson, young Deveaux went into the baggage car. There was a washout at a very small creek just beyond Kingville.

The baggage car was wrecked and he and his grandson killed.[13]

There are many other stories, rumors and versions of the details of the accident.

-The passenger compartment was crowded and because Colonel Singleton was a gentleman, he and his grandson gave up their seats to others and went to the baggage car to travel.

-The Colonel and his grandson went into the baggage car to examine some of the baggage.

-Cigar smoke in the car was too much for the Colonel and he got up to move to the baggage car and was stopped by a railroad official, even though he practically owned the railroad and got free rides. Offended, he pulled out a wad of cash and offered to pay his way.

-Colonel Singleton was robbed and killed.

-Marion Singleton Deveaux, the Colonel's daughter and mother of Robert, was also onboard the fatal train ride.

The newspapers pursued the story, focusing on the cause of the accident and explaining where Colonel Singleton and his grandson were on board the train.[14]

According to these accounts, the entire section of the railroad line had been rebuilt after the fall flood washouts and the timbers of the trestles were sound. Much heavier trains than the one the Colonel and his grandson were on passed this section of track safely on a daily basis; an even heavier train had passed the accident site one half hour before the Colonel's ill-fated train. Why it gave way is a mystery.

Colonel Singleton and his grandson Robert were buried in a double grave at the Singleton Family Cemetery. The inscription of the gravestone read as follows:

IN THE SAME GRAVE COVERED BY THIS STONE, REST THE REMAINS OF COLONEL RICHARD SINGLETON AND

ROBERT MARION DEVEAUX, HIS GRAND-SON, WHO
TOGETHER DIED IN AN ACCIDENT, ON THE SO.CA.R.R.
THE DAUGHTER OF ONE AND THE MOTHER OF THE
OTHER, ERECTS THIS MONUMENT; TO THEIR MEMORY

Not everyone was saddened by the passing of Colonel Singleton.
Dr. Samuel Leland was a neighbor of Matthew Singleton's, a
physician who did some medical work for the Singletons, and a
small landowner. His diary records comments critical of the
Singletons, and on the day Colonel Richard Singleton died he
wrote, "Dick Singleton is dead.   No comments." [15]   (In the
original diary there is a great space between the two statements. I
suspect, that he chose the option of better to say nothing, than to
speak ill of the dead.)

PART NINE

HIGHS AND LOWS

Chapter 76-Singleton Family Plantations

At the time of Colonel Richard Singleton's death in 1852, Singleton family wealth including the Broüns and the Moores family members was at its zenith. Its nineteen South Carolina plantations and properties, including the plantations put in trust by Colonel Singleton's father John, were spread over tens of thousands of acres worked by well over a thousand slaves. The plantations ranged from Albemarle in the west to Cane Savannah in the east, (a distance of approximately thirty-six miles) and from The Ruins in the north to True Blue in the south, (a distance of approximately twenty-four miles). Some of the plantations were contiguous like Fork and Kensington, Midway and Home Place, and Shiver and Deer Pond, but most were not.

Singleton Family Plantations Map)

The following list also does not include the following properties—Hemlocks in Flat Rock (owned by Matthew and Martha Singleton), the Hyde Park, N.Y. home bought by Rebecca Singleton and Mary Martha Singleton McRae, Flatwoods Plantation (inherited by Mary Singleton McDuffie Hampton from her father), and the Colonnade cottage at White Sulfur Springs. The Pines/Summer Seat and Gilman(s)/the Summer Residence are also not included because they aren't plantations.

Locations and Acreages of the Plantations, Properties

Sumter County- 11,322 Acres (This does not include 2,000 unnamed acres from the will of John Singleton.)

400	The Ruins
3,000	Melrose
4,000	Cane Savannah
1,767	Midway
2,050	Home Place
105	The Summer Residence/Gilman(s)
??	Fulton(Cotton Factory)

Clarendon County- 15 Acres

15	Cuddoes /Cuddoes Pond (originally Sumter district)

Richland County- 19,170 Acres

3,500	Albemarle
2,200	Big Lake
1,930	Gadsden
400	Raiford(s) Creek
840	Deer Pond
1,300	Shiver
??	Scott
??	The Pines/Summer Seat
5,000	Kensington/Headquarters
4,000	Fork

-Calhoun County- 5,553 Acres

5,553	True Blue (originally Orangeburg District)

Total Acreage- 36,060 Acres (fifty-six square miles)

This is a conservative estimate. The total may have been as much as 40,135 acres (sixty-two square miles) or more. The estimates are based on incomplete records 160 or more years old, but they do convey the magnitude of the acreage.

For comparison's sake—Manhattan Island's land mass is twenty-two square miles. Walt Disney World sits on a forty-seven square mile plot of land. Washington, D.C. has a total land mass of sixty-one square miles.

Singleton Family Slaves in 1852

Kensington	250
Fork	232
True Blue	245
Home Place	62
Midway	?
Fulton	49
Cuddoe's Pond	55
Melrose	?
The Ruins	?
Gadsden	17
Albemarle	300 (from Albemarle & Raiford's Creek?)
Raiford's Creek	?
Big Lake	?
Deer Pond	?
Shiver	78

1,288 total   (Does not include Midway, The Ruins, Raiford's Creek?, Big Lake or Deer Pond, whose numbers are unknown)[1]

Chapter 77-Colonel Singleton's Estate and Will

The value of Colonel Singleton's estate alone, excluding real estate, was $480,506.00. His total plantation acreage amounted to 18,500 acres (29 square miles)—value unknown. In terms of economic power, his estate would be worth $2,720,000,000 today.

Inventory and Appraisement of
Estate of Colonel Richard Singleton

Plantation	Item	Worth
Home Place	Furniture, fixtures & contents	$15,923.50
	Negroes and personal property	$38,658.00
	51 (+11*)Slaves	*$30.852.00*
Fulton	Negroes & personal property................	$24,076.00
	49 Slaves	*$22,206.00*
Headquarters (Kensington)		
property...	Negroes and personal $139,948.00	
	250 Slaves	*$122,450.00*
Fork	Negroes and personal property...................	$114,568.00
	232 Slaves	*$104.500.00*
True Blue	Negroes and personal property............	$120,914.50
	245 Slaves..........	*$111,950.00*
Gadsden	Negroes and personal property...............	$10,850.00
	17 Slaves	*$10,850.00*
All other personal property, bonds, notes, cotton, etc		$15,568.00
	Total...	**$480,506.00**
	855 Slaves......	*$402,808.00*
	Slave % of Value 83.83%	

*Eleven Slaves found at Home Place, but not from there, were counted as part of the Inventory and Appraisement. (Appraisement was a period term for appraisal.)[2]

Terms of the Will

Colonel Singleton's will was similar to his father's, giving the bulk of his estate to his sons only for their lifetimes. Real ownership would only pass to his grandsons. He left Home Place plantation (2,050 acres on both sides of the great Charleston Road) with its slaves to his wife; and at her death to their eldest son, John Coles Singleton, his life interest only. (Only fifty-one slaves were at

Home Place at the time of the Colonel's death. There couldn't have been very much land under cultivation at that time, unlike

what Mrs. Anne Royall had observed 20 years earlier.) He also left his wife his summer residence in the Sand Hills (Gilman) plus 105 acres of pine land attached. By the time of Colonel's own death, both his wife and son, John Coles Singleton, had preceded him in death, causing the inheritance to go to John Coles eldest son, Richard Richardson Singleton (1840-1900), when he came of age. In the meantime, John Coles Singleton's widow, Bonnie, handled his estate.

Colonel Singleton also left the Gadsden plantation purchased from Wade Hampton II to John Coles and also affirmed John Coles's legal right of ownership of the property on Raiford's Creek with its slaves. He also bequeathed to John Coles his gold mounted double barreled gun imported by his father, Captain John Singleton, and his gold watch. (This was probably the same gold watch that had been placed in Richard Singleton's coffin.) Colonel Singleton's blooded horses were to be divided between John Coles and his brother, Matthew Richard.

In addition to a half share of the thoroughbreds, Colonel Singleton left Headquarters (Kensington) Plantation with its slaves to Matthew Richard Singleton for his lifetime only, to be passed on to his sons who would own the property. He also gave Matthew Richard his two silver mounted double barreled guns.

True Blue and Fork Plantation properties with all their slaves were to be kept together and managed by his executors to benefit his wife (deceased at the time of his death) and daughters, Marion and Angelica. At the death of Colonel Singleton's wife, True Blue was to go to Marion and Fork to Angelica. These were life interests only. Real ownership was to pass to the children of Marion and Angelica. Any slaves in excess of 200 at True Blue and Fork were to go to John Coles.

In the initial draft of the will, the slaves in excess of 200 at True Blue and Fork were to be divided equally between John Coles and Matthew Richard. At the end of the will, that passage is struck and changed so all the slaves over 200 at both locations were to go to John Coles. This amounted to forty-five slaves from True Blue and thirty-two slaves from Fork. The will stipulated that the slaves were to be "taken off" in families.[3]

The change in the will, done in 1848, may have been recognition by Colonel Singleton of what appeared to be the more critical immediate need of John Coles to deal with his debts. John Coles's widow, Bonnie, was forced to sell off the Gadsden plantation of 2,100 acres, and also seventy-one slaves in an equity sale after his death to cover his debts. These slaves are probably the ones referred to in Jacob Stroyer's account of John Coles's slaves being "sold south." Many of these slaves were probably from True Blue and Fork originally.

Doing the Inventory and Appraisal

Three executors were designated in Colonel Singleton's will: John Coles Singleton, Matthew Richard Singleton, and the Colonel's good friend, Benjamin Franklin Taylor. John Coles had died in September and Benjamin Franklin Taylor the previous May. At the time of Colonel Singleton's death, the only living executor was Matthew Richard, so the entire work load fell on him.

Within a week of Colonel Singleton's death (December 3, 1852), action was being taken on the estate. Matthew was designated as administrator and sworn by the probate court to give a "full and perfect" inventory and appraisal and credits of Richard Singleton's estate to the court within six months; that is by May 3, 1853. The court charged Matthew Richard Singleton with the responsibility to see that the inventory and appraisals were done thoroughly and accurately.[4] As executor, Matthew had to do a full accounting of assets and to pay bills. Even the cash found on Colonel Singleton's person, $63, and the amount found in his desk, $324, was detailed.[5] (At this time the average unskilled farm worker or production worker in the U.S. was earning about $85 a year.)

Matthew Richard sent teams of three or four men to the various plantations to do full inventories and appraisals of everything of value on the Colonel's plantations.

Importantly this included the slaves, who were by far the most valuable "asset" in the estate. One crew did Home Place and Fulton. They gave no slave a "$0" value, although three slaves were given the value of $1. They also detailed some slaves in terms of relationships like "wife of" or "children of." This differed from some of the other Singleton plantations.

The inventory and appraisal team at Gadsden also did not value any slaves at "$0" value. The True Blue team gave twelve slaves a "$0" value. The team that did Fork and Kensington valued sixteen slaves at Fork at "$0" and at Kensington eighteen slaves were given a "$0" value.

An unexplained anomaly of the inventory at True Blue is that there are squiggly lines with a distinctive start and stop point next to most of the names in groupings from one to eleven. Most of these groupings begin with a man's name. Perhaps that this was an intentional effort to recognize these groupings as families or relations to fulfill Colonel Singleton's desire that any slaves in excess of 200 on True Blue and Fork were to be taken off by families. Twenty-three of the names on the list have no squiggly marks and I believe they were unrelated individuals.

At the Kensington six slaves have a first and last name listed. That was unusual. Slaves were usually listed only by first names. True Blue was the only other Colonel Singleton plantation where a slave was listed by first and last name and there was only one there.

Slaves with special skills were singled out with their skills listed next to their names: boat hand, shoemaker, patroon of boat, carpenter worked at wheelright shop, driver, blacksmith. The mobile force of skilled slaves who moved from one plantation to another as needed were at Home Place at the time of the Colonel's death. There was a carpenter foreman, three carpenters, a carpenter apprentice, a bricklayer, two sawyers, and three unclassified apprentices.

The Stain of Slavery

In all these inventories and appraisals, the slaves are listed strictly as another form of property. At Home Place the slaves are listed right after blankets and right before the contents of the dining room. At Fork, they are listed on the same page as tools, horses, mules, livestock and crops. At True Blue, they are listed with the mules and livestock and at the Kensington, on the same page with the mules.

Slavery is the elephant in the room in any discussion of the antebellum South and nowhere more so than in South Carolina. Anyone who writes about the antebellum period has to wrestle with this issue. For me, it became more than an issue to be written about at the end of a long day of reading through documents while doing research for this book. I came to the Inventory and Appraisement of the Estate of Richard Singleton. I read through page after page of individual slaves listed by name, some with descriptive comments like old, dead, little, big, sold. Values were placed next to each name, including $0. There were "x's" placed next to thirty-six names at the Kensington. The last "x" on the last page was written very faintly, as if by reluctant decision. (What did they designate? To be sold?) It all brought tears to my eyes. Slavery is the underlayment of the plantation story, always there, always troubling.

Inventory & Appraisement

Amount bot forward		Amount bot forward	
Mitchell	300	Sie	300
Robt	400	Fanny Bluff	800
Cuffy	100	Nancy	300
Harriette	200	Sarah	150
Alex	100	Joe	100
Gill	1000	William	1000
Harriet	200	Daniel	1000
Glasgow	000	Anderson	1000
Andre	1000	Lewis	1000
Peggy	800	Jake	000
William	500	Caty & child	1100
Daniel	350		
Vina	250	*Mules*	
Sorianna	100	Eliza	150
Esther	800	Phoebe	75
Mary	650	Kit	130
Nanny	350	Buck	125
Sue	200	Diana	150
Minerva	100	Linda	125
Monday	000	Liza	150
Molly	000	Leddy	125
Rachel	1000	Clara Fisher	150
August	1000	Henry	75
Toney	000	Caroline	125
Venus	100	Jenny	100
Ezekiel	500	Nelly	150
Moses	800	Spread Eagle	50
Linda	800	Sterling	60
Randal	150	Catharine	75
Charley	800	Hester	150
Thomas	100	Jem	100
Judy Cuff	250	Nelly	150
Andry	1000	Nebs	140
Jack	1000	Sue	150
Lizzie	400	Valentine	150
Amount carried forward		Amount carried forward	

Page from Headquarters/Kensington Appraisement Sheet

Slaves at Headquarters / Kensington 1852

Diana	Rebecca	Francis
Shadrack	Nancy Pash	Phoebe
Joshua	Mary Mountain	Bella
Mary Ann	Manda	Dick
Little Diana	Elvira	Katy
Caroline	Reuben	Abram
Meshac	Binah	Jane
Prince	Harry	James
Phillis	Dolly	Maggy
Jake	Hannah	Diana
Eliza	Linda	Phoebe
Marg	Ellen	Harry
Wilcher	Nora	Hardy
Jumma	Catherina	Gabriel
Caesar	Botta	Hilliard
Rina	Azarine	Jim
Simon	Nelly	Miley
Sarah	Hagar	Tena
Jimmy	Rose	Thomas
Harriet	Duke	Jeannet
Joe	Patience	Pompey
Tilla	Ellis	Binah
Dubtin	Grace	Josh
Phillis	Jonas	Phoebe
Monday	Isaiah	Louisa
Bristol	Jim	Big Jack
January	Abby	Fate
Maria	Clarissa	Cuffy
Moses	Washington	Smart
Judy	Old Fanny	Big Martha
Pach	Washington	Hebe
Levina	Bess	Abram
Gilbert	Amy	Zack
Letitia	Elizabeth	Bacchus
Sam	George	Man
Jane	Neila	Peggy
Hester	Snow	Fanny Croft

Page 1

Hester	Orlando	Jack	Toney
Benjy	Mary	Jonas	Venus
Binah	Orlando	Dorinda	Ezekiel
Loman	Josey	Cudjo	Moses
Soloman	Cato	Priolean	Cinda
Phillis	Jeremiah	Rose	Randal
Robert	Emeline	Davy	Charley
Johnny	Murray	London	Thomas
Lucy	Jeffrey	Sarah	Judy Croft
Stepney	Town Sam	Edwin	Henry
Lamfry	Flora	Will	Jack
Lucy	Jackey	Chloe	Scipio
Hector	Betsey Ann	Lydia	Sie
Daphne	Celia	Footy	Fanny Bluff
Matty	Billy Moore	Jake	Nancy
Nelson	Leah	Catherina	Sarah
Bowman	Priscilla	Mitchell	Joe
Clarinda	Ned	Caleb	William
Big Jim	Ben	Cuffy	Daniel
Lingo	Renty	Maritta	Anderson
Tom	Kitty	Alex	Lewis
Big Sue	Kit	Bill	Jake
Molly	Chloe	Harriet	Caty & child
Limus	Celia	Glasgow	
Flora	André	Andre	
Charles	Sarah	Peggy	
Peter	Ned	William	
Becca	Christiana	Daniel	
Hector	Charlotte	Vina	
Tenah	Epsey	Jorianna	
Katy	Little Sue	Stephen	
John	Judy	Mary	
Patience	Sie	Nanny	
Silvia	Harriet	Sue	
John	Betsey	Minerva	
Rachel	Job	Monday	
Anthony	Martha	Molly	
Caesar	Cuffy	Daniel	
Rachel	Esau	August	

Page 2 [6]

Inventory Complete

By the January 15th, 1853, only six weeks after the process was initiated, the plantation inventories and appraisements were complete, well ahead of schedule. There seems to have been urgency to take quick action on the debts, keep the estate intact, and the plantations operating. Matthew Richard Singleton was also able to file a "true return on the estate of Richard Singleton" detailing all estate assets meeting the deadline of May 3, 1853. For the rest of his life, Matthew managed his father's estate, paying off his father's debts and expenses, as well as recording the sale of commodities and collection of debts for the profit side of the balance sheet. As executor he simultaneously dealt with the estate provisions of his grandfather, John Singleton, who had put part of his estate into trusts for his daughter, Mary McRae, and the surviving Broün grandson, John Peter Broün.[7]

Chapter 78-A Word on Matthew Richard Singleton

The emotional toll of dealing with the death of his father and brother within two months must have been a heavy burden for Matthew. He had his hands full as executor of his father's estate at the same time he was embarking on the renovation and expansion of the Headquarters Plantation house that would become the Kensington mansion. It was a large and costly undertaking. In addition, I'm sure he was also aiding the widow and children of John Coles as they were navigating the aftermath of his death. As executor and only surviving son of Colonel Singleton, Matthew was also being bombarded (I don't think that's too strong a word) with correspondence regarding his father's estate and enterprises within weeks of his father's death. One week after Colonel Singleton's death, Matthew received a letter from one of his father's best friends and brother-in-law, Andrew Stevenson, offering condolences saying that he is "overwhelmed" at the loss— but also wanting to know about the Colonel's will.[8]

Matthew received demands for payment, a request to return a loaned slave who was unsuitable as a cook, and handled the myriad other details of his father's vast holdings. (It would take generations to clear the debts and obligations from Colonel Singleton's estate.) In addition to all this, his sister, Marion, reached out to him for help as she and her husband struggled over control of her assets.

Chapter 79-The Converses in Trouble

As part of his will, Colonel Singleton bequeathed to his daughter, Marion, the profits of the True Blue plantation for life. Marion and her husband, the Reverend Augustus Converse, argued over control of her assets, including the profits from True Blue. She turned to her brother Matthew and other relatives and friends to try to regain control. In April of 1853, the Church of the Holy Cross accepted the resignation of the Reverend Converse. His interests were elsewhere.

By all accounts, the behavior of the Reverend Converse began to change dramatically. Increasingly bitter disagreements ensued between the marriage partners as the struggle for power continued. It is reported that Marion increasingly went on long visits to relatives in New York, Philadelphia and Virginia as well as other parts of South Carolina to escape her husband.

Marion's family increasingly saw Converse as a "tyrannical, sanctimonious, short tempered scoundrel." Some have suggested that alcohol may have played a part in the increasingly abusive actions of Augustus Converse. Matters came to a head in January of 1854, when in the course of a violent argument at The Ruins, Converse forced Marion into his room, locked the door behind them and began loading a gun. Marion ran out onto the veranda and leaped to the ground below, where slaves drawn by her screams, took her to their quarters to protect her from her rampaging husband. Converse punished the slaves for their actions.

Shortly thereafter, he attacked Marion again. This time she fled the house bruised, battered, and bleeding, seeking shelter in a cotton house with one of her daughters. Converse pursued them to the location and looked for a hammer and nails to seal them inside. Realizing what was going on, Marion and her daughter ran into the cotton fields and hid themselves in the cold rain until her husband gave up the pursuit. Again aided by slaves and a neighbor, they eventually made their way across the Wateree River to safety at her True Blue plantation, some thirty miles away.

Marion took her husband to court. In a legal filing in 1854, Marion accused Converse of threatening her with a "hammer or hatchet" to get her to sign over rights involving True Blue plantation. The community took notice and in 1855 the Episcopal Church, the denominational governing body of Church of the Holy Cross, "degraded" his ministry [defrocked him], after finding him culpable of the "unprovoked and cruel beating of his wife."

In 1856, Marion brought suit to legally separate from her husband, regain her property and resume using her first husband's name—Deveaux.

In court, Converse argued that he could not abide that…"all his rights as a husband were subordinate to her claim"… and also that her actions had undermined his authority over the slaves and finally that her family was guilty of…"unwarrantable interference in his domestic concerns." The court found in his favor and he retained control of The Ruins and its income. On appeal, the court continued to uphold Converse's side, but ordered that he give half of the land's income to Marion. In sum, the courts found in Converse's favor according to the law, but condemned his behavior toward his wife as "revolting".

Finally, in 1857, a legal settlement was reached between Augustus Converse and Marion. He agreed to vacate The Ruins and all claims to her person and estate for a payment of $24,250, a huge amount at the time.

To pay off Converse, Marion turned to family and friends for help and they responded generously. Although divorce was illegal in South Carolina at the time, Marion was granted a legal separation. She resumed her first married name, Deveaux, continued managing the True Blue plantation, and took up residence back at The Ruins with her youngest daughter. Having learned a painful lesson, Marion specified in her own will that her property was to go to her daughters for their "sole and separate use" during their lifetimes. Later, when one of her daughters, Anne Peyre Deveaux Moore, married her second husband, Richard I. Manning, he had to purchase True Blue plantation from his wife and her sister in the 1880's to establish ownership.

In 1860, Augustus Converse died and was buried in the graveyard of the Church of the Holy Cross where he once was Rector as well as a respected member of the community. He rests at the foot of a large headstone.[9]

Marion moved onto the True Blue plantation, leaving her eldest daughter, Anne Peyre Deveaux Moore and her husband, John Burchell Moore, to live at The Ruins.

Marion died in 1867 and is buried in the Singleton Family Cemetery in a grave near the entrance with a simple headstone, recently placed, marking her grave.

(Of all the Singleton family plantation homes, only The Ruins and the Kensington survive to the present day.)

PART TEN

THE KENSINGTON MANSION

Chapter 80-Designing the Mansion

In the summer before Matthew's father, brother and nephew died, in a time of low cotton prices, floods, and debt pressures, Matthew and Martha began to transform their basic Georgian style two-story home into something special: the Kensington mansion.[1] To do that, they engaged the pre-eminent architects in South Carolina at that time, the firm of Jones and Lee.

Matthew and Martha shared a great interest in European culture. Matthew had been to Paris and appreciated French culture. He had seen the Louvre and the Fontainebleau Royal Palace. Both buildings would influence his thinking on what he wanted in his home. Many of the design features utilized in the Kensington could be seen within a thirty mile radius of Paris.[2] Edward C. Jones and Francis D. Lee had designed and constructed well known commercial and church properties in Charleston and elsewhere.[3] Many of their works reflected an Italianate style with its distinctive, dramatically arched windows. This look was included in the Kensington design. Jones and Lee had remodeled many buildings, but designing and constructing a private home was something new for them. Locally, Jones and Lee had just completed work on the Church of the Holy Cross in Stateburg.

The architectural style of Jones and Lee was exotic and eclectic, something different from the ordinary, a good match for what Matthew had in mind. The architects were being called upon to design something unique and distinctive. The Kensington mansion would be different than anything else in South Carolina or the entire South. No Greek Revival Style with white pillars in front for Matthew. It would be just what Matthew wanted—European style. The Kensington mansion was conceived in Europe, mid-wifed by Singleton power and wealth, and birthed in the Midlands of South

Carolina.

Matthew's love of all things French broke with his father and grandfather's tastes, who were complete Anglophiles. Paris was the epitome of culture and refinement in the 1800's. It is clear that Matthew was profoundly influenced by what he saw and experienced in the *Old World*.[4]

Chapter 81-Building the Mansion

Construction work commenced in 1852 and was completed in late 1854 or early 1855. Edward D. Jones was the primary designer and Francis Lee built it. Matthew, hands-on owner with very distinctive ideas, wanted to be involved every step of the way. Because he was often not on site, either spending time at his home in Flat Rock, 165 miles away, or pursuing his far-flung horse racing interests, communications had to be carried on primarily by letter. Jones and Lee had trouble understanding exactly what Matthew wanted done. They were also frustrated in getting him to make decisions, or saying one thing, then changing his mind, then denying it later. Disagreements arose on the type or gauge of materials to be used. They sometimes found it difficult to get approvals on ordering materials and the other myriad details of renovation and construction. Matthew Singleton also dealt directly with subcontractors, not just through Jones and Lee, adding another layer to the difficulties.[5]

The existing house was cut in two. One section of the house was moved to one side and the two sections were jacked to form two wings. Then the soaring center section with a Mansard Style square domed roof was built in between the sections.[6] The roof design was very similar to the distinctive roof at the Louvre and the Fontainebleau Palace. French influence is strong.[7]

The Louvre

The Kensington's exact architectural style remains up for debate even today. The National Historical Register of Historic Places designates it as Italianate Revival. John Califf, the architect who did an analysis of the Kensington before its restoration in the 1980's, believes that the style of the house is French Renaissance with Italian country influences.[8]

Under the direction of Mr. Lee, work proceeded. He probably brought in master craftsmen to supervise the skilled slave laborers from the Kensington and the "mobile force", a group of slaves owned by the Singletons, skilled in crafts such as bricklaying, carpentry, etc. that moved from Singleton plantation to plantation as needed.[9] John Califf believes that "most of the construction work, including the highly skilled masonry, plaster work, and wood carving at Kensington was done by slaves." [10]

Local materials were used whenever possible. Access to timber, like the kind now found in what is now the nearby Congaree National Park, provided lumber. Some materials were imported to the property and some were obtained on the property. "Building materials for Kensington, cypress and river rock," and possibly the clay for the bricks, "came from the Wateree River and its swamps." [11] Colonel Singleton's estate inventory showed a stockpile of 120,000 bricks on the Kensington property. (The remains of a brick kiln still exist on the Kensington property near the river.)

The house was built on a foundation of brick, masonry and river rock (sandstone). The walls of the ground floor level or basement were mostly brick and some fieldstone. The upper stories were constructed of wood. The main structural supports were hand planed cypress timbers. Evidence of the hand planing of the timbers is still on view in the basement of the Kensington. Heart pine was also used as a main structural material. It is very strong, durable, and insect resistant, but highly flammable. In a fire, structures utilizing heart pine went up like a torch. (Several Singleton family plantation houses using this material suffered this fate, including Home Place, Midway, Fork and True Blue. When the Fork plantation house burned down in the 1930's, reports say that the fire could be <u>heard </u>two miles away in Eastover.)

Chapter 82-Painting the Mansion

The exterior was covered in brick and coated with stucco. It was painted with a sanded, stone gray or drab warm gray color, and grooved to produce the visual effect of masonry of a French chateau.

Grooved stucco over brick example

This included the chimneys and the basement. The window sashes were painted white and the shutters a darker gray. A dark reddish brown (Spanish brown) was chosen for the roof and dome. The front and back steps, as well as the pedestals of the large columns of the porte cochère were painted brown stone and the overhead ceilings of the piazzas and the colonades were painted lead white.[12]

I believe that during the post Civil War Period another exterior paint scheme was applied, more of a classic Victorian look. "The body of the house, siding and columns were a purple-gray or blue gray. The dome, roofs, and wood trim were maroon, and the shuttters were a peacock green. Yellow-gold accents on the columns and balustrades added further exotic allusions." [13] Some evidence of this paint scheme can be seen in the only known photographs of the Kensington taken prior to the twentieth century. These pictures were taken at a Singleton family gathering after the death of Martha Singleton in 1892. It is believed that the Hamers, later owners of the Kensington, painted over the Victorian paint job with white. This would also be the color chosen for the restoration.[14]

The exterior doors had a grained oak look. The mahogany front door was faux painted to look like oak and varnished to show off the appearance of natural grain. This was a typical look in European country homes at the time. The original Kensington front door still has that look.

"The interior walls and plaster details, including door and window frames were to be painted in lead white zinc or white French zinc."[15] The marble mantels in the dining room were white; the others in the house were "shades of amber" and left unpainted. "Much of the interior woodwork was to be painted blue gray." [16]

Everything was done to create a light and airy interior.

PART ELEVEN

MATTHEW PASSES THE TORCH

Chapter 83-Trouble

In the midst of building the Kensington and dealing with everything else, Matthew had other problems. He had a history of bad health. At fifteen, he had contracted a congestive chill (probably malaria) that killed his twin, Richard. His aunt, Sallie Stevenson, had noted his poor health at twenty-one when he was a military attaché in England. In the mid 1840's, Matthew was directed by a Doctor Buckner to spend the summer at Red Sulphur Springs for treatment of consumption (tuberculosis).[1] He was not well.

Even the weather was causing problems. The same floods of 1852 that had damaged the crops of John Coles and Colonel Singleton had also affected Matthew's. The following years, 1853 and 1854, had brought severe droughts causing low yields and crop damage eroding his finances in the midst of the huge capital outlay for the building of the Kensington.

Matthew was saddled with debts big and small and creditors were clamoring to be paid.[2]

Jacob Stroyer wrote about the effect all this had on Matthew Singleton.

> …Master stood security for a northern man, who was cashier of one of the largest banks in the city of Charleston. This man ran away with a large sum of money, leaving the Colonel [Matthew) embarrassed, which fact made him very fretful and peevish. He'd been none too good before to his slaves, and that made him worse, as you knew that the slave holders would revenge themselves on the slaves whenever they became angry. I had seen master whip his slaves a great many times, but never so severely as he did that spring…[1854]. One day before he went to his summer seat

[Flat Rock], he called a man to him, stripped and whipped him so that the blood ran from his body like water thrown upon him in cupfuls, and when the man stepped from the place where he had been tied, the blood ran out of his shoes. He said to the man, 'You will remember me now, sir, as long as you live.' The man answered, 'Yes, master, I will.'[3]

An indication of just how bad the debt situation had become is in a "Deed of Assignment" conveyed to Thomas S. Magg of Charleston on July 3, 1854, directed at Matthew Singleton. It detailed the transfer of ownership of forty-three slaves, including highly skilled and valued slave craftsmen, as well as twelve racehorses, carriage horses, riding horses and a pony. One of the racehorses was John Hopkins, a prize racehorse of Matthew's, a gelding, whose only return of investment for Matthew could be on the racetrack. John Hopkins did win a purse of three hundred dollars in the last race that Matthew entered earlier in the year.[4] (A Deed of Assignment is a legal agreement under which assets of an insolvent debtor are assigned to a trustee to be sold and the proceeds distributed equitably among the creditors. The assets are no longer owned by the debtor, although actual physical transfer of the assets has not taken place.)

Chapter 84-Matthew Passes Away

On August 18, 1854, just as the Kensington was nearing completion, Matthew Richard Singleton died while he was at the Hemlocks, his mountain home in Flat Rock. He was only thirty-six years old. He left his wife of ten years with three small children to raise—aged nine, eight, and three.[5] The final completion of the mansion, the handling of his creditors and the future was left to Martha Singleton.

By the time of his death, Matthew Richard Singleton owed fifty-three different creditors: thirty-seven in South Carolina and sixteen in North Carolina. Given the financial pressure he was under, it was rumored by some at the time that he had killed himself. However, he is generally believed to have died of a lung ailment, probably consumption (tuberculosis). The day after Matthew's death, Dr. Leland wrote in his diary, "The vast property accumulated by the father [Richard] proved a curse, rather than a blessing to the sons." [6]

While in Switzerland accompanying the Van Buren family, Matthew's niece, Mary Singleton McDuffie wrote to Martha Singleton. In a letter dated Sept. 1, 1854, she offered funds to assist her Uncle Matthew. It was too late to help.[7] During the last few months of his life, Matthew had acted as her agent, trying to sell 4,000 acres and 230 slaves in Abbeville, South Carolina that she had inherited from her father, George McDuffie.

Chapter 85-Reactions to Matthew's Passing

During his last years, there are indicators that Matthew Singleton underwent a spiritual introspection. A close friend or relative (it's not clear who) sent a letter to Mattie Singleton shortly after Matthew's death, saying how Matthew had discussed religion with her during his last illness and he "felt that something was wanting beyond this world's pleasures to make a man really happy." She also related that she had chided him for breaking the third Commandment (Thou shalt not take the Lord's name in vain), during the previous summer and he had admitted that it was "ungentlemanly" and that he regretted it. She went on to say that when she saw him this last summer, he had overcome the "habit."[9] Matthew's obituary in the Charleston Courier describes him as "modest and retiring in his temper and simple in his habits" as well as "sincere, humane and generous…singularly considerate of the feelings and interests of others." It also said that Matthew had undergone a spiritual awakening toward the end of his life and was repentant for his sinfulness.[10] (For Matthew's complete obituary, see Appendix.)

Several months after his death, a family friend from New York wrote a consoling letter to Mattie, regarding his death. "Your poor dear husband had every attention, everything that could be done and he had his mind and was aware of the situation and now is happy and at rest and though you must grieve still, dear, you have your little children to fill up your heart." [11]

Jacob Stroyer also commented on Matthew's death and its aftermath.

> When they brought his remains home all of the slaves were allowed to stop at home that day to see the last of him, and to lament with mistress. After all the slaves who cared to do so had seen his face, they gathered in groups around mistress to comfort her; they shed false tears, saying, 'Never mind, missis, massa gone home to heaven.' While some were saying this, others said, 'Thank God, massa gone home to hell.' Of course the most of them were glad that he was dead; but they were gathered there for the express purpose of comforting mistress. But after master's death mistress was a good deal worse than he had been. [12]

A neighbor of the Singletons, Mrs. Keziah Brevard, wrote in her diary of slave's real feelings towards their masters, as opposed to the outward appearance usually presented. "Many an hour have I laid awake in my life thinking of our danger." The fear expressed by Mrs. Brevard was also mentioned several times by Mary Boykin Chesnut in her "Diary From Dixie" Mary Chesnut also mentioned a friend and a cousin who had been killed by their slaves. [13]

Chapter 86-Martha Takes Charge

After the death of Matthew, Martha did have the advice and assistance of family and friends such as Wade Hampton III, but it is clear that she took charge. Matthew had often been absent from the Kensington and Mattie had been left to direct its operations. When her father had become so mentally ill that he could not manage his own business affairs, she, along with her mother, had taken over doing that. These experiences would stand her in good stead.

In his last will and testament, Matthew left his "whole estate real and personal" to Martha to manage and appointed her sole executrix of his estate.[14] It indicates his high level of confidence in her abilities. He did not do as his father had done, naming three males as joint executors of his will.

Upon Matthew's death Martha was faced with a multitude of issues: managing a 5,000 acre plantation with hundreds of slaves, handling creditors clamoring for their due, settling land disputes with her neighbors, managing her father-in-law's estate, and dealing with internecine family legal disputes. Many of these issues would consume her for the next twenty years; while she was also raising three young children.

An example of her "take-charge" ability is her handling of a dispute between Mr. Clark, an overseer of hers, and another employee of hers, Count de Choiseul, the French Consul at Charleston and friend and neighbor of hers in Flat Rock. This exchange began a month after Matthew's death, and involved a road building project on her property in Flat Rock, North Carolina. Rather than writing directly to Martha, Mr. Clark, an employee of Martha's, had written to a friend of Martha's, Mr. King, to resolve his disagreement with Count Choiseul regarding who was in charge.[15]

On receiving word of this from Mr. King, Martha would have none of this and clearly asserted *her* authority by writing directly to Mr. Clark, rather than using her friend Mr. King, as an intermediary. She upbraided Mr. Clark for usurping her authority and also declared that his actions had weakened her authority with the slaves who had witnessed the dispute between him and Count de Choiseul. *That* was serious business in ante-bellum South Carolina.

Martha clearly took the side of the Count in the dispute whom she had hired to oversee Clark's work. She dismissed Mr. Clark from her employment. She wrote, "I cannot allow you to dictate from which friends I shall or shall not receive advice and assistance. As your views and mine the duties and position of a gardener differ so widely, I shall let no occasion for your services an other [sic] year." [16]

Martha Singleton did all of this within six weeks of Matthew's death. This exchange of letters took only seven days: the first letter from Clark to King, the letter from King to Martha, and her letter dismissing Clark instead. No hesitation.

Mary Boykin Chesnut, a friend of Martha's, commented in her *Diary From Dixie* :

> Mrs. Mat Singleton uses English as pure as that of Victoria Regina; such clean-cut sentences, every word distinctly enunciated. She is the delight of her friends, the terror of her enemies. Sometime those words dropped one by one with such infinite precision are drops of vitriol [highly caustic]! (There is some debate as to who the last part of the quote refers to: Martha Singleton or her, sister-in-law, Mrs. John Coles "Bonnie" Singleton. Either way, the Singleton women of that generation were nobody to be trifled with.)[17]

Chapter 87-Martha's Debt Management

Matthew and the Kensington had been heavily in debt. Martha was responsible for dealing with it and providing for her three children. She also had the memory of her grandfather, Francis Kinloch Sr., losing the original Kensington plantation in Georgetown due to debt.

The widow Singleton sold off whatever needed to be sold off to meet the demands of the thirty-seven creditors in South Carolina and the sixteen creditors in North Carolina. Assets included land, her partial interest in the Farmer's Hotel in Flat Rock and slaves, but only those who were not part of Colonel Richard Singleton's estate. They were to go to his grandchildren (Matthew and Mattie's sons) when they became of age as stipulated by the Colonel's will. Only those owned by Matthew could be sold. She sold off thirty-eight slaves for $15,831. She also sold $2,300 worth of furniture, $1,260 worth of land (400 acres), securities, all of Matthew's remaining racehorses, some carriage horses, and mules.

Martha paid "out of her own funds" $2,958.55 to sixteen North

Carolina creditors. This indicates that she *had* her own funds. She was not totally dependent on Matthew's provision. Thirty-seven South Carolina creditors were to be paid off in 10% installments on $75,688.43. Martha paid $7,569 as a first installment in 1855.[18] She was still involved in probate court with Matthew's estate as late as July of 1857, almost three years after his death.

There were still-dangling legal and debt issues with Colonel Singleton's will and estate. As Matthew had been the executor of Colonel Singleton's estate, Martha assumed responsibility for these as well. Ironically, Colonel Singleton had not provided for his son's wives in his will, but left provision for his son's wives up to his sons.[19] In 1858, six years after Colonel Singleton's death, Martha had to deal with a note and mortgage from 1846, signed by Colonel Singleton for $5,000. The suit had been brought against the estate by Colonel Singleton's nephew, John Peter Broün, who lived in Alabama.[20] Other issues from Colonel Singleton's estate would continue to bedevil Martha well into the 1870's.[21]

Chapter 88-The Mansion & Grounds Completed

In late 1854 or early 1855, in the midst of Martha's dealing with debt and economizing, the dream—the Kensington mansion—was completed. The mansion was approached from the old McCord's Ferry road along a gradual upwardly sloping driveway of almost half a mile. Lined with live oaks, it brought the visitor into a fifty acre park surrounding the twenty-nine room, 12,000 square foot mansion. Due to the many mature trees to the front of the mansion, a full view could only be experienced as the visitor made the final approach.[22] People had never seen anything like it; what a view it must have been.

The head of the driveway became an oval bringing the visitor into the shelter of a massive port-cochère (covered carriage entrance). This consisted of four columns linked by Italianate arches topped by a balustrade (a rail of balusters or posts). On the top of the columns were rams heads, probably selected to reflect Matthew Singleton's interest in African broad-tailed sheep. Above the port cochère were three windows. (The one in the center is faux, to balance the design.)

Interior Description

After climbing twelve steep steps to the threshold, one entered the house through a massive solid mahogany door, faux painted to look like oak. The door was nine feet tall, four feet wide and two inches thick with a crest (a plow, the symbol used by Matthew's grandfather on glasses made for him by English craftsmen) carved into the lintel above the doorframe. The door was sided by panels of imported glass. The high windows above the door, provided natural light onto the balcony. Light flooding through the many windows created a light and airy interior.

On entering the main entrance hall one's attention was immediately drawn to the soaring two-and-a-half story view to the skylight forty-three feet above it. Besides providing light, the skylight could be opened to allow heat to escape in the summer producing a cooling airflow. The distinctive squared off Mansard style balustrade-topped dome roof with the skylight was the most striking feature of the mansion.

The layout of the house was cruciform (cross-shaped) with three wings. To the right off the entrance hall was the ladies' sitting room and to the left is the gentlemen's parlor. In general, the left side of the house was Matthew's and the right, Martha's.

Side hallways led to bedrooms off the main entrance hall. The ceilings of the halls and rooms were adorned with carved cornices and chandelier medallions. Mirrors and niches for statuary and flower boxes were placed along the walls.[23]

The main entrance hall led straight back to a smaller hallway, with six large niches for statuary. This hallway led into the dining room: a large room (14' X 29') with a vaulted barrel ceiling, nineteen and a half feet high, topped with a massive plaster cast decoration.[24] One of the family descendants later said that as a child when she looked up at it she always thought it looked like icing on a cake.

From recollections by visitors and descriptions of furniture scattered among descendants, the original furnishings were probably heavy First Empire (Napoleonic) pieces. It is also said that there were many paintings on the walls of the central hall, but their subject matter is unknown.[25]

A door off the south hallway led to a hidden narrow stairwell to the upper story and balcony. Nearby, another stairwell led to the ground floor and winter kitchen.

The upper story contained the children's bedrooms, schoolrooms and quarters for the governesses or teachers of the Singleton children. The balcony overlooking the main hall "was richly adorned with paintings and potted plants." It was edged by a decorative iron railing of an "unusual and impressive Anthemion leaf motif from classical architecture" that had been cast in New York.[26]

The balcony was a favorite gathering spot for the ladies to sew and talk, making use of the natural light from the skylight above and the upper story windows. It also provided them with a view of what was happening on the floor below. The children used the balcony to do their schoolwork.

Special Features

The house had sixteen fireplaces and five closets. Having closets was very unusual at that time. Hangers had not been invented, and people usually stored their clothes in wardrobes.

It is said that Mrs. Singleton's side of the house had:

-Seven different pull bells for servants in her bedroom, denoting different needs.

-A bathroom in an alcove in her bedroom, the first indoor bathroom in Richland County, with a tin tub and shower attached to it. This included in the Jones and Lee design plans.

-During the winter, hot water was produced down below in

the winter kitchen. When the cook was heating up breakfast, a cast-iron tank filled with water situated behind the fireplace was heated. It was then pumped upstairs, using a kind of force pump, to a tank above the bathroom.

-Family members have also reported that there was a 100 gallon copper tank on the roof that the summer sun would heat. The warm water was piped down so warm baths could be taken.

The ground floor or English basement, as it was known, contained the winter kitchen, servant's quarters and food storage facilities and possibly a room used as a jail for recalcitrant slaves. It also contained a stuccoed, domed, double brick-lined 10,000 gallon cistern set into the floor of the basement. (Actual holding capacity is 9,644 gallons. It is forty-six feet long, over seven feet wide, and seven feet in height, accessed by two hatches.) It was used to catch rainwater from the house gutters for general household use and to furnish potable water to the residents.

Grounds

On the back side of the house facing the Wateree River is a portico (porch with a roof supported by columns). It could be accessed through full length sashed French windows in the dining room that could be used as pull-up doors or from stairs leading up from the grounds behind the house. The floor boards at the corners of the portico radiated out, forming sunray patterns.

The portico overlooked a formal English garden that was situated directly behind the home. It was "laid out in a spoke design and containing both native and exotic trees including water oak, magnolia, cedar, haw [crabapple] and holly." [27] The garden contained 100 rose bushes, camellias, lilacs and syringia, "centered around a circular plot, bordered by a boxwood hedge." The circle was cut into quadrants by paths leading "to the north and south between the rows of magnolias, and to the east towards the river through orchards of crabapples and smaller exotic trees."

The landscape plan, like the house plan, had definite French influences. "The open park in front, alignment parallel to the river, formal garden behind, and native groves of trees to either side were typical of French palaces." [28]   From the rear portico, one was offered a gently sloping view down to the bank of the Wateree River, a mile and a half distant and beyond. This greenway was lined by a double row of trees.[29] The river itself could not be seen, because it was below line-of-sight, but one would have been able to look across the river to the ancestral family plantation properties of Matthew's father, grandfather and great-grandfather, sloping gradually up from the Wateree River. (To get a sense of what the view from the Kensington once was, one can drive east along Vanboklen Rd. (Hwy. 263) toward Highways 378/76 and look across an open field in a southeasterly direction toward the Wateree River valley and beyond.)

Southeast of the mansion, located about a half mile away, were the slave quarters, referred to "the street" or "the quarters." The Kensington property at that time included fifty buildings: forty slave cabins and thirteen outbuildings, including barns, corncribs, a cotton warehouse, saw and gristmill, blacksmith shop, and a brick mill. At the riverside was a ferry, docks and barns.[30]

George Egleston Woodruff described the Kensington as he knew it in his youth: "a splendid plantation…worked 50 plows and owned hundreds of slaves. Her [Martha Singleton's] Negro settlement was laid off like a town, 10 houses to a row with shade trees between; about 50 houses all whitewashed and from a distance looked like a real town. As children when we went there we were awestruck with her elegant home in spacious grounds of 40 or 50 acres, rows of live oaks, beautiful shrubbery, flowers, vines, hollies and magnolias, large trees bending with sweet smelling yellow jessamine". [31]

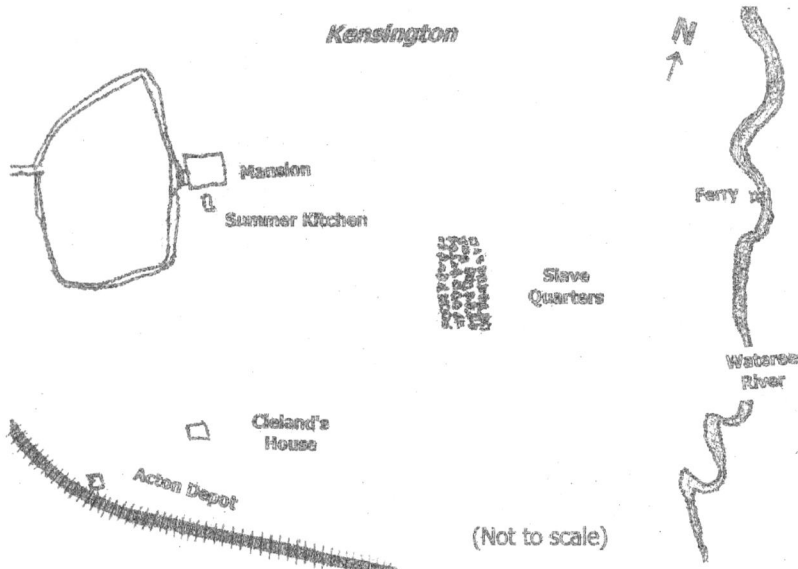

Kensington Plantation Drawing

Chapter 89-Martha Turns Things Around

Martha Singleton managed the Kensington largely on her own without reliance on male family members. This was not typical of Southern plantation widows. The Kensington was known as an efficiently run plantation. Martha Singleton recognized the importance of having effective overseers. Given the size of the Kensington slave population there were probably three or four. Martha Singleton hired William Turner to replace another overseer. In his memoir, Jacob Stroyer discusses at some length his run-ins with William Turner. He describes him as a "very bad man", being repeatedly whipped by him, and how he got even.

When Martha sold the racehorses, Jacob Stroyer lost his prized job of working with them, as did other slaves associated with horse racing. Most of them were sent to work as field-hands including Jacob Stroyer, but largely because of his persistence and ability to read (an illegal but valuable skill), Martha Singleton allowed him to work as a carpenter. This was against the wishes of Mr. Turner who had sent him back to the fields. Jacob had gone directly to Martha Singleton, over the head of Mr. Turner, so to speak, to settle his grievance.[32] She took a hands-on approach in dealing with more than household slaves and did not leave even job assignment issues solely to the discretion of overseers.

Iconoclastic Businesswoman

Besides dealing with debts and managing the day to day affairs of the plantation, Mattie began to make significant changes in what was being raised on the Kensington plantation. She shifted from an overwhelmingly cotton orientation to a much more diversified mixture of crops while at the same time increasing animal production. This ran counter to what was being done by many other Richland District planters at the time, who were increasing their reliance on cotton.

Martha was also expanding her landholdings at the same time as the number of farms in Richland district decreased by more than half between 1850 and 1860. Most of these were small landowners. By 1860 the Kensington property had expanded to 6,600 acres from 5,000 at the time of Matthew's death.[34]

Another difference between Martha and most of her neighbors was the increase in the number of her slaves. Between 1850 and 1860 there was a large decrease in the slave population of the Richland District. Martha increased her slaveholding from 281 at the time of Matthew's death to 465 by the 1860's.[35]

She continued to make other improvements on the property. She had the grist mill on the property converted from water to steam power to improve its capacity. She did this with the aid of Wade Hampton III in 1860. It required a large capital investment on her part of $2,250. She was also responsible for supplying all the labor to do the project.[36]

Agricultural Census

Commodities	1850 Matthew	1860 Mattie
Acres Improved	2600	2800
Acres Unimproved	2400	3800
Total Acreage	5000	6600
Cash value of farm	$30,000	$100,000.00
Cash value of implements	$1,050.00	$3,000.00
Horses	15	6
Asses and mules	28	36
Milch (milk) cows	25	50
Working oxen	0	4
Other cattle	80	200
Sheep	60	200
Swine	217	500
Value of livestock	$7,500.00	$8,000.00
Bushels of wheat	0	100
Bushels of Indian corn	7000	10,000
Bushels of oats	3500	500
Pounds of rice	0	300
Pounds of tobacco	0	0
Ginned cotton bales 400 lbs each	405 (162,000 lbs)	350 (140,000 lbs)
Pounds of wool	160	100
Bushels of peas and beans	600	1500
Irish potatoes	15	0
Bushels of sweet potatoes	3000	8000
Pounds of butter	300	500
Tons of hay	52	200
Gallons of molasses	0	1160
Value of home manufacture	$250.00	$200.00
Value of animals slaughtere	$400.00	$1,000.00

Comparison Chart 1850 and 1860)[33]

Chapter 90-Things Were Looking Up

As Martha was taking steps to turn around the fortunes of the Kensington, events beyond her control aided her efforts. There were no floods and droughts like there had been in 1852, 1853 and

1854. Cotton prices rose from 10¢ a pound through most of the 1840s and early 1850's to 15 cents a pound by 1857.

In 1856, Martha was able to order a new carriage from New York through her sister-in-law, Angelica, for which she paid $300, boxed and shipped. It was not an economy model. There were four seats inside as well as the coachman. It also had silver ornaments applied to japan'd glass panel edges. Angelica had difficulty in finding exactly what Martha wanted, but she ordered it from the Brewster Carriage Company in New York, the finest makers of carriages in nineteenth century America. She changed the color that Mattie wanted from blue to black.[37] Angelica didn't tell her why. (The Astors had the exclusive right to blue with the Brewster Carriage Company.)

PART TWELVE

THE CIVIL WAR

Chapter 91-Antebellum Wealth Picture

On March 4, 1858, on the eve of the Civil War, former Governor of South Carolina and sitting Senator, James Henry Hammond, famously declared, "Cotton is King." It was the war cry of the South and on the face of it, he appeared to be right. Overwhelmingly, as a region, the South had the highest per capita income in the country.

South Carolina's economy rested on a agricultural system, relatively unchanged for 150 years: "staple crops produced for world markets by enslaved black labor." [1] South Carolina, though she had slid from first in cotton production by state in 1820 to seventh in 1860, still ranked third behind Mississippi and Louisiana in per capita wealth in 1860.

Most of Southern wealth was in human property—slaves. In South Carolina, it's estimated that up to two-thirds of a slaveholder's wealth was in slaves and one-third in other assets. (Slaves were over 80% of Colonel Singleton's estate, for example.) Among South Carolina districts (counties), Sumter was ranked first and Richland eighth in per capita income.[2] On the eve of the Civil War, the South and the Kensington had never been more prosperous. That was about to change.

Chapter 92-The Civil War Comes

The Civil War changed everything for the South, the Singletons, and the Kensington, but the fighting did not come to the South Carolina interior where the Kensington was located until the last few months of the war. Even before that, however, the extended Singleton family and the residents of the Kensington plantation were not left unscathed by the war and the times.

During these early Civil War years, tragedy stalked Bonnie, the widow of John Coles, and their daughters. Rebecca Coles Singleton, the second oldest daughter, was called Decca and was a beauty with blue eyes and wavy, reddish gold hair. An accomplished dancer, she was extremely vivacious and charming in manner.

Mary Boykin Chesnut, close friend of Bonnie's, commented that "Decca was the worst in love girl she ever saw." The object of her affections was Colonel Alexander Cheves Haskell. He urged "her to let him marry her at once" since "in war times human events" and "especially life are uncertain". [3] She finally consented and they were married in September of 1861, spending a honeymoon of several days in Richmond before he returned to his duties. Colonel Haskell spent Christmas of 1861 with Decca in Columbia. It was the last time he saw her. Their daughter Rebecca was born in June of 1862.

Mary Chesnut wrote in her diary:

> Decca is dead. That poor little darling! Immediately after her baby was born, she took it into her head that Alex was killed. He was wounded, but those around had not told her of it. She surprised them by asking, 'Does anyone know how the battle has gone since Alex was killed?' She could not read for a day or so before she died. Her head was bewildered, but she would not let anyone else touch her letters; so she died with several unopened ones in her bosom. Decca's mother, Bonnie Singleton, fainted dead away, but she shed no tears… In a pouring rain we went to that poor child's funeral – to Decca's. They buried her in the little frock she wore when she engaged herself to Alex, and which she again put on for her bridal about a year ago. She lies now in the churchyard, in sight of my window.

It was many weeks before Alexander Haskell heard of his wife's death. Chesnut wrote, "Alex has come. I saw him ride up about dusk, and go into the graveyard. I shut up my windows on that side. Poor fellow." [4]

Alexander Haskell was wounded four times during the Civil War, the last time on October 7, 1864. He was left for dead on the battlefield after being shot in the head. A Union soldier took a gold ring off his little finger and promised to return it to Colonel Haskell's family. Shortly afterwards, Colonel Haskell was picked up by a Confederate scouting party and taken to a hospital. He recovered after the loss of an eye.[5]

After the death of Decca, Bonnie adopted and raised her granddaughter, Rebecca. Rebecca visited her father, Colonel Haskell, once a year after he remarried.[6]

Thirteen years after Colonel Haskell's wounding, a letter was placed in the *Charleston News and Courier* seeking to return the ring to its rightful owner. Colonel Haskell answered the letter, and the ring was returned to him.[7]

Decca's sister, Mary Carter Singleton, was described by diarist Mary Chesnut as

> ...exquisitely beautiful, cold, quiet, calm, lady-like, fair as a lily, with the blackest and longest eyelashes, and her eyes so light in color some one said 'they were the hue of cologne and water'. ...The effect is startling, but lovely beyond words.[8]

Mary Carter Singleton married the Reverend Robert Barnwell several years before the war. During the war, Reverend Barnwell ministered to the Confederate sick and wounded. He contracted typhus in Charlottesville, Virginia (Albemarle County) and died on July 25, 1863. Mary died within forty-eight hours along with their newborn baby, unaware of her husband's death. Chesnut wrote in her diary,

> Husband, wife, and child were buried at the same time in the same grave in Columbia. And now, Mrs. [Bonnie] Singleton has three orphan grandchildren. What a woeful year it has been to her.[9]

Chapter 93- Midway's Fate

In 1862, the same year that Decca died, Midway plantation, former home of Captain John Singleton, was owned by Mrs. Mary Martha McRae, his daughter, although she was hospitalized in a Philadelphia insane asylum at the time. J. Pringle Smith, a attorney from Charleston, rented the property to have it planted.

Mr. Smith put an overseer in charge and he was allowed to sleep in the house. It is said that while drunk, the overseer went into the English basement ground floor, lighting his way using a fat lighter torch (a piece of pine with a high dried sap content). He then laid it down on a pine table. After passing out, he awoke to find the table ablaze. Without attempting to put out the fire, he staggered out of the house and watched the entire house and all the furnishings go up in flames. Only the six foot high stone foundation of the home, along with the stable and carriage house complex survived the fire.[10]

Mary Carter Singleton Dwight, great great granddaughter of Captain John Singleton, lived in another dwelling on the property in 1870's. Years later she wrote that as children, she and her brother, John, "…thought it great fun to climb up to the top of some of the remaining six-foot high basement rock formations of the old burned mansion and jump off." [11] (Nothing remains of the Midway mansion today, except a marker along Highway 261.)

Chapter 94-A Wedding Story

On August 21, 1862 Henrietta Aiken, daughter of one of the wealthiest men in South Carolina, Governor William Aiken Jr., married Andrew Burnet Rhett.[12] The wedding took place in Flat Rock, North Carolina at Hill Side, the home of Martha Singleton. One of Henrietta Aiken's bridesmaids was Julia Rutledge. Both bride and bridesmaid were relatives of Martha Singleton.

Mary Boykin Chesnut told a story about the wedding in *Diary From Dixie*.

We could for a while not imagine what Julia [the bridesmaid] would do for a dress. My sister Kate remembered some muslin she had in the house for curtains, bought before the war, and laid aside as not needed now. The stuff was white and thin, a little coarse, but then we covered it with no end of beautiful lace. It made a charming dress and how altogether lovely Julia looked in it!

...A candle left burning in the bridal chamber during the wedding ceremony caught a drapery on fire. With the aid of the English maid and the servants of Mrs. Aiken and Martha Singleton, the fire was put out without disturbing the wedding ceremony being performed below, while a storm raged outside with high winds, rain, thunder and lightning. Everything in the bridal chamber was burned up except the bed, and that was a mass of cinders, soot, and flakes. [13]

(In *Gone With the Wind* there is a scene when Scarlett O'Hara uses curtains to make a dress just like in the wedding story. Margaret Mitchell, author of *Gone With the Wind*, would have had access to *Diary from Dixie*, one of 200 books she purchased for her research.)

Chapter 95-Cleland Enlists

Cleland, Matthew and Martha's eldest son, enlisted in January 1863, with Company E, 1st South Carolina Infantry (Charleston Battalion). Barely eighteen, he served on the staff of Major Andrew Barnet Rhett.[14] He served for the duration of the war as a private. He participated in several actions in South Carolina, including the defense of Fort Wagner that was charged by the 54th Massachusetts. (This unit was made famous in the movie "Glory"). Part of his service was on detached duty with the Signal Corps, where he served at Fort Sumter and Sullivan Island in Rhett's battery. He served until the end of the war, surrendering with Joseph E. Johnston's Army in North Carolina.[15]

Chapter 96-Angelica's Part

Angelica lived in New York City during the Civil War. She had to balance her loyalties to her Southern birth family and her Northern married family. Here, views diverge as to her actions during the Civil War. One view is that she only sent blankets and medical supplies to Confederate prisoners of war held at the infamous and deadly Elmira, New York prison. There is even a story that the Confederate government made efforts to confiscate her property in South Carolina.

On the other hand, according to a direct family descendent, Eliza Singleton Barron Macauley, Angelica sent scarce and otherwise unavailable items to family members in South Carolina by any means necessary. Angelica sent children's shoes, virtually unavailable in the South during the war. Macauley says they "were gratefully received." She also mentions in the same passage that all money sent from Angelica was invested in Confederate bonds.[16]

Chapter 97-Jacob Stroyer Wounded

According to Jacob Stroyer, during every year of the war fifteen Kensington slaves were sent to work on Confederate fortifications in South Carolina. Jacob Stroyer was one of those. He, along with other slaves from the Kensington, was sent to Charleston on two separate occasions.

On his second trip to Charleston, in summer of 1864, he, along with fourteen other Kensington slaves were sent to work at Fort Sumter during a time of heavy Union Naval shelling. Of the total of 360 slaves sent to work on the fort only forty would survive.[17] Stroyer mentions one of the Kensington slaves his own age being killed. Out of a group of fourteen or fifteen who sought shelter in a lime house during the bombardment, only the two who didn't make it in survived, including Jacob.

Jacob's companion's leg was broken, Jacob was wounded by a shell fragment, which injured his right eye and cut his lower lip.

He returned to the Kensington to recuperate and stayed there until freedom came with the end of the war.[18] (After the war, he headed north to further his education, became a pastor and revered figure in Salem, Massachusetts. For more on Jacob Stroyer, see Appendix.)

Mattie continued to manage the Kensington throughout the war with the critical help of overseers and slave drivers. They were so important that she paid $500, an overseer's yearly salary, to the Confederate Quartermaster's office to exempt one of her overseers, Robert Newsome, from military service. [19]

Chapter 98-Sherman Rampages through South Carolina

The interior of South Carolina largely escaped the ravages of the Civil War until February of 1865. After Sherman's March through Georgia, he turned north to South Carolina to to link up with Grant's army in Virginia. What Sherman's Army did in South Carolina is a story that is not well known outside of South Carolina, with the possible exception of the burning of the capital, Columbia. Sherman's March to the Sea, through Georgia, is much better known, but the level of wanton destruction of homes, private property, looting and in some cases, torture and murder, was unprecedented among the major armies during the Civil War. The gloves were totally off, although Sherman and some other officers paid lip service to the premise that they were not.

Sherman's personal fury was directed against the proud aristocratic planter class, for whom he seems to have developed an intense animosity. Wade Hampton III was singled out by Sherman for a special loathing.

A letter written by Sherman to the Union Chief of Staff, General Halleck, on Christmas Eve of 1864, describes the mood of the Union Army.

> The truth is the whole army is burning with an insatiable desire to wreak vengeance upon South Carolina. I almost tremble at her fate, but feel that she deserves all that seems

in store for her.[20]

In a letter written to Ulysses S. Grant just prior to the start of his march through South Carolina, Sherman describes his feelings,

> I do sincerely believe that the whole United States, North and South, would rejoice to have this Army turned loose on South Carolina to devastate that state, in the manner we have done in Georgia.[21]

Another Union officer spoke to a Georgia woman about the fate that awaited South Carolina.

> You think the people of Georgia are faring badly, and they are, but God pity the people of South Carolina when this Army gets there, for we have orders to lay everything in ashes – not to leave a green thing in the state for man or beast. That state will be made to feel the fearful sin of Secession before our army gets through with it. Here our soldiers were held in check…but when they get to South Carolina they will be turned loose to follow their own inclinations.[22]

Shortly after Sherman began his march through South Carolina, Lieutenant Colonel Hooper of the 54th Massachusetts, observed,

> Sherman destroys everything that stands in his line of march, – rice – mills, houses, fences. All through this country, as far as it can be seen, pillars of black smoke rise … The saying is that 'when Sherman gets through South Carolina, a crow can't fly across this country unless he carries rations with him.' [23]

General Judson Kilpatrick, head of the Union Cavalry, known unaffectionately by his men as "Killcavalry", reputedly sent a message to General Sherman, that "We have changed the name of Barnwell [South Carolina] to Burnwell." [24]

Responding to a South Carolina woman's pleadings that her sick son's room not be disturbed, a Union officer replied, "I can promise nothing. Every restraint is removed from our men in South Carolina." [25]

A newsman travelling with Sherman's army commented,

As for the wholesale burnings, pillage, devastation, committed in South Carolina, magnify all I have said of Georgia some fifty fold, and then throw in an occasional murder...[26]

From an unnamed source: "When we came through South Carolina, if we couldn't find a house to burn, then we set the woods on fire." There are other diary entries by Union soldier that express their joy at seeing the woods on fire in South Carolina.

Colonel Oscar Jackson, commander of the 63rd Ohio Regiment, wrote in his diary:

We have given South Carolina a terrible scourge since we left Pocotaligo [the jumping off point of the South Carolina march]. Our army...moving in a belt of from 30 to 70 miles...have destroyed all factories, cotton mills, gins, presses and cotton; burnt one city, the capital, and most of the villages on our route as well as most of the barns, outbuildings and dwelling houses, and every house that escaped fire has been pillaged...Their bacon, cattle, hogs, horses and poultry, to say nothing of the *dogs* [my italics] which we always kill, have been entirely cleaned out, and all wagons and carriages were either taken along or burnt. There was a recklessness by the soldiery in South Carolina that they never exhibited before and a sort of general 'don't care' on the part of the officers.[27]

The "war on dogs" by Sherman's army was a strange phenomenon that occurred on the march in South Carolina. It is mentioned in a number of Union soldiers' accounts. Colonel Jackson explained:

When on our march through South Carolina we had a spite at dogs because blood hounds were used to recapture our soldiers after they had escaped the southern hell – holes for prisoners and we were determined that no dog should escape, be it cur, rat dog or blood hound; we exterminated all. The dogs were easily killed. All we had to do was to bayonet them.[28] Household pet dogs suffered the same fate according to a number of eyewitness accounts.

A Michigan soldier wrote, "In South Carolina, there was no restraint whatever in pillaging and foraging. Men were allowed to do as they like, burn and destroy." [29] Wholesale looting was the unofficial order of the day.

One of Sherman's staff officers, an aide-de-camp, Brevet Major George Nichols, describes what was done and the attitude that engendered it.

> The well-known site of columns of black smoke meets our gaze again; this time homes are burning, and South Carolina has commenced to pay an installment, long overdue, on her debt to justice and humanity. With the help of God, we will have principal and interest before we leave her borders. There is a terrible gladness in the realization of so many hopes and wishes. This cowardly traitor state, secure from harm, as she thought, in her central position, with hellish haste dragged her Southern sisters into the cauldron of secession...where our footsteps pass, fire, ashes, and desolation follow in the path.[30]

In commenting on slaveholders in South Carolina, Nichols writes, "I firmly believe that we are God's instruments of justice, and that they are at last called to account for this shameless crime." [31]

Nichols goes on,

> Columbia will have bitter cause to remember the visit of Sherman's army. Even if peace and prosperity soon return to the land, not in this generation nor the next – no, not for a century – can this city or the state recover from the deadly blow which has taken its life. It is not alone in the property that has been destroyed – the buildings, bridges, mills, railroads, material of every description – nor in the loss of the slaves...It is in the crushing downfall of their inordinate vanity, their arrogant pride, that the rebels will feel the effects of the visit of our army. Their fancied unapproachable, invisible security has been ruthlessly overthrown...I know that thousands of South Carolina's sons are in the army of the rebellion; but she has already lost her best blood there. Those who remain have no homes. The Hamptons, Barnwell's, Simses, Rhetts , Singletons, Prestons, have no homes.[32] (The Singletons were related to the Hamptons, Barnwells, Rhetts, and Prestons.)

One Iowa Union soldier wrote in his diary on leaving Columbia, "The once pleasant town of Columbia is now nothing but a massive smoldering ruins. Everybody is glad that the town is burnt but the inhabitants." [33]   Sherman's men burned down Wade Hampton III's plantation home, *Millwood*, at the edge of Columbia.[34]

Millwood Ruins

Albermarle and the Singleton Silver

Adjacent to Millwood was the Albemarle plantation which had once been owned by John Coles Singleton; it was also put to the torch. In 1862, John Coles Singleton's widow, Bonnie, had sold Albemarle to George Trenholm.[35]   He was a banker, shipping magnate and blockade runner during the Civil War. (According to one researcher, he is the real life model for the Rhett Butler character in Margaret Mitchell's *Gone With the Wind*. For more on George Trenholm, see Appendix.)

To protect the Home Place silver from the expected approach of Sherman and the Union army, most of it had been sent to the Albemarle property for safekeeping, not realizing where Sherman was headed. Although Bonnie Singleton had sold the bulk of the property, she had retained forty acres and a dwelling. The Home Place and Albemarle silver were buried in three separate locations, each at the point of a triangle. Sherman's men found one box which contained some of the Home Place silver. Realizing the fine quality of it, they thought there must be more. An overseer was questioned and denied that there was any more, but after being hung up by his thumbs, he revealed the location of a second box, which contained the rest of the Home Place silver. It appears that the Albemarle silver was not found by the looters.[36] (According to a family descendent, the Albemarle silver was bartered and sold off piece by piece during the 1930's to provide food and pay medical bills for a disabled descendant of John Coles and Bonnie Singleton who lived in Camden, South Carolina.)

To South Carolinians, "whether or not Sherman gave an actual order to burn Columbia became an academic matter." [37] Sherman testified in a deposition after the war, "Though I never ordered it, never wished it, I never shed many tears over the event..," saying he believed it hastened the end of the war.[38]

Seventeen-year old Emma LeConte expressed the response from white South Carolinians to the wanton destruction in South Carolina, in general, and Columbia. in particular. On February 19th, two days after the burning of Columbia, she wrote:

> "When they [Sherman's troops] are gone, I will walk out of the Campus and see it all—yet how I dread it! Poor Columbia! Sometimes I try to picture it to myself as it now is, but I cannot. I always see the leafy streets and lovely gardens—the familiar houses. I cannot imagine the ruins and ashes to save my life. How I hate the people who have done this!" [39]

As to the desolation brought to South Carolina, General Sherman was called to testify in a post-war cotton case:

> Q: Were you at any time before crossing the Savannah

River, or before reaching Columbia, aware of a spirit of vengeance—a desire of vengeance—animating your troops to be wreaked upon South Carolina?

A: (Sherman) I was; the feeling was universal; and pervaded all ranks.

Q: Officers and all?

A: Officers and all; we looked upon South Carolina as the cause of our woes.

Q: And thought she thoroughly deserved strong treatment?

A: Yes, sir; that she thoroughly deserved extirpation.[40]

In the 1880s in a final slap at South Carolinians, Sherman wrote to a friend that the people of Georgia "bore their afflictions with some manliness," but in South Carolina, "the people whined like curs." [41]

Chapter 99-The Great Escape

How did the Kensington escape the ravages of Sherman's army, which destroyed the Kingville depot and rail line only five miles south of the Kensington and laid waste to so many private homes?[42]

As the story goes....

When Martha received word that Sherman's army was close by and threatening the Kensington, she hid what she could, sent the livestock into the swamp, and loaded up a wagon with what few valuables they could carry. Her thirteen year old son, Richard was sick with the measles and placed on a pallet in the back. Along with her mother, Mary I'on Kinloch, and a driver, they set off for the Summer Seat, a summer residence in the Sand Hills. Being three and a half miles northwest of the Kensington, off the main road, it provided a better refuge.

Part way, Mrs. Kinloch told Martha to stop and to let her out. She said she was going to return to the Kensington and see if she could protect it. With no one there, she was sure it would be burned down as so many other plantation houses had been on Sherman's march. Knowing that her mother had made up her mind, Martha agreed to go on with her son, Richard, to the Summer Seat.

Mrs. Kinloch returned to the Kensington and situated herself in the front women's parlor, which looked out on the Kensington driveway to the main road. To steady her nerves, she began reading the Bible, the passage from the book of Matthew that says, "Blessed are the merciful, for they shall receive mercy."

Shortly after, she heard hoof beats coming up the drive and saw a young Union officer at the head of some Union cavalry. He dismounted, came to the front door, and knocked. Mrs. Kinloch greeted him at the front door and asked him what he wanted. He replied that he had received orders to burn down the Kensington and that he planned to do so. He asked her who else lived there. She told him she was a widow and this place was all she had, that she wouldn't leave and that he'd have to burn the house down around her. The young man tried to persuade her to leave, but finally gave up, telling her that she reminded him of his own grandmother and that he would spare her house even though he was violating his orders. He rode off.

Shortly afterwards, a contingent of Wade Hampton's cavalry rode up looking for Yankee house burners and asking if any had been there. The Confederate officer in charge reputedly said to Mrs. Kinloch, "We were informed that a house burner had come here." She reputedly replied, "A young man was here a while ago, but as you can see, he did not burn the house."

Mrs. Kinloch engaged the cavalrymen in conversation. Being February, it was terribly cold and she offered them some buttermilk as refreshment. They accepted. Finally they asked her directly where the Yankees had gone. She waved her hand vaguely in the direction of Columbia, not being much help at all. They rode off in hot pursuit in the wrong direction. "Blessed are the merciful for they shall receive mercy." [43]

Mary I'on Rutledge Kinloch

Mrs. Kinloch may have saved the young Union officer not just from a fight with Confederate cavalry, but from a hanging. Due to the increasing bitterness at the destruction and home-burning, including his own, Wade Hampton, head of Confederate forces in South Carolina, had issued an edict saying that any Yankees caught burning homes would be hung. That happened on several occasions and Sherman promised his own retribution. Cooler heads prevailed before the matter got totally out of hand.

Chapter 100-Potter's Raid

When Sherman swept through South Carolina, his forces stayed to the west of the Wateree River, on the Kensington side of the river. The east side of the Wateree, which included Manchester, Home Place and the first Singleton family properties, had escaped the wrath of the Union army. However, after bypassing this area, Sherman became aware of large amounts of Confederate railway rolling stock, food, and military supplies in the area east of the Wateree. Recognizing this, he directed that a force be sent immediately to lay waste to these resources.

In his order to General Edward E. Potter, Sherman said, "those cars and locomotives should be destroyed if to do it costs you 500 men."[44] Potter was given command of a pieced-together force of some 2,500 men, to accomplish this mission as soon as possible. Potter set out on April 5th from Georgetown, South Carolina for the Sumter district side of the Wateree River. As Union troops drew closer to Home Place, the china and glassware were buried by a house slave. During part of the campaign, General Potter made his headquarters at Home Place.[45] The division, which included the 54th Massachusetts, (of the movie *Glory* fame), camped in a grove of trees on the plantation grounds. Even though Home Place was occupied by Union troops and searched for treasure, none of the china and glassware was lost.[46]

The force did as ordered, destroying locomotives, rail cars, railways, foodstuffs, bales of cotton, and cotton gins, but did not engage in the wholesale burning of homes as Sherman had done on his march through the rest of South Carolina. Potter's primary mission was to destroy the rolling stock and supplies. The raid continued with sporadic fighting up and down the district from Stateburg to Camden and back to the Manchester area with the Confederates shuttling their rolling stock back and forth to escape the Union forces.

Finally, on April 20th, Potter's force, having hemmed in the remaining rolling stock at and around the Middleton Railroad Depot on the Singleton Plantation, set about their destruction. Spread over two miles were fifteen or sixteen (possibly up to forty) locomotives and 245 (some say 248) railcars loaded with military supplies and foodstuffs. They were set ablaze. As the flames reached the ammunition, gun powder and shells, they detonated over the course of hours with tremendous explosions, sending projectiles in all directions. That night, the 54th Massachusetts bivouacked on the Home Place grounds.[47] The next day, Potter's entire force began a return to their base at Georgetown, leaving the Home Place mansion intact.

PART THIRTEEN

POSTWAR

Chapter 101-The Economic Impact of the War

The end of the Civil War brought the end of slavery. It is estimated that over fifty percent of South Carolina's capital investment in 1860 was in slaves.[1] That was all gone. For the Singletons, the loss was even greater. Referring to Colonel Richard Singleton's estate in 1853, almost 84% of his wealth, excluding real estate, had been in slaves. Martha Singleton had also invested heavily in slave labor, increasing her slave population from about 250 to 465. Emancipation and defeat eliminated all slave "capital" in one stroke.

By 1867 land values in South Carolina had declined sixty percent. Approximately one-third of South Carolina's military age white males—a desperately needed work force—had also been killed during the Civil War.[2]

Chapter 102-Early Postwar Life at the Kensington

When Mrs. Kinloch returned to the Kensington mansion to save it, the plantation was deserted. All the slaves had left the property or hidden themselves. At the end of the war almost all former slaves left their home plantations, at least initially, to experience freedom for the first time. It seems to have been a rite of passage to really know you were free.

There was some land distribution to freedman, but many returned to their home plantations or neighboring plantations. The Kensington was no exception. Within the next year or so, it appears many former slaves had returned. It's easy to understand why. It was what was familiar and it had been home. The freedmen really had known no other type of life and in most cases didn't have the skills or means to relocate to the North and to feed themselves and their families.

"The Great Migration" really began in the twentieth century, when blacks moved in their millions to take advantage of economic opportunities in the North and to flee the "Jim Crow" conditions of life in the South.

Mattie's mother, Mary I'on Lowndes Kinloch, having saved the Kensington, died the fall of that same year, 1865. This left Martha to carry on alone, until both her sons returned to help in the running of the Kensington plantation.

In 1866, Richard attended the school of Mr. Hugh S. Thompson in Columbia; his tuition was paid in bushels of wheat.[3] He then enrolled at the Virginia Military Institute (V.M.I.), but was forced to return home in 1868 due to lack of funds.

Cleland had attended school at St. Timothy's School in Baltimore before he returned home to enlist in the Confederate army. In 1867, a schoolmaster from the school sent a letter to Martha in 1867 requesting payment for Cleland's past schooling. He apologized for asking for payment *again* and said he couldn't forgive the debt, but would settle for a payment of $100, assuming some loss. The actual amount due from 1861 was $116.97.[4] There is no record of her response.

Cleland returned to the Kensington shortly after the war. In a letter of July 27, 1869 Mrs. Singleton reported to her attorney, James Simons, that Cleland was unable to pay the taxes on "our Richland property."[5]

To illustrate the change in Kensington economic fortunes, see the chart on the next page.

Agricultural Census

Commodities	1860 Before the War	1868 After the War
Acres Improved	2800	(215 acres planted)
Acres Unimproved	3800	
Total Acreage	6600	6600
Cash value of farm	$100,000.00	0
Cash value of implements	$3,000.00	$80.00
Horses	6	2
Asses and mules	36	8
Milch (milk) cows	50	38
Working oxen	4	2
Other cattle	200	0
Sheep	200	42
Swine	500	18
Value of livestock	$8,000.00	0
Bushels of wheat	100	11
Bushels of Indian corn	10,000	900
Bushels of oats	500	18
Pounds of rice	300	0
Pounds of tobacco	0	0
Ginned cotton bales 400 lbs each	350 (140,000 lbs)	7000 lbs
Pounds of wool	100	0
Bushels of peas and beans	1500	18
Irish potatoes	0	0
Bushels of sweet potatoes	8000	36
Pounds of butter	500	0
Tons of hay	200	0
Gallons of molasses	1160	0
Value of home manufacture	$200.00	0.00
Value of animals slaughtered	$1,000.00	$45.00

Comparison of farm production 1860 and 1868)[6]

Chapter 103-Sharecropping at the Kensington

At the Kensington, the sharecropping system initially replaced slavery as the farm labor system. The following are details of a Freedman's Contract from the year 1867 between Cleland Singleton and thirty-two freedman sharecroppers. Duties, obligations and compensation are enumerated. Many of the names on the contract are the same names as those who had been slaves at the Kensington. Three of the names are Stroy, probably relatives of Jacob Stroyer. (After the war many members of the Stroyer family changed their name to Stroy.)

Employer Responsibilities

- Employer agrees to treat freemen with justice and fairness, furnish quarters on the plantation, and allot each freedman four acres of land to be planted and firewood gathering privileges in designated areas.

- Compensation—Shareholders will receive one third of the corn, potatoes and peas and one third of the net proceeds of the ginned cotton.

- Employer will provide one peck [eight quarts] of grain or meal per week without charge and three pounds of bacon per week to be charged at market price to be deducted from laborer's share of the crops at the end of the year.

- Employer will provide work animals and their feed.

Freedmen Responsibilities

- Freedmen to do daily tasks of the plantation.

- Freedmen will start work at sunrise and will get one and a half to two and a half hours per day for meals depending on the season.

- Freedmen to be fined for lost time and absences, up to and including forfeiture of share of crop, but will be compensated for time worked.

- Freeman must use due diligence in caring for tools, "be kind and gentle to work animals," and will be fined for carelessness or neglect of same.

Shared Responsibilities

- If additional hands are needed "to keep the grass down" or additional hands are needed during harvest, the shareholders must pay their share of the cost.

- Freedmen shall keep stock and poultry where permitted by employer and out of the crops. Out of bounds violations will be fined for each offense.

- All fines go to employer and shareholders, "in relation to their relative shares."

Contract, Penalties and Compensation

- Contract is for one year.

- All violations of the terms of the contract or the rules and regulations of the employer subject the laborer to dismissal and forfeiture of his share and will receive four dollars per month for a full hand, less advances.[7]

Chapter 104-Martha's Ongoing Legal Problems

Besides dealing with the change of fortunes at the Kensington, Martha Singleton was embroiled in legal and family wrangling.

In November of 1867, she writes about her anguish that an uncle of hers in New York is claiming the right to possess some of her family portraits in a lawsuit , R. L. Livingston v. Martha Singleton, executrix.

> I cannot tell you how it grieves me to part with these portraits, which seem to me a very part and parcel of home, and as a connection for my children with my past and my people! And to think that they should be carried off to adorn

Yankee homes, where they will have no value save as works of art.[8]

(Robert Livingston was the husband of Mary Singleton McRae Livingston, daughter of Powell McRae Jr., who was banned from White Sulphur Springs by Matthew Singleton's father, Colonel Richard Singleton, many years before.)

Later, Martha was involved in a lawsuit with another uncle, Charles T. Lowndes, her mother's brother. The lawsuit was filed in May 1876 by Martha Singleton against her uncle, alleging mishandling and misuse of trust funds for Martha's mother which would devolve to Martha as sole survivor of her mother's estate. She filed the complaint, calling on him for an accounting of his actions and doings as trustee. The case was heard by the South Carolina Supreme Court in the November term of 1877, Singleton vs. Lowndes. The case finding was twenty-seven pages long. It appears that the court found in her favor, but her compensation is unknown.[9]

Chapter 105-Where Martha Spent Her Time

During these early postwar years Martha Singleton divided her time between the Kensington and Flat Rock. At Flat Rock she was surrounded by relatives and friends. She also often visited her aunt, Harriet Lowndes Aiken, in Charleston. Matthew and Martha's social network of friends and family seems to have been focused more on Flat Rock and Charleston, rather than locally in Richland and Sumter Counties.

Chapter 106-The Singletons Across the River

Singletons continued to live across the river in Sumter County, the initial settlement location and home to three generations of Singletons. Richard Richardson Singleton (1840-1900) and John Coles Singleton Jr. (1844-1919), sons and heirs of John Coles Singleton Sr. (1813-1852) had served in the Civil War as members of the 2nd South Carolina Cavalry, part of Hampton's Legion. After the war they moved onto the ancestral Singleton properties at Home Place and Melrose.

The brothers married their second cousins, who were sisters, the daughters of John Peter Broün, grandson of Captain John Singleton (1754-1820). They were married in a double marriage ceremony in 1868. Richard Richardson Singleton (1840-1900) married Annie Hinman Broün and John Coles Singleton Jr. (1844-1919) married Harriet Singleton Broün. Richard, the eldest son of the eldest son of Colonel Richard Singleton, inherited Home Place plantation, including the "mansion...completely furnished, with wonderful glass fronted presses full of beautiful cut glass, also marvelous dinner and tea sets etc." [10]

Initially, both young married couples lived together at Home Place. Within a year, John Coles Jr. and Harriet, soon-to-be parents of Mary Carter Singleton Dwight (1871-1958), left Home Place and moved to Melrose, the former residence of their great great great grandfather (third great grandfather), Matthew Singleton (1730-1787).[11]

Treasures in the Attic

As a new bride, Annie H. Broün Singleton began exploring her new home. In the attic she found a dozen and a half maple dining chairs in perfect condition and others in slightly broken condition. It was what remained of the set of twenty-four dining chairs once owned by Colonel Richard Singleton. She found other items as well: a double dinner stoneware set of twenty-four dinner plates, two soup tureens, and accessory pieces. They were from the English pottery founded by John Davenport in 1793, who served the Royal Family.

Annie Singleton also found a strange white flannel mask shaped like a hood and pierced with eye holes. Dolley Madison, a cousin and frequent guest at Home Place years before, had a beautiful complexion that was "a source of wonder to all who knew her." Angelica Singleton's former maid, by then an old woman, told the new bride that Dolley Madison used to "sit by the hour in the attic in that sweat box of a mask for her complexion's sake." [12]

Grandmothers

Mary Carter Singleton Dwight, granddaughter of John Coles Singleton Sr., daughter of John Coles Singleton Jr., and author of her family memoir, *A History of My Long Life*, wrote about her two distinctly different grandmothers: Abby, who had married John Peter Broün and Bonnie, who had married John Coles Singleton, Sr.

She wrote that her Grandmother Broün, originally from Connecticut, had a "wonderful mind and a superb education…brought up to be a New England school teacher". Mary wrote that her grandmother "could only see one side" of an issue. When she had made up her mind there was no changing her mind to see "the other side." She was also a superb housekeeper and cook and a very practical Yankee. During the four years of the "Confederate War," she knitted a sock a day for the Confederate soldiers.

> My grandmother Singleton differed completely from my grandmother Broün. She was considered a perfect blonde beauty and was a typical society woman with lovely manners. She taught me many of the amenities of life; namely, always to be gentle and kind to everyone; when on a trip never find fault or to fuss if things were unpleasant; also, when visiting to enjoy all that was done for your comfort or entertainment and express your thanks.

Mary Carter Singleton Dwight went on to say:

> Here's an illustration of the different outlook of these grandmothers, the one a thrifty Yankee, the other a lavish Virginian. Bonnie always said, 'Mary, never eat up everything on your plate at meal times. Leave a little as manners to show that you are not greedy.' On the other hand, Grandma Broün said, 'Mary, never take more on your plate than you can eat and be sure to eat it all as it is wasteful to leave food uneaten.' This made me act differently when at table with one of the other grandmother, but later I stuck to the Yankee grandmother's teaching on that question.

And in a final comment on the grandmothers:

> I think he [father-John Coles Singleton Jr.], was her
> [Bonnie's] favorite son and he was certainly devoted to her.
> But she never thought anyone good enough for her sons. So
> she and my mother and Aunt Annie never got on well
> together.[13]

Family Woes

Mary Carter Singleton Dwight described her family's situation:
"As he [her father, John Coles Jr.] returned from the Confederate
Army with nothing, he barely could make ends meet. We had none
of the luxuries and barely the necessities during our childhood;
however we were a very happy loving, care-free family and only
Mama seemed to miss all she had been accustomed to until the war
swept it away." [14]

After the war, the widow of Powell McRae Jr., Julia May McRae
Oelrichs, brought suit against the heirs of the Colonel Richard
Singleton estate to settle her long-standing grievance.[15] Richard
Richardson Singleton was forced to sell Home Place, the mansion
and most of the plantation property to settle the lawsuit. He was
able to retain a small piece of the property and built a smaller
home there, similar in style to Home Place, that he named
Blackwoods. He was able to move all the Home Place furniture,
books, glass presses, etc. there before Home Place was sold.[16]

Martha Singleton wrote to her son Cleland around the same time,
regarding Richard Richardson Singleton:

> "Your Uncle Dick [Richard Richardson Singleton] was in
> town a week and such a picture of woe I never saw. He
> seems to have lost all his strength & power of action,
> morally I mean. He mopes and sighs in the most dreadful
> manner." [17]

Home Place burned down in 1876. According to Mary Carter
Singleton Dwight, her uncle Richard Richardson Singleton viewed
this with a certain satisfaction.[18]

Upon his death in 1900, 703 items of the family heirlooms that
Richard Richardson Singleton had retained from three generations

of Singletons—Matthew (great great grandfather), John (great grandfather), and Richard (grandfather), were sold at auction at the Fifth Avenue Art Galleries in New York City. Blackwoods burned down a few years later, joining the other Singleton homes that suffered a similar fate.

Chapter 107-Angelica, Last of the Golden Generation, Dies

Angelica died in New York City on December 29, 1877. She had outlived her husband by three years, all her siblings, as well as many of her nephews and her beloved niece, Mary McDuffie Hampton. The only Singleton-related family attendees at her funeral, other than her sons, were the daughter and widow of Powell McRae Jr. : Mrs. (Mary Singleton McRae) Robert Livingston, and Mrs. (Julia May McRae) Oelrichs.

Both Mrs. Livingston (Powell McRae's daughter), and Mrs. Heinrich Oelrich (Powell McRae's widow) had sued Colonel Singleton's estate which had included Angelica. The suit by Mrs. Oelrich had caused the sale of Home Place as well as imposing a huge debt burden upon Colonel Singleton's children and heirs. Mrs. Livingston had sued Martha Singleton to gain possession of the family portraits. Nevertheless, Mrs. Livingston with her second husband, Robert J. Livingston, was seated in the mourner's row along with Angelica's three sons.[19] Angelica was buried alongside her husband in Woodlawn Cemetery in the borough of Bronx, New York City.

Chapter 108-The Brothers

According to the will of Colonel Singleton, the Kensington property was to pass to his grandsons, Richard Singleton (1851-1921) and Cleland Kinloch Singleton (1844-1920), but the deed transfer of ownership and partition of property did not occur until 1879. At that time Cleland was thirty-four years old and Richard was twenty-seven years old, well past the age of legal majority necessary to divide the property. (Why? I believe they tried to share it at first.)

Richard Singleton married Virginia Eliza Green in 1873 and brought his new wife to live at the mansion. According to a family descendant the newlyweds brought their wedding gifts home in one shoe box.[20] Helen Coles, Richard's sister, had married Eliza Green's brother, Allen Jones Green, in 1868. It appears that Richard and his wife, Helen Coles and her husband, Martha Singleton and Cleland were all living on the Kensington property in the early 1870's. Richard's new wife Eliza seems to have developed a close relationship with her mother-in-law, Martha. Richard and Eliza would have seven children together and appear to have been a close-knit family.

The relationship between the brothers, Richard and Cleland, began to unravel. The exact when and why is not clear, but the following letters trace the change. Captain A. Burnett Rhett, Cleland's commanding officer in the war, and a mutual friend of Richard and Cleland, wrote to Cleland about cockfighting, an interest of both brothers, and his impending visit to the Kensington.

> Charleston, S.C. June 22, 1875
>
> Dear Cle,
> We will leave Charleston on Tuesday next [29th June] in the "night train", & hope you will meet us all right. I will send you two hens by Express to-morrow. Tell Richard that I will take the match up with pleasure. [Wm.?] Aiken asks me to say to Richard that he thought him a better business man -- more prompt—
>
> > Yrs. in Haste
> > A. Burnet Rhett[21]

(The intent of the "better business man" comment is not clear, but the bantering, challenging tone to the letter is common among men around sports. The letter indicates Richard and Cleland were on speaking terms in the summer of 1875, at least as far as Mr. Rhett knew.)

Two months later, Martha wrote a four page letter to Cleland. The first part discussed family and friends in Flat Rock, her weight and the marvels of "modern" transportation. The second part focused on Cleland's relationship with his brother, Richard, and provides a hint of the growing schism between them. She wrote:

> I had a long and very pleasant letter lately from Eliza [Richard's wife]. She complains of seeing so little of you and that, tho' Allen [Helen Coles Singleton Green's husband] dines with them on Sunday, you will not. Pray my dear son, do not let any coldness grow up between you. It would distress me more than I can say. And little as Richard may say, I know [her underline] he feels it deeply. We are poor enough God knows, in worldly form, but we may be rich in love and affection, which are worth money many times over.[22]

One year later Richard sent a letter to his brother Cleland, who lived on part of the Kensington property, less than a half mile away from the mansion where Richard lived. When and why this residency change took place is unclear. It was written on letterhead stationery with the heading: *Richard Singleton Dealer in General Merchandise*

> Dear Cle, I enclose herewith a list of all the tenants on the place and have divided them to the best of my judgment, but should you however be not satisfied I beg you….make a new list and send to me at your earliest convenience. I would also suggest that you make some arrangements to get your rent in, as some of your tenants are ready to pay up. I really do not have time to attend to it. Another matter I wish to call your attention to is that I wish to keep house to myself this winter. I am willing to take either one of the two houses on the plantation or part of the main dwelling. For some reason I suppose known to yourself, you have not spoken to me for twelve months. If I am in the wrong and you had told me what I had done I could have then apologized. But before heaven I do not know what has caused your displeasure. To say this has pained me is useless as you must know that yourself. Do not understand by what I have written that I do not want you at my house, for I should always be most happy for you to be there but as my guest as it is my house [underlines are Richard's]. Please let me hear from you soon and fully.
>
> Yrs Richard Singleton [23]

Partition

Two years later, in 1878, Richard Singleton instructed attorney, Louis Le Conte, to contact Cleland Singleton to get the Kensington property divided and partitioned between the brothers.[24] The properties were surveyed and the property partitioned and probated in January of 1879. The Kensington property (6,692 acres) was on both sides of the Wateree River. In general, Richard got the northern half of the property and Cleland the southern half. The property (3,160 acres) on the west side of the Wateree (the mansion side) in Richland County, was partitioned with Richard getting 1,585 acres and the mansion and Cleland getting 1,575 acres.[25] The property (3,532 acres) on the east side of the Wateree in Sumter County was divided in a similar north and south fashion, each brother receiving 1,766 acres.[26] After the partition of the property, the rancor between the brothers continued. It is said that the brothers did not speak to each other for ten years. (Eventually, the brother's Richland side properties would be sold to new owners, but what happened to the brother's Sumter side properties, a total of 3,532 acres, is unknown.)

In a final land disposition in 1879, Martha gave some of her land to her daughter, Helen Coles Singleton Green.[27] She had previously given some of her landholdings to Cleland and Richard.

Chapter 109-Helen Coles Singleton Green (1846-1924)

A neighbor of the Singletons, George Egleston Woodruff, in his memoir, *Boyhood Sketches*, written in his old age, described Helen

Singleton as "the most beautiful girl I ever saw". [28] Helen Coles Singleton appears to have been a small woman. Martha's mother was described as small and I conjecture that Mattie was the same as well as Helen Coles. Initially she lived on the Kensington property, but moved to Columbia with her husband Allen and their children about 1880.

Helen Coles ended up with many of Angelica's heirlooms in her possession. In the early twentieth century she lent several of these items to the Smithsonian:

- A marine blue velvet skirt and waist with lining and hoops worn by Angelica while acting as Hostess of the White House.

- An embroidered laced handkerchief of unusual size marked S. A. (for Sarah Angelica) Singleton. It was part of her trousseau.

- A white satin fan with ivory sticks with Angelica's monogram painted upon it in bright colors.

Chapter 110-Cleland Singleton (1844-1920)

Cleland Kinloch Singleton was the eldest son of Matthew Richard, but he didn't get the mansion and seems to have been the less successful of the two brothers, at least in worldly terms. He was definitely the less ambitious. He lived an almost shadowy, reclusive existence. Very little is said about him in family accounts. He had friends, but seems by and large to have lived an isolated life. Martha wrote a letter to Cle, as he was known by his friends and family, on September 26, 1873: "I have been so troubled at your loneliness..." Martha then apologizes for not writing more, but that she found her "own life so dull and monotonous" that she felt it was "not likely to raise your spirits." [29]

Cleland was a great lover of books and literature—an interest he shared with his mother and the rest of his mother's family, the Kinlochs. This interest would be noted in his obituary. Cleland never married and or had children, but his sister, Helen Coles Singleton Green, gave birth to a boy in 1872 and named him

Cleland Singleton Green.

Cleland's House

Cleland lived in a house a half mile south of the oval driveway of the mansion along the main north/south plantation road, on his half of the original Kensington property. It is thought by some that Cleland built the home, but according to Richard's letter of September 8, 1876, there were already two houses on the property.[30] Cleland's may have been one of them.

Cleland's house was a structure of three rooms, built on stilts with the living quarters above ten feet or more. (This helped avoid mosquitoes as they generally stay below 25 feet.) Flooding may have been a consideration also.

Cleland's house was unique in at least one other way, at least on the Kensington property. According to a story, a man came to the Kensington mansion and asked if Cleland Singleton was there. A servant told the salesman that he was not and that he lived in the house down the road with the "flour sieves" (screens) on the windows.

Cleland's house

Photographs taken in the summer of 1892 show clearly there are no screens on the windows of the Kensington mansion. There is no indication that there were screens on the windows until the twentieth century.

Cleland Stories

Cleland was an active outdoorsman and loved to hunt. He was interested in dogs, too, and along with his brother, Richard, was an avid cock fighter.

According to stories, passed down for generations from friends and family, Cleland liked to hunt with a double barrel shotgun, but a companion of his never saw him shoot it. The same person also said that Cleland drank and would be drunk for a week. A direct family descendent said that when Cle was questioned about his lifestyle, he answered that he had been at Fort Sumter and he could do anything he wanted with the rest of his life.

It is also said that Cleland didn't go out into the fields to supervise the work. Cleland stayed in the house and had a long spyglass that he would use to see what was going on in the fields. Cleland was in the Signal Corps during the war and a spyglass is one of the instruments that he would have used. Cleland's house was on a ridge that sloped away toward the fields. The elevated living quarters would have provided a good viewing location.

The Columbia Daily Register of December 28, 1880, reported that a fire at Cleland Singleton's plantation, destroyed "a stable and barn, two mules and a lot of seed cotton and fodder." The Christmas night fire was most likely caused by fireworks which were a common local practice at the time.[31]

Cleland's Household

In the 1880 Census, Cleland is listed as head of household and a white farmer. Emmeline Anderson (38 years old) is listed as a black cook, and her children, Flora (15 years old) and Jennette (13 years old) are listed as black servants.

In the 1900 and 1920 censuses, Cleland is listed as a white farmer and head of household. In these two censuses, Henrietta Scott is listed as a servant, categorized as black in 1900 and mulatto in 1920. In the 1920 census, Henrietta Scott's sister, Charlotte, is also listed as a servant and mulatto. Henrietta Scott was born in 1862/3, and was twenty years Cleland's junior.[32]

It is believed that Cleland and Henrietta had a long-term romantic relationship and would have married had not inter-racial marriage been illegal in South Carolina at that time. Neither Henrietta nor Cleland ever married and there were no children.

Chapter 111-Richard Singleton (1851-1921)

Richard was a planter and businessman. His letterhead stationery in the mid-1870's said, *Richard Singleton Dealer in General Merchandise*. In a publication of the Gazetteer of Richland County, 1879-1880, he is listed as postmaster and merchant.[33] He lived a much more conventional and outgoing life than his brother. Although he farmed his half of the Kensington, he seems to have been most successful in the mercantile trades.

He also served one term in the State Legislature in 1882 as a political ally of Wade Hampton III, but he did not find it a "congenial occupation." [34] He was swept out of office along with many other representatives of the South Carolina aristocracy, to be replaced by members of "Pitchfork" Ben Tillman's Populist supporters. Richard Singleton was also appointed a Lieutenant-Colonel on Governor Hugh Thompson's staff, thus continuing a family tradition of Colonels, going back to his great great grandfather, Matthew. (Governor Hugh Thompson had been a teacher of Richard's when he attended school at the Columbia Academy in the 1860's.)

Richard Singleton was active in his local community and later in Columbia. He was involved in church governance, served on grand juries and various civic committees and was later President of the Columbia Club. The contrast with his brother, Cleland, who was private, reclusive and shunned the public spotlight, could not be more stark.

Chapter 112- The Kensington Lifestyle

After the war the Kensington mansion became a refuge for friends and family members whose homes had been lost in the war as well as a gathering place of entertainment for family and friends. It was common for guests to stay from the Christmas season to the beginning of the Lenten season in February. The household not only consisted of family members and guests, but also a governess for the children and the storekeeper who managed the commissary utilized by the sharecroppers.

Eliza Singleton Barron Macaulay, a direct descendant of Richard Singleton, described the post war daily routine and lifestyle at the Kensington.

Rachael, known affectionately as the Duchess because of the high turban that she wore on her head, "was in the kitchen each morning by 6 a.m. to serve an early breakfast to the storekeeper and Richard Singleton before he did his morning inspection ride around the plantation…About 9 AM an elaborate leisurely breakfast was served to the whole family." After breakfast the children went upstairs to the school room with the governess for their studies. The lady of the house, Eliza Green Singleton, took her key basket, opened the storerooms and smokehouse, and "measured out the ingredients for the meals she had planned for the day." The Duchess stayed working in the kitchen with only "a short break in the afternoon until after a hot supper was served." Sunday was the only exception when a cold supper was prepared so Rachael could attend church.

Mrs. Singleton was also involved in overseeing the house servants and gardeners as well as attending to the minor medical needs of both black and white residents of the Kensington, as had been the case in antebellum times

The dining room was the main location of family gatherings for generations. After supper the family gathered there. It was the largest and the driest room in the house and warm in the winter with fireplaces at either end. Family members used the room to play cards, discuss the news of the day or read. The large mahogany dining table was covered with a green cloth making it ideal for playing cards or other activities. The room also contained a sofa and additional chairs. Newspapers, Harper's Magazine, and "new books which were ordered from New York" (unavailable in Charleston or Columbia) were always given to the Colonel first. In his easy chair, he sat reading the newspapers and magazines. He had the habit of sitting on them until he finished reading them before passing them on to other members of the family. In the corner behind his chair was a small rocker upon which his youngest child, Eliza, known as Daisy, often sat, sharing his lamp light and reading her book.

Governess Sallie Gillespie (Miss S) and Eliza (Daisy) Singleton

"The children were all taught to ride" and owned their own mounts. They were instructed by the horse master, Jesse, to ride well and to take care of the horses. Every afternoon a sun-down bell was rung, signaling that it was time to return to the house before sunset. All the horses knew what that meant and no matter how hard the young riders tried to extend their rides, the horses would not be dissuaded and would return to the barn.[35]

Richard Singleton was the cousin and godfather of Mary Carter Singleton Dwight. She relates how,

> Often as a child I would run over with Papa [John Coles Singleton Jr.] to spend the day at Kensington. The trains ran very conveniently, leaving Wedgefield [on the east side of the Wateree River] at 10 a.m. and returning at 5 p.m., after a ten mile trip mostly across the Wateree swamp and river. The train stop was at the Acton station [half mile from the

197

mansion]. I remember many delightful stays there from childhood on through the years.[36]

Mary Carter Singleton Dwight and her cousins, Marie and Elise, daughters of Richard Richardson Singleton, were invited for a weekend at the Kensington. Mary noticed that the two little girls of Richard's were wearing button shoes with buttons on the inside. Their nurse said that the shoes were changed from one foot to the other every day. Mary thought it odd and never received an explanation. (Seventy years later when Mary Dwight wrote her memoir, she still puzzled over the *why*.)[37]

Social Life at The Pines

After the war, there were no more summers at White Sulphur Springs for the Singletons. The Summer Seat, also known as The Pines, the place where Martha Singleton had fled to avoid Sherman's men, served as a family summer home during "the sick season". Its location in the Sand Hills several miles from the river and swamps with their malaria and mosquitoes provided a welcome respite. It was a large, comfortable cottage-type house with a broad front porch, which was fully equipped with joggling boards, hammocks and rocking chairs. Inside was a wide hall running the length of the house. As the Singleton children and their friends grew up, the hall was used as a dance floor for social events and as a dancing school.

The Pines/Summer Seat

Chapter 113-The Passing of Martha Singleton

After the Kensington property was divided between her sons, Martha Singleton lived with her daughter, Helen Coles Singleton Green and her family. She moved with them when they relocated to Columbia.[38]

Martha spent her remaining years teaching and enjoying her three grandchildren. The Green Family lived at the northwest corner of Sumter and Pendleton, adjacent to the "Horseshoe", heart of the University of South Carolina campus. (Much of the research done for this book was done at the South Caroliniana Library, home to many of Martha Singleton's letters. The Library is one block from the location of Martha's daughter's house, which no longer exists.)

In the spring of 1892, typhoid fever struck Martha Singleton at her daughter's home. Richard Singleton and his wife Eliza went to the Green's home to be with Martha during her illness.[39] They dashed off a note in pencil to Cleland, on May 17th, imploring him to come quickly to his mother's bedside who was gravely ill. Richard's wife, Eliza, wrote the bulk of the letter, heading it "Dear Cle" and ending with "Affectionately, E.G.S." [Eliza Green Singleton].

Richard added,

> I can get no expression from Doctor or nurse of how long she can last & don't think they know—But think you best come up by S.C. RR tonight or certainly on early train tomorrow. RS [40]

Martha died on June 13, 1892 at the age of seventy-four of typhoid fever. She had lived more than twice as long as her husband, Matthew Richard, who died at 36. Martha's obituary read in part,

> ....she lived a life that was beautiful in the extreme. She was a brilliant, sympathetic, and attractive woman, who endeared herself to all with whom she came in contact.

Her sons Cleland and Richard and her grandson Cleland Singleton Green accompanied her body was to the gravesite. She was laid to rest beside her husband in Flat Rock, at St. John in the Wilderness

Cemetery.[41] (Edward C. Jones, the architect who had designed the Kensington, also designed the St. John in the Wilderness Church. For Martha Singleton obituary, see Appendix.)

Martha left a personal estate of twenty-one shares of Charleston Gas and Light stock and less than $5,000, to be divided equally among her children.[42]

The only photographs known to exist of the Singleton-owned Kensington and of Singleton family members on the property are from 1892. They were taken shortly after Martha Singleton's death. In her memoir, Mary Carter Singleton Dwight mentions that she is "…standing in one of the three bedroom windows on the front in one of those pictures." [43]

Kensington in 1892

Richard Singleton Family on Kensington Front Steps
Back Row (L-R):
Virginia Taylor(13), Mary Lowndes (17),Lillian (12)
Middle Row (L-R):
Eliza Green Singleton, Richard Singleton, Governess Sallie "Miss
S" Gillespie, Eliza (Daisy) Singleton (6)
Front Row: Dog (name unknown), Matthew Singleton (15)
Lucy Pride (8) not pictured.

Chapter 114-Matthew Richard Singleton (1877-1910)

Matthew Richard Singleton was the only son and male heir of his father, Richard Singleton. Matthew's father, Richard, had attended the Virginia Military Institute (VMI) after the War, but had been forced to drop out and return home when there wasn't enough money to continue his education. In 1895, when he was 18 years old, Matthew Richard enrolled at the Citadel, the South Carolina military school, following in the military education footsteps of his father.

Just a few weeks before his projected graduation in 1898 and just prior to the outbreak of the Spanish American War, Matthew Richard, along with twenty-three of his senior classmates, out of a total of thirty, were expelled for what has been described as an "ill-fated attempt at Espirit de Corps". A total of sixty-four students, which comprised about half of the entire student body was expelled in what became known as the Cantey Rebellion.[44] Matthew Richard returned home to the Kensington and joined his father in the farming and merchandise business.

PART FOURTEEN

THE SINGLETON ERA ENDS

Chapter 115-Festive Wedding Occasions

The twentieth century dawned auspiciously for Richard and Eliza Green Singleton's family with three of their children getting married in its first decade.

In 1900, Matthew Richard married Charlotte Cantey Johnson of Camden. A small house was built for them north and east of the mansion on the Kensington property.

In the spring of 1907, Eliza (Daisy) Singleton married a prominent attorney from Columbia, Charles Henry Barron. Eliza was known as Daisy all her life. A family nurse gave her the nickname saying she was "as pretty as a daisy". "She had dark hair and green eyes and was very tall and beautiful" and was known as "the belle of the county". [1]

Daisy's marriage to Charles Barron was a huge social event with a special train running from Columbia to Acton station, just south of the Kensington, bringing 200 guests. Carriages and wagonettes (horse-drawn open wagons for passenger transport) met the guests at the station and brought them up the avenue to the mansion's front steps where they were greeted by the proud father of the bride to be.

The mansion's interior was festooned with wedding-roses and every imaginable flower in every conceivable location. The wedding was held in the main hall with the bride and groom entering from the two wings. After the ceremony, old sherry and champagne punch in abundance were offered and a meal of several courses was served. The special train returned to Columbia at midnight with many of the guests; and for those who remained, the house party broke up the next day.[2] (For more on the Singleton - Barron wedding, see Appendix.)

The following year, another sister, Lillian Singleton, married Thomas Coker, Jr. of Hartsville in another festive wedding.

Chapter 116-End of an Era

The year 1910 brought great change for Richard Singleton, his family and the Kensington. Besides farming, he owned a store in Eastover. In partnership with Julian Byrd, Richard capitalized the Farmers and Merchants Bank of Eastover in the amount of $25,000, and served as its first president. Eastover, by 1910, was the only incorporated town in Richland County besides Columbia. (The bank building is now on the National Register of Historic Places.)

While Richard Singleton was finalizing the details of the incorporation of the bank, his son, Matthew Richard Singleton, died unexpectedly on January 14, 1910. According to his obituary, Matthew Richard had been in ill health for the last few years of his life and died of pneumonia.[3] He joined the long list of other Singleton male adults who didn't live past forty: John Peter (1775-1800), John Coles (1813-1852) and Matthew Richard (1817-1854), as well as all three sons of Angelica Singleton Van Buren. (It has been suggested that there was an inherited congenital lung defect present in the family genes that particularly affected male members of the family. Other than the perils of childbirth, the Singleton daughters seemed to have fared much better.)

Matthew Richard Singleton was well-liked, loved sports and hunting and was known as "Matt". A memorium published in *The State* newspaper two months after his death, fondly remembered his affable nature and the loss that his friends and family suffered.[4]

With the death of his son and heir, the spirit seems to have gone out of Richard. Within the year, on December 29, 1910, he sold his portion of the Kensington property, including the mansion, to his friend, Robert Pickett Hamer, Jr, for $75,000.[5] A Singleton family legend maintains that the Kensington was lost to Mr. Hamer as the result of a wager on a cockfight. Mr. Hamer would never live at the Kensington.

Mary Carter Singleton Dwight wrote,

> My last visit there [Kensington] was a sad one, some months after Matt's death, when they [Richard and Eliza] had decided to sell the house and plantation and move to the Sand Hill summer home [the Summer Seat / The Pines] which they were having heated, the upstairs completed, and made comfortable as a winter home. They felt that Matt's death from pneumonia was due to his life at the plantation, so near the swamp, and that malaria had undermined his constitution and so caused his death.[6] (According to a family descendant: After Matthew's death, whenever his widow, Charlotte Cantey Johnson Singleton, drove past the Kensington mansion, she would avert her eyes or shield her view of the mansion with a fan. She could not bear to look at it.)

Richard Singleton retired from business in and around Eastover and after a sojourn at the Summer Seat/The Pines, he and his wife, Eliza, moved to Columbia, where they lived out the rest of their lives.[7] Richard continued to take an active part in business and community activities in Columbia.

A family descendent said of Eliza Green Singleton that she was "small in stature but very imposing in spirit, always wore formal dresses with high collars"… but when she went to the country, her Sand Hills [The Pines] home, the "dress code" was off and "she changed to gingham dresses." [8] Mary Carter Singleton Dwight maintained a close relationship to her cousin Eliza. She wrote that Eliza preferred The Pines to her Columbia home and spent as much time there as possible, even in the years when she became an invalid.[9]

Richard and Eliza celebrated their forty-fifth wedding anniversary in 1918 with Richard's brother Cleland in attendance. "The day was celebrated quietly and within quarantine limits with a family dinner", noted *The State* Newspaper. (A health quarantine was in effect in Columbia at the time.)[10]

Chapter 117-Passing of Cleland Singleton

On May 19, 1920, Cleland Singleton died of pneumonia, at the age of 75, at the home of his sister, Helen Coles Singleton Green, in Columbia. He chose to be buried in Charleston in Magnolia Cemetery, away from his parents, brother and sister, but in the same cemetery as thirty-eight other Kinlochs.[11] (Edward C. Jones, designer of the Kensington and the chapel of St. John in the Wilderness Church, in whose cemetery, Matthew and Martha Singleton were buried, also drew up the plans for Magnolia Cemetery in 1850 where Cleland Singleton was buried.)

Cleland's obituary described him as

> ...a gentleman of shy, retiring disposition who shrank from conspicuous activities and publicity, content to spend his leisure in reading solid literature. He was a man rarely [unusually] well-informed and his conversation and companionship were delightful to the members of his circle of friends.[12]

All of Cleland's real estate went to his sister, Helen Singleton Green, for her natural life. Upon her death it was to be divided between her sons, Cleland Singleton Green and Walter T. Green. The will also provided for payment to his brother Richard Singleton for any monies due on a mortgage for his Kensington property. One year after the death of Helen Singleton Green a sum of $5,000 was to go to Richard Singleton (1901-1978), grandson of his brother, Richard Singleton, and grandnephew of Cleland. All personal property was left to Cleland Singleton Green and Walter T. Green.[13] It is also believed that Cleland Singleton paid for Henrietta Scott's niece's (Eppie-House Smith) college education at Allen University in Columbia, South Carolina.

Chapter 118-Passing of Richard Singleton

Thirteen months after Cleland's death, on June 30, 1921, Richard Singleton went to Ashville, North Carolina for treatment of a heart condition. He died of heart failure the same day he arrived.

Duncan Ray, a lifelong friend, wrote a sketch about him in his obituary: "One of his most notable achievements was the redeeming of his home from ante-bellum obligations, incurred by his grandfather [Colonel Richard Singleton]." He also characterized him as a "true southern gentleman".[14]   Richard Singleton, was buried alongside his wife, in Zion Episcopal Cemetery in Eastover along with five of his six daughters and his only son.

Chapter 119-Tragedy

A year after Richard Singleton's death, tragedy struck the family of his daughter, Daisy Singleton Barron.

Daisy's husband, Charles Henry Barron, was one of the best known businessmen in South Carolina, a senior member of the law firm Barron, Frierson, McCants and Elliott. He had served as assistant attorney-general of South Carolina in 1906, and as an attorney for American Export and Import Corporation, Liberty National Bank, Division Counsel for Atlantic Coast Line Railroad, Counsel for American Railway Express Company and the Pullman Company. He was also President of Carolina Bond and Mortgage Company and Director of Liberty National Bank. During World War I, he served as State Chairman for the Victory Liberty Loan campaign.

On November 14, 1922, Charles took his own life with a self-inflicted gunshot to the head. Mr. Barron's hat was found about four feet from where he lay. He had left a note in his hat, carefully covered with a handkerchief. The note was written in pencil on the back of an old letter.

"My life insurance is the only way I have to pay those I owe. I have done my best."
 (Signed)   "Chas. H. Barron"

"Be sure to get return premiums on policies less than a year old."
(Signed)   "C. H. B."

"Please ask my good friend, J. E. Belser, to have my loyal friend and partner, J. Nelson Frierson, appointed administrator. My estate is solely liable for the firm debts as all others were on a salary basis and know nothing of my troubles or the conditions of finances."

(Signed)   "Chas. H. Barron"

11-14-22 [15]

He left his wife Daisy, and three children, aged fourteen, thirteen and ten. Daisy moved in with her widowed mother and lived with her until the children were grown.[16] Upon her retirement, Daisy Singleton Barron (1886-1968), a much beloved librarian at Columbia High School from 1923-1951, advised "every young girl to choose a profession or vocation while she is still young; you never know when it may be necessary for you to support yourself or your family." Upon her death, Daisy was buried alongside her husband, Charles Henry Barron, in Columbia at Elmwood Memorial Gardens cemetery.

PART FIFTEEN

NEW OWNERS

Chapter 120-The New Kensington Owners: The Hamers

Robert Pickett Hamer Jr., the new owner of the Kensington, was one of the largest and wealthiest landowners and farmers in South Carolina.[1] He was described as a "human dynamo", active in politics, having served in the South Carolina House of Representatives and twice chosen as Executive Committeeman of the South Carolina Democratic Party. He was being prominently mentioned as a possible future Governor. He was a handsome man, even suitable for the present media age. Desiring to be closer to Columbia than his native Dillon County, he was prompted to buy the Kensington property of his friend, Richard Singleton, so that he could run for governor and entertain properly, in proximity to the state capital, so the story goes.

Robert Pickett Hamer Jr.

In August of 1912, Mr. Hamer was attending a Democratic Party Executive Committee Meeting in Columbia and was overcome by the heat. He was taken to Saluda, North Carolina in the mountains to recover. He arrived there on August 31st. He passed away from heat prostration nine days later.[2] Robert Pickett Hamer Jr. was only forty-nine years old, seemingly in robust health. He never had the chance to reside at the Kensington.

Robert Cochrane Hamer

It was left to Robert Pickett Hamer Jr.'s son, Robert Cochrane Hamer, at age 21, to take over the management of the 1,500 acre Kensington plantation as well as overseeing the management of two other Richland County properties for his minor sisters. He and his new wife, Janie Porcher Dubose Hamer, resided at Kensington mansion for the next thirty years.

Robert Cochrane Hamer

One of the first changes he made was to install screens on all the windows. This was done to keep out the mosquitoes, because the discovery had been made that mosquitoes were the carriers of malaria. Malaria had been the bane of those residing close to the swamps and rivers. Many planter families had moved to higher elevations in the summer to escape the "sick season".

The Hamers also installed electricity, modernized and extended the indoor plumbing, and updated the water system with a gasoline motor driven water pump system. A huge ice box was installed in the "English" basement and 300 pound blocks of ice were delivered from Eastover once a week.[3]

Chapter 121-The Kensington Properties Reunited

At first, the Hamers only owned the half of the Kensington that Richard Singleton sold to Robert Pickett Hamer Jr. After Helen Coles Singleton Green's death in 1924, Cleland's property passed to his nephew, Walter Taylor Green. He lived there with his family until 1925, when he sold it to the Hamer family for $29,100.[4]

With the purchase, the original Kensington plantation property was reunited for the first time since the brothers divided it in 1879. Fifteen hundred and seventy-five acres from the Cleland Singleton estate were added to 1,585 acres from Richard Singleton for a total of 3,160 acres. It is said the overseer of the Hamer property took up residence in Cleland's former home. During the 1920's, the stilted open basement was enclosed to create a two story dwelling and in the 1930's, the house was remodeled. Robert Cochrane Hamer's son, Robert Pickett Hamer III, also lived there with his wife for a time.[5]

Cleland's House After Remodel

Chapter 122-Hamer Childhood Memories

The Hamers used one of the rooms upstairs in the mansion as a library. It was called the book room. The balcony space across the front of the house was used as the school room because it was much wider than the six to eight foot width of the other three sides of the balcony. The ornate iron railing that overlooked the main hall on the balcony was a caution. The children were admonished to never touch it for fear of falling through it or over it. Their friends who were visiting had to be similarly instructed before they were allowed upstairs to play.

During their tenure of thirty years at the home, the Hamers found it practical to live primarily on the main floor of the house. The open two and half story (forty-three feet) entrance hall was almost impossible to heat in the winter; and with the exception of winter holidays and special occasions, no real attempt was made. The children would dash quickly across the central hall from one heated room to another to keep warm.[6]

One Christmas, the Hamer children, Robert, Beverley and Jane, received a gift from their parents. Bob received a handwritten note from his father saying, "Dear Bob, If you have time look in your Daddy's stable, Santa"

Bob found a pony with one blue eye and one brown eye who he immediately named Spot. The girls received notes also. Beverley received a pony cart and Jane a pony harness. They promptly formed a partnership! Later in the year on a hot fall day, they "began to quarrel over whose turn it was to drive." Bob declared the partnership dissolved, unhitched the cart, took off the harness and rode Spot bareback to the Big House. Jane picked up the sweaty harness, draped it over her shoulders and began trudging her way back home. The cart was too heavy for Beverley to pull so she just sat in the cart and cried. Very shortly, their father straightened Bob out, retrieved the girls, got peace restored and the partnership reactivated.[7]

Beverly, Bob, Jane, and Spot

Jane, Robert, and Beverly Hamer

The Hamer children and their guests at the Kensington often played the game they called "Going to Heaven" on the steep front steps of the house. One child would be chosen the leader and stand on the top step. All the other children would start at the bottom step. The leader would hide a small stone in one fist or the other, changing it from hand to hand to make it difficult for the other children to guess its location. When the leader was done doing that, the other children would take turns guessing which hand the stone was in. If they guessed correctly they could move up one step. If not, they had to stay where they were. The first one to reach the top made it to heaven. That one then became the leader and the game started over.

Chapter 123-Farming

The Hamers farmed the land, raising cotton; but depressed prices, the devastation wrought by the Boll Weevil, as well as the depletion of the soil wrought by raising cotton didn't help. They tried many things to diversify, some more successful than others. The Hamers tried a variety of labor methods to work the Kensington land—tenants, sharecroppers, and wage earners.[8] They raised acres of asparagus. One year they raised carrots and sold them to horse trainers in Columbia. They also raised peanuts, soy beans, lespedeza (a type of legume like peas or beans, often grown for forage, but also used for soil enrichment), crotalaria (used as a soil builder, but poisonous to cattle) among others. One year they planted five acres of onions, but prices got so low that they weren't worth harvesting, so they were left in the fields. The onions left in the fields in the summer heat produced an aroma not to be forgotten. The Hamers did not have company for a while after that. Although the Hamers introduced mechanized farming equipment; over time, farming proved unprofitable.[9]

Chapter 124-Description of the Grounds

At the time of the Hamers, a large grove of about nine acres of trees surrounded the Kensington mansion and the house that had been built for Matthew Singleton. Seven huge magnolias were part of this grove. By this time, the avenue leading to the highway was populated with hollies and hickories.

Behind the Big House was a "...large rose garden laid out in a circle with a shoulder high hedge of beautiful shiny green eponymous. It was divided into four beds by the walks bordered with jonquils and old-fashioned yellow narcissus. There was a tremendous Japonica bush—tree really—in one corner." Once, one of the Hamer girls climbed it, got scared and cried for her Momma to come get her down. One of the workers had to be summoned to get her down safely. "The four flower beds were filled with old fashioned roses." Of particular note were "fragrant pink Duchess roses and the very hardy red Louis Philippe's." (This is reminiscent of Angelica's visit to the court of Louis Philippe in the 1830's. Were they planted by Matthew Richard Singleton with the King in mind?)

"There were also huge bushes of syringa, several kinds of spirea and breath of spring. There was flowering pomegranate, an aromatic bay tree, the Granddaddy grey-beard tree and a large trellis covered with yellow Jessamine. The borders of the garden were boxwood and the lane to the Mr. Matt's [Matthew Singleton's] house had boxwood on each side. [The above plantings may very well date to the time of Matthew Richard Singleton (1817-1854).] There were also huge red and white oleander bushes," believed to have been planted by Mrs. Hamer.

Between the Big House and Cleland Singleton's house, to the south and southeast, were the stables, the barns, the smoke house , the cotton gin, the commissary, and the Street, the old slave quarters. During the Hamer time, only a few of the farm workers lived on what had been the Street—the lot man who took care of livestock, the gardener and cook's family. The other farm hands lived in houses scattered about the property close to the acreages they farmed.[10]

Sporting Life

Hunting was a big pastime, especially quail hunting. Mr. Hamer was careful to see that the quail population was not over-hunted, but maintained at a sustainable level. A fox hunt was reputedly held on the grounds in the 1930s. Robert Cochrane Hamer and his son, Robert Pickett Hamer III, were active horsemen. Son Robert showed horses as well as rode a jumper in tournaments and raced successfully. Both Robert Cochrane Hamer and his son, Robert, participated in tilting tournaments, sometimes called ring tournaments, in the 1920s and 1930s. (Tilting, also known as lancing, began in antebellum times and continues until the present day. Riders attempt to put their lance through a small wooden circle while riding at speed. The tournaments are conducted in the manner of medieval jousting tournaments.)[11]

Kensington during the 1930s

Chapter 125-The Government Buys the Kensington

By the end of the 1930s, the three Hamer children had grown up, gone away to school and gotten married. Only Robert Cochrane Hamer and his wife Janie remained in the Big House. Mr. Hamer suffered a serious illness in 1940 and when the opportunity to sell the Kensington arose, he sold the entire 3,160 acres to the U.S. Government's Farm Security agency for $95,000 on May 20, 1941.

The property was to be used to resettle people displaced by the Santee-Cooper River project.[12] It is said that the property was sold with the understanding that the Big House was to be maintained and used as the administrative office for the agricultural cooperative being established there.

The government purchased additional adjoining acreage to the Kensington that brought the total to some 6000 acres. The displaced farmers were to be given 100 acre plots, according to one source. A few months later, the United States was plunged into World War II and the resettlement project never really took place at the Kensington, although stories persist that a few people were relocated there.

Chapter 126-The Last Private Owners: The Lanhams

After sitting vacant for four and a half years, the Kensington mansion, along with 3,300 acres was sold by the federal government to the James Christie (J.C.) Lanham family on December 10, 1945. The price is believed to be $61,000. The Lanham family thus became the last private owners of the original Kensington property. J.C. Lanham married Edith Hill Lanham, and they had four sons—J.C. Jr. (Jimmie), Butler, Edward Lee and Melvin. Three of the four are pictured below in a picture with J.C. Lanham.

J.C. Lanham and sons: (L-R) J.C., Jr. (Jimmie), Edward Lee, and Calbriath (Butler)

The Lanhams turned the property into a successful agricultural operation once again, running a large cattle operation and raising soybeans. Cattle herd estimates run anywhere from 1,000 to 2,000 head.[13] Many farm hands were required. The youngest son Melvin Lanham, recalled seeing a very long wooden table, specially built for the purpose, with stacks of coins laid out on it to pay off the hands. It is said that J.C. Lanham Sr. had a prize bull that won a stock contest in Dallas and that he sold a half interest in the bull for $50,000.

Not everything was coming up roses however. There were severe droughts in 1952, 1953 and 1954. One hundred years before in 1853 and 1854 it had been the same for Matthew Singleton. The 1952-1954 droughts were so severe that pine needles were picked up, mixed with molasses, and fed to the cattle. They didn't start a combine for harvest for three years.

The mansion had sat vacant and unattended during the war years. The Lanhams did not occupy the mansion. They used the mansion as a storage location for farm equipment, fertilizer, and animal feed. Instead, the family built a brick ranch style house at the junction of the oval drive and the driveway to the highway.

The iron railing from the balcony of the mansion was taken down and installed on the front porch of the ranch house. A picture of the youngest son, Melvin and his mother, next to the porch railing is below.

Melvin with his mother

Melvin's mother died when he was only five years old. His African-American nanny, Elizabeth Deveaux, known as Mother Deveaux, pretty much raised him after that. She was a preacher and took him to church with her. When he grew up, Melvin preached at African-American churches, including the Prayer and Bible Church, located just south of the Kensington. He and his wife, Sandy, became members of the Prayer and Bible Church and he served on the board of trustees. Melvin also converted the central hall of his home, The Pines (the former summer seat of the Singletons), to use as a chapel. (See next page.)

Central Hall Chapel

Melvin's father, J.C. Lanham Sr., grew up several miles from Senator Strom Thurmond in Edgefield, South Carolina. Senator Thurmond used to visit J.C, Lanham at the Kensington on a regular basis, usually three or four times a year. Mr. Lanham always instructed the cook to get out the whiskey when Senator Thurmond was coming. Melvin Lanham, J. C.'s youngest son, said that he got shooed away when Mr. Thurmond came to visit, because his father and Senator Thurmond wanted to talk. Melvin said they would sit on the porch of the ranch house with their feet up on the Kensington railing and drink whiskey. J.C. said that Strom Thurmond could eat more biscuits that any man he'd ever seen and always with blueberry preserves. Strom Thurmond called J.C.—Christie, as did many of his other friends. J.C. told the cook to always have food available—biscuits and cornbread as well as sweet tea, pies and cakes for any visitors that might stop by. He didn't care if it went bad. He just wanted it available at all times.

PART SIXTEEN

PRESERVATION AND RESTORATION

Chapter 127-Preservation Efforts

As the years went by, the mansion fell into more dilapidation and ruin. Voices began to be raised, lamenting the situation and expressing a desire to somehow preserve and restore this historical and architectural treasure of antebellum South Carolina. Someone described the mansion in those days as a "sad widow" or an "impoverished blue blood".

Before restoration Porte Cochere

On February 18, 1956, Mary Carter Singleton Dwight noted that she received from an old schoolmate "two pages from the magazine section of *The State* with pictures and descriptions of the sad fate and former glory of Kensington which, through all the years had been like a second home to me." She goes on to lament the sad fate of all the Singleton mansions, the only other survivor being The Ruins. She wrote, "Of all the Singleton homes Kensington was the most elaborate and beautiful and no one who was ever entertained there could help feeling a great admiration and love for it." [1] (Mrs. Dwight passed away three years later, not living to see what was to come.)

Beginning in the 1960's, the preservation effort began to pick up steam. A citizen's group, The Committee for the Preservation of the Kensington, was constituted in the late sixties. The Historic Columbia Foundation became involved, coordinating historical research about the Kensington. A number of proposals were put forth, including a plan to make the Kensington the headquarters of what would become the Congaree National Park. Another idea was to make Kensington part of the Poinsett State Park across the Wateree River. None of these ideas came to fruition; but through the efforts of the preservationists, the Kensington was placed on the National Register of Historic Places in 1971, one of the first rural properties in South Carolina so designated. It was also listed as the number one priority for restoration in the Central Midlands region of South Carolina.

Before Restoration Front view

An article entitled "Kensington: The Plantation Escaped

Sherman's Torch, But Is Losing Its Battle Against Time", in *The Sandlapper*, a widely circulated tourist magazine, brought statewide attention to the situation in April of 1971. The article had a picture of fourteen-year-old Melvin Lanham sitting on a tractor in front of the old mansion, as well as pictures showing the dilapidated state of the mansion's exterior and interior and an account of how the Kensington had escaped Sherman's torch. Melvin had became the unofficial caretaker, historian and tour guide for anyone that wanted to see the old deserted Kensington mansion. He continued to be actively involved with the Kensington and its preservation until his death in 2012.[2]

Before Restoration Side View

Also in 1971, The *Victorian Society in America*, a national organization dedicated to historic preservation of nineteenth century heritage, published an article in their newsletter about the Kensington, adding to the groundswell of interest in preserving it.

Ann Jennings wrote an article in *The State* in 1977 entitled "Kensington: An Uncovered Treasure"

> …today, the magnificent house, built in 1852, is losing its battle against the ravages of time, vandals and

neglect…Kensington is there, a treasure lurking beneath the vines, crumbling plaster and the stored hay that fills its halls and rooms. For all of us who share a concern and pride for South Carolina's natural and historical heritage, Kensington represents a special chance to save a piece of this past.[3]

Nancy C. Fox, Historic Preservation Planner for the Central Midlands Regional Planning Council of the South Carolina Department of Archives and History, had been involved in placing Kensington on the National Historic Places Register. In an article published in the *Columbia Record*, she was interviewed about the Kensington. She described its architecture as "absolutely unique", a mixture of several styles with unusual eclectic features, and "very Avante garde." She said the Kensington "represents the extreme sophistication and cosmopolitan tastes of the Singleton family" and "the interior of the Kensington contained the finest ornamental plaster work seen outside of Charleston." [4]

Finally, in 1980, Triad Architectural Associates of Columbia was commissioned to do preliminary architectural research and the site work of the Kensington mansion.

Chapter 128-The Road Back

"I'll never forget walking into that place the first time. There were pigeons flying all around…Up under the dome were snakes and dead animals and hay…and poop from all kinds of birds." –John Califf, architect for Triad Architectural Associates.[5] "The mansion, used for storage, was full of grain, hay and rusting farm equipment."

From an interview with John Califf:

> I had been doing historic preservation work for a couple of years. The property had become controversial. They'd heard the paper company was going to buy it. There was no documentation. There were no measured drawings of it. If it burned down, they'd have photographs. They asked me to do measured drawings of what was there. So, I worked up a cost of what it would cost to do that and they didn't have any

money. So…we'll give such and such, just to do the plans just for the record. In the Central Midlands Planning Commission there was an ad-hoc committee. They had a preservation committee—Nancy Fox of the Department of Archives and History was in on it and they had a citizen's group. And so I went out there and started measuring. We got so interested in it we started doing the elevations. We did the whole shebang, kind of beyond what little bit they paid for the plans. Got swept up in it? Yes.[6]

Russell Maxey, in a story for *The State* newspaper described the scene:

Today, Kensington still stands lonely and ghostly silent—a shambles of its former glory. Stripped of its fancy, carved woodwork, marble mantles, wrought iron handrails and some of its ornate plaster work, it is in sad shape. The broken skylight has allowed the rains to have their way with ceilings, walls and floors. Its rooms are filled with farm implements, feed bags and Melvin's memories of yesterdays.[8]

Chapter 129-The White Knight Arrives Just In Time

In June of 1981, Union Camp, later known as International Paper Company, purchased the Kensington property from the Lanham family in order to build a paper mill.[7] It is believed that they paid $2.5 million to the Lanham family. Union Camp also agreed to restore the Kensington to its former grandeur and to maintain it.

Kensington Just Prior to Restoration

The first step taken by Union Camp for preservation and restoration was to protect the house from further weather damage by sealing off openings to the outside, including sealing up the skylight and erecting a cyclone fence around the building to keep out vandals. A fire alarm and security system were also installed. Ten acres surrounding the mansion were to be set aside as part of the preservation and restoration effort.

Prior to restoration the National Park Service conducted a detailed survey called the Historic American Building Survey (HABS). All of the nineteenth century structures except for the mansion, the Matthew Singleton house (built around 1900), the plantation store (the commissary) and the summer kitchen had been lost. An existing slave cabin on the property was not noted in the report. All the outbuildings including the summer kitchen, the Matthew Singleton residence and the Lanham residence were scheduled for demolition as part of the restoration effort. The report also noted that the formal gardens east of the house had been removed and leveled for cultivation.[9]

All of the existing secondary buildings on the property were demolished as planned, including the Lanham home, but the summer kitchen was preserved as was the Matthew Singleton house.

Chain Gang Road House

The small house of Matthew Singleton (1877-1910) located north and east of the mansion was moved off the property to a location on Chain Gang Road. It was modified to include a second story and its roofline altered, but it was never occupied. It still exists today at that location, although in an abandoned and dilapidated condition.

Chapter 130-Restoration Begins

The stabilization and restoration process began in September of 1982. The house appeared to be in woeful shape, having been open to the elements for forty years and put to hard use for farm equipment and grain storage. The skylight in the dome over the main entrance hall was broken. Rain and snow had poured in, damaging the floor. Most windows were brokcn and the shutters were dysfunctional. All but the marble mantles in the dining room had been carried off, and much of original plaster ornamentation was damaged, broken, or missing.

The wooden downspouts hidden in the exterior walls had become clogged over time and water had leaked into the walls creating damage as far as twelve feet from the spout locations. Family members who lived in the Kensington commented that it had always been a wet house. Many more downspouts would have been required to handle the flow of rainwater. Why so few? One speculation is that Matthew Singleton was under severe financial pressures at the time and may have been reluctant to "go the extra mile". Another is that the architects, Jones and Lee, had designed mostly commercial buildings and may not have been familiar with the hidden downspout design needs.

Ralph Boyd, an engineer for Union Camp, was given the job of Project Director for the restoration. For him it became a labor of love. He joked in a conversation with me that he had "drawn the short straw" in being given the job among other Union Camp engineers. He also said that he believed that the reason he had been selected for the job was that woodworking and cabinetry was a hobby of his. Union Camp had never attempted a restoration like this one, but it became a resounding success with family and community members, full of praise for a job well done in preserving and restoring the grand old lady. In 1984 the Historic Columbia Foundation gave Union Camp one of its highest awards for its work in preserving the Kensington.

The Task at Hand

After the initial stabilization process the real work began. Ralph Boyd said in regard to the downspouts, the Kensington was "designed to fail." The four downspouts were completely inadequate for the amount of runoff. One of functions of the downspouts had been to furnish potable water. Once they were removed during the restoration, it was thought that the 9,644 gallon cistern in the basement would empty and go dry, but it did not. After the rain gutters were removed, the site manager at the time reported that within three days, water had filled the cistern again. The logical explanation is that it is spring fed. Today, the crystal clear water level in the cistern varies from six inches to four feet.

The window sills were extensively water-damaged; ninety percent had to be replaced. Sixty percent of the support beams in the house had to be replaced, probably weakened by the tons of grain and farm equipment that been stored there. The house had to be jacked up in order to complete the task of replacement.

Entrance to dining hall from the main entry hall

Most of the ornate plaster work in the main entry hall was non-existent or damaged. During a tour given after the restoration was complete, a gentleman admitted to the tour guide that as a young boy wandering in the vacant mansion, he had thrown rocks at the plasterwork breaking off chunks with his marksmanship. The good news for the restoration was that enough original pieces remained so that molds could be made to replace the originals and the entire effect of the original regained.

The original terne (steel, coated with a lead-tin alloy) roof also needed to be replaced. The company that had made the original terne roof was still in business and the restorers were able to purchase new terne roofing from the same company.

There was still disagreement as to the original paint color with some historians believing the original color was purple-gray, trimmed in maroon, with peacock-green shutters and yellow-gold accents on the columns and balustrades. As noted earlier, according to 1853/1854 orders for paint, the exterior was to be painted a sanded stone gray over the stucco to achieve the look of stone in a French country house. The interior was to be white zinc. Initially, restoration manager Ralph Boyd thought the house was painted blue-gray with teal-green shutters. During the restoration process, paint chips and wood samples were sent to professionals in Philadelphia for an analysis to try to get a definitive answer. Ralph Boyd was sure that that would settle it once and for all, but of course it did not. People still disagree. The restoration team decided to go with white on the exterior with gray accents and red on the dome.

Ralph Boyd said the interior color scheme, in two tones of cream, was based on the Owens-Thomas House in Savannah, rather than trying to duplicate the original paint scheme. During the restoration process, the balcony railing that had been removed and placed on the Lanham porch was restored to its rightful place on the Kensington balcony. Heating and air conditioning was installed to protect the mansion from temperature variations and to make it suitable for year round visitation. According to Mr. Boyd, the actual restoration construction took one year and cost up to $1,000,000.[10] The Kensington was officially dedicated on May 10, 1985 and opened to the public.

Front of the Kensington "Port Cochere" after restoration

Chapter 131-Maintenance and Education

After the restoration was complete Union Camp/International Paper, as part of the ongoing effort to preserve and maintain the Kensington mansion and property, paid all the ongoing expenses (estimated at $60,000 a year) including energy costs and security.

In 1985, the Kensington mansion was made available for tours on a limited, appointment-only basis for groups of twenty or more. Tours lasted from fifteen to thirty minutes and were conducted by Union Camp employees.

Chapter 132-Furnishing the Mansion

When the Kensington was first opened for tours there was no furniture in the house. Robert Lee Scarborough, grandson of Robert Pickett Hamer Jr.(1863-1912), considered the Kensington a second home, having spent many hours at the Kensington with his cousin Bob, Robert Picket Hamer III. Mr. Scarborough had an extensive antique furniture and decorative arts collection of some 2,750 pieces, including linens and textiles. He reached an agreement with Union Camp to furnish one of the rooms at the Kensington with Victorian period pieces from his collection.

Chapter 133-Restoring the Trees

As part of the restoration process, Union Camp planted magnolias along both sides of the driveway from McCord's Ferry Road (U.S. Hwy. 601) to the oval drive of the Kensington. The trees recreated a beautiful entrance corridor to the property.

In 1989 Hurricane Hugo swept through South Carolina and left its mark on the Kensington property. Approximately 100 trees, including many live oaks, were destroyed. An observer said some of the roots of the massive trees stuck twelve feet up out of the ground. Several years later, Mr. Scarborough offered to donate oak trees to replace those that had been lost. They were planted in 2002.

Chapter 134-The Scarborough-Hamer Foundation

In 1996, the Scarborough-Hamer Foundation was formed under the direction of Mr. Scarborough and began a partnership with Union Camp. After Union Camp merged with International Paper Company in 1999 this relationship continued. Mr. Scarborough agreed to furnish the entire main floor of the mansion with pieces from his collection of furniture and the decorative arts and the Foundation agreed to "provide tours of Kensington for the general public...". [11]

The governing board of the Scarborough-Foundation consisted of Scarborough, Hamer, Singleton and Stroyer (now shortened to Stroy) descendents as well as other community members. The Foundation also saw their role as "preserving and interpreting the history of the Kensington, Lower Richland and Sumter Counties and providing educational programs" to that end.[12]

The Kensington was one of the few antebellum homes in the area open to the public.

Tours were conducted by the Foundation four times daily, at 9:30, 11:00, 1:00 and 2:30 on Thursday, Friday and Saturday. The Kensington was decorated for the Christmas Season and there was a special Christmas Open House conducted in early December in which refreshments were served, volunteers were dressed in period dress and carriage rides were available. The mansion was closed during the months of January, February and August.

On Display

Very few original Singleton family pieces remained in the mansion. Approximately twenty-two items belonging to Singleton family members were on display, making them approximately one percent of the total collection at the Kensington, according to Carl DuBose, Kensington site manager. It is estimated that five to ten percent of the items on display were from the Singleton and Hamer families. Most of the rest were scattered among family members. The Richland County Library in Columbia has an original Singleton bookcase from the Kensington on display. It is 9'3" wide, 9'10" tall. The remainder of the objects in the mansion belonged to the Scarborough-Hamer Foundation.

People continued to donate and loan relevant artifacts to deepen and expand the Kensington story. For example, in the past few years, Matthew Richard Singleton's field desk and silver dining service were donated, as well as the wedding china of Janie DuBose Hamer, who married Robert Cochrane Hamer in 1912. A large portrait of Helen Coles Singleton Green, daughter of Matthew Richard Singleton, was donated and still needs restoration. Various items like the mourning shawl of Martha Singleton were loaned for periods of time.

The Mansion and the Summer Kitchen were on display. A slave cabin still exists on the Kensington property. The cabin measuring 48 1/2' x 16' is divided into two dwellings. A chimney in the middle indicates where the cooking and heating source would have been. There is an ongoing desire to preserve it and at one time there was a desire to move it closer to the mansion where it could be displayed.

Chapter 135-Final Thoughts

When Melvin Lanham died in 2012, he was laid to rest close by his nanny, Mother Deveaux, in the predominately African-American Prayer and Bible Church cemetery. Melvin was a last private owner of what had been Kensington plantation and Elizabeth (Mother) Deveaux bore the last name of a slave-owning family. This somehow helps resolve the story for me.

The Kensington is currently (as of November 2015) closed to the public due to water damage. The Scarborough-Hamer Foundation Collection is in storage and it is unlikely that the collection will again be displayed in the Mansion. The Foundation is actively seeking a location where its collection can be displayed and enjoyed by the public.

How do you end this story? There is no end; it's ongoing.

Appendix Contents

The Appendix is an "Everything Else" section. It includes more information about people, places, things, etc. mentioned in the narrative and other items of interest.

Appendix

People

Robert W. Andrews (1790-1887), a lifelong resident of Stateburg and Sumter, South Carolina, was known as "The Walker." His walking feats were prodigious and life long. He lived a long, vigorous, adventurous life of ninety-seven years. He fathered twelve children beginning at age fifty-two and the last when he was seventy-seven.

He was restless, never staying in one place or job too long, but always returning to his home in South Carolina. As a young man he had developed, as he put it, "a love for a roving life." During his life he worked as a teamster, itinerant peddler, shipbuilder, seaman, butcher, honey businessman, stage driver, hotel owner and manager, slave catcher (hired by William Ellison on one occasion), plantation overseer, owner of wild cattle in the Wateree swamp, bounty hunter, horse trader, omnibus (horse-drawn enclosed bus) owner, veterinary surgeon in the Confederate Army, chief of police in Sumter, and militia captain, among other occupations.

As a young man, he walked from Charleston to his home in Stateburg, a distance of 103 miles, accomplishing this in thirty-two hours. He left Charleston at 10 o'clock in the morning and arrived at his home at 6 o'clock on the afternoon of the following day.[1]

On one occasion he walked from Sumter, South Carolina, stopping along the way in Washington, Baltimore, Philadelphia, New York City, New Haven (Connecticut) and ending up in Portland, Maine. He made these lengthy journeys a number of times. In his nineties, he walked from Sumter to Jacksonville, Florida, then on to New Orleans and back to South Carolina. Over his lifetime he walked thousands of miles, averaging twenty to twenty-five miles a day. In his last years he was accompanied by his trusty dog, Fido. By the last decade of his life he had became a national figure and was interviewed by reporters in many of the towns and cities he passed through. People would stop him along the way just to meet him and shake the hand of the great pedestrian. During the last year of his life he walked from Sumter, South Carolina to Boston, Massachusetts and expressed a desire to walk across the continent to the Pacific. That is one journey he did not make.

Robert Andrews and Fido

He wrote an autobiography entitled *The Life and Adventures of Capt. Robert W. Andrews,* published in 1887, detailing his life. (Available free online or through Amazon.)

P.T. Barnum (1810-1891), flamboyant showman, circus owner and promoter extraordinaire, bought the 7,000 acre Goodwill Plantation in 1888 for his granddaughter, Julia Hurd Clarke. It was located just north (according to some sources, south) of present day Highways 76 and 376 on the west side of the Wateree River, some six miles north of Kensington. Julia and her husband, Henry P. Clarke, already owned another plantation near Eastover.

It is said that the Barnum circus animals, including elephants, wintered at the Goodwill Plantation for six years and that the elephants were led down along a path just north of the former Singleton land (the Fork Plantation) to the Acton Railway depot just south of Kensington, for transportation to exhibitions. Remnants of the trail remain today. (See photo below)

In an earlier area connection, P.T. Barnum began his show life in Columbia. He was the advance agent for Napoleon Turner's Circus in 1837. The company disbanded in Columbia; Barnum reorganized it and took the circus on a route through the Southwest, beginning his career as a Circus owner.[2]

Barnum was an ardent Union supporter during the Civil War. When Jefferson Davis was captured by Union Troops at the end of the war, allegedly, though wrongly accused, of wearing his wife's clothes to avoid detection, Barnum immediately telegraphed Secretary of War William Stanton that he would pay $500 for "the petticoats in which Jeff Davis was caught." The press soon caught wind of this. White Southerners were not amused by the aspersion cast upon their Confederate leader. After the war, Barnum's travelling circus shows usually avoided the South.

Reputed Elephant path

Edward Coles (1786-1868) was Colonel Richard Singleton's brother-in-law. As a young man Edward Coles, a Virginian and son of a slaveholder, resolved to free his slaves, but kept this from his father and family.

From 1810 to 1815, Edward Coles served as the private secretary of President James Madison. Dolley Payne Madison, wife of the President, was also his first cousin. In 1811, while visiting the Northeast, John Coles met former President John Adams. Adams and Jefferson, one-time friends, had become estranged over political differences. Edward Coles is given credit for helping to rekindle the friendship between these two Founding Fathers. Adams and Jefferson died on the same day—July 4th, 1826, fifty years to the day of the adoption of the Declaration of Independence which they had both signed. Adams's last words were of Jefferson.

Edward Coles, being a confidant, friend, and correspondent of Thomas Jefferson, wrote to him in 1814, asking Jefferson to take a public stand to end slavery in Virginia. Jefferson refused, while at the same time urging Edward Coles to stay in Virginia and work for the end of slavery.

John Coles had other plans. He made a tour of Kentucky, Indiana and Illinois in 1815. He revisited Illinois again in 1818, searching for land to purchase that would be suitable for himself and the slaves he proposed to free.

Edward Coles left his plantation in Virginia in the Spring of 1819, travelling separately from his slaves (6 adults and 11 children), who came by wagon to allay suspicion about his future plans. They joined together in Pennsylvania. West of Pittsburg, Coles announced their immediate freedom and his plan to provide 160 acres of land to each household head in Illinois. They all journeyed by flat boat via the Ohio River to Southern Illinois.

Illinois State Capitol Mural

This scene of the Cole's freeing his slaves is commemorated in a mural that is located on the first floor (south hall) of the Illinois State Capitol Building.

In May of 1819, after arriving in Edwardsville, Illinois, Coles, in addition to the 160 acres he had promised to each family head, also provided employment for those he had freed. President James Monroe, another friend slaveholder and neighbor of Coles from Albemarle County Virginia, appointed him as Register of Lands, a position he held from 1819 through 1822.

In 1822, Edward Coles became the second Governor of Illinois serving until 1826. During these years there was an attempt to legitimize slavery in Illinois, to circumvent the Ordinance of 1787, prohibiting slavery in the Northwest Territory (of which Illinois had been a part). John Coles was instrumental in maintaining the anti-slavery provisions in the Illinois constitution.

Coles ran unsuccessfully for the U.S. Senate in 1831 and decided to leave the state, moving to Philadelphia. At the end of that year he visited James and Dolley Madison at their home. James Madison expressed his desire to free his slaves, but in a way that would still provide for his wife Dolley. Madison died without freeing any of his slaves, all of whom were left to Dolley.

Edward Coles maintained a close relationship with his brother-in-law, Colonel Richard Singleton, over the years. In a letter that Colonel Singleton sent to his son, Matthew Richard Singleton, a few month's prior to his own death, he laments that due to his own ill health he will not able to make a trip to Philadelphia from White Sulphur Springs to thank Edward Coles for the kindnesses he had extended to his sister, Mary Singleton McRae, who was institutionalized in a mental institution in Philadelphia.

William Ellison (1790-1861) was born a slave in South Carolina. He purchased his own freedom in 1817 when it was still legal in South Carolina to do so. He became a free black entrepreneur in Stateburg, South Carolina. His primary business was the manufacture of cotton gins. His product was well respected, believed by many to be superior to Eli Whitney's original design. Ellison sold his gins not just area-wide, but to customers in other states in the South as well. He also repaired gins, a lucrative business, given the volume of hard use they received. He was the "go to" person for his services for most of the area planters. He had extensive business contacts with the Singletons, including Rebecca Singleton (widow of Captain John), Colonel Richard, Matthew Richard and John Coles Singleton. He was also a blacksmith, landowner and slave owner. By 1860, he owned 900 acres and sixty-three slaves. He owned more slaves than any other black person in South Carolina and more than 90% of all slaveholders in the United States.

Ellison successfully conducted a business as a black man in a slaveholding culture. He always walked a fine line between the demands of needing to be paid for services rendered to white planters and the ever-present danger of overstepping his bounds, appearing to be "uppity," and all the dangers that entailed for *any* black man in South Carolina, slave or free.

As a reflection of his confidence in his own ability to maintain that fine balance, he successfully brought suit in a South Carolina court against a white man. Another indication of his acceptance in the white community was that in 1835 he was able to purchase the home of Stephen D. Miller, former Governor of South Carolina, and father of the famous Civil War diarist, Mary Boykin Miller Chesnut. Due to a law passed in 1822, all free blacks in South Carolina had to have a guardian, a white man who would vouch for him. Dr. William Wallace Anderson, a close neighbor, family doctor, and friend, vouched for Ellison.

Mr. Ellison was also the only black person to be accepted as a pew renter at the Church of the Holy Cross, church home of some of the wealthiest planters in the area, including Colonel Richard Singleton. His pew was at the back under the organ, but he was on the ground floor, not in the balcony with the poor whites and slaves. His daughter was later married in the church. When he died in 1861, he was buried in his family cemetery instead of the Church of the Holy Cross Cemetery.

William Ellison's family supported the Southern cause during the Civil War. His grandson, John Wilson Buckner, served in the 1st South Carolina Artillery in a company of local men whose officers knew that he was black. Although it was illegal for blacks to serve in the Confederate forces, he was accepted by his comrades because of the Ellison family reputation and commitment to the Southern Cause. He was wounded in the battle for Fort Wagner, on July 12, 1863, fighting against the 54th Massachusetts, the black regiment made famous in the movie, "Glory." At his funeral in 1895, he was eulogized as a faithful soldier by his former commanders.[3]

George McDuffie (1790-1851) married Mary Rebecca Singleton, Colonel Singleton's daughter, and was a force in South Carolina politics for many years. He was widely known as a powerful orator, serving in the state legislature and later as a Congressman, Senator, and Governor of South Carolina.

Born in Georgia, from a background of modest means, he was educated at South Carolina College (later University of South Carolina). McDuffie, considered a man of superior intellect, caught the attention of Senator John C. Calhoun of South Carolina and became his personal friend and political protégé.

As a sitting U.S. Congressman, McDuffie became embroiled in a bitter political and personal dispute with Colonel William Cumming in 1822, ultimately leading to a series of duels. The dispute involving McDuffie concerned the highly charged political issue of state's rights and attracted widespread national attention. President Monroe tried to intervene to end the dispute; both John Quincy Adams and Andrew Jackson felt it important enough to make note of it in their personal journals.

Seven meetings (duels) between Cummings and McDuffie were arranged. They met four times and shots were exchanged on two of these occasions. During the first duel, McDuffie's arm was broken; and during the second, he received a pistol ball that lodged near his spine, remaining there for the rest of his life. It caused a painful permanent limp and affected his temperament in the negative, as noted by his contemporaries. The lingering effects of the wound were said to have contributed to his eventual death.

George McDuffie is buried under a prominent marble monument in the Singleton Family Cemetery, erected by his father-in-law and friend, Colonel Richard Singleton. The epitaph reads "The History of His Country is the Monument of his Fame;" The figure of a man is carved into the stone next to the epitaph.

Mrs. Anne Royall (1769-1854) was a true American original, one of the first female American journalists and the first female to interview a President of the United States. She had tried to interview President John Quincy Adams, but he had been reluctant to do so. The President was known to take daily, early morning nude baths in the Potomac River. Mrs. Royall went to the site and sat on his clothes to maintain his attention until she was finished with her questions. President Harry Truman loved to tell the story. It may not be true, but what makes it believable is that it seems to run true to her character. She constantly demonstrated fearlessness, single mindedness, and determination to pursue her goals; she was dismissive of cultural conventions.

After the death of her husband in 1797, and losing a lawsuit with his family for her share of the estate, she began to travel, taking copious notes of her observations. She determined to become a writer. In typical and uniquely American fashion, she reinvented herself as a writer, publisher, and social and political commenter, publishing her first book at fifty-seven years old.

In 1829, she became involved in a dispute with her Presbyterian neighbors in Washington, D.C. She was charged, tried, and convicted of being a "common scold and disturber of the peace," becoming the only person in American history to be so convicted. The common-law punishment for this offence was "ducking," for which purpose a ducking chair had been constructed on the grounds of the Naval Yard. Instead, however, she was fined ten dollars, which was paid by two reporters from a Washington newspaper, *The National Intelligencer*.

After her conviction, she left Washington and travelled throughout the South, where she encountered the Singleton Plantation in 1831. She published a number of travel books, started two newspapers; *Paul Pry* in 1831, and *The Huntress* in 1836. She became a feared, reviled and/or respected muckraker (a searcher and exposer of real or apparent misconduct, corruption, scandal in public life) in Washington D.C. She relentlessly sought out government corruption and injustice in any quarter, and sought to expose them by any means at her disposal. She had friends and many enemies. When this little, plump, older woman turned her piercing blue eyes on people, they quaked in their boots; because she would say and write anything that she thought, undeterred by the genteel manners that were expected from a woman at the time.

Even though he found her pesky, grudging respect came from John Quincy Adams. He referred to her as a "virago [a woman of strength or spirit] errant in enchanted armor." Others called her a "virago", meaning a shrew(a loud tempered, scolding woman).

Susan B. Anthony characterized her as a "living curiosity of Washington." It is no wonder that P.T. Barnum, the great showman and promoter, wanted to put her on a lecture tour even though he himself had been lambasted by her.

H.L. Mencken, himself a social and political commentator and often-caustic critic in the 1920s, referred to Mrs. Anne Royall as the "grandmother of the muckrakers." Anne Royall's biographer said that "For more than thirty years Anne Royall was a Voice, a strident Voice, crying out for national righteousness — at a time, too, when nearly all other American women of the pen were uttering themselves in sentimental verse or milk-and-water prose." [4] Mrs. Anne Royall lived an uncompromising, iconoclastic life, and died in 1854 at age 85. She is buried in the Congressional Cemetery in Washington, D.C.

Jacob Stroyer

Jacob Stroyer (1846? -1908) wrote a memoir entitled *My Life in the South* that detailed his life as a slave on the Kensington plantation and is the most complete record of life at antebellum Kensington. He was born and raised as a slave on the plantation and later became a pastor and leader of the Colored Mission in Salem, Massachusetts.

His date of birth is often given as 1849, but a more likely date is 1846. Stroyer himself gave dates of 1846 and 1849 in different editions of his memoir. For him to have experienced all that he did as a young boy that is recorded in his memoir, he would have had to have been born earlier. In 1901 a newspaper report gives 1846 as his birth date. The origin of the name Stroyer is unclear; but it is a surname of Jacob's father William, which could not be used in public. (In the time of slavery, only the master's last name was allowed.)

The name Stroyer was shortened to Stroy in the local area shortly after the Civil War. Red Stroy was one of the founders of St. Phillip AME (African Methodist Episcopal) Church, located just south of the Kensington. Several Stroy family descendants are active members of the Scarborough-Hamer Foundation Board, which administered the restored Kensington in partnership with the property owner, International Paper Company.

When Jacob Stroyer was wounded at Fort Sumter in September of 1864, the shell came from Fort Wagner, which the 54th Massachusetts, the *Glory* regiment, had attacked several months before. After the Confederates were forced to abandon the fort, Union troops occupied it, using it to bombard Confederate positions.

After the war ended, Jacob Stroyer made his way to Charleston and eventually to Worcester, Massachusetts, where he enrolled at the Worcester Academy to further his education. In 1876 he also was ordained a lay preacher in the African Methodist Episcopal Church. He was known as a great storyteller and "spellbinding preacher." Continuing his education, he studied at the Talladega Theological Seminary in Alabama for four years as a part-time student, beginning in 1879. He then studied at Oberlin Seminary from 1886-1889.

He published his memoir, *My Life in the South*, in 1879, followed by an second edition in 1880 and a greatly expanded version in 1885, and later editions in 1890, 1891 and 1898. He personally sold copies of his book for twenty-five cents a copy to finance his education and his dream to help his brethren in South Carolina. Numerous newspaper advertisements and personal notices in Massachusetts, New Hampshire, and Vermont announced that he was in town to sell and discuss his book.

On Monday, June 3, 1901, the *Boston Herald* published his previous day's sermon notes which focused on the recent celebration of Memorial Day.

Mr. Stroyer said of the Union soldiers in the Civil War,

> Theirs was a good fight because it was upon the broad basis
> of liberty for humanity. The result of their warfare was the
> saving of the Union, the freeing of 4,500,000 slaves, and
> freeing the masters from the condemnation of conscience
> which it cost for holding fellow beings in servitude.[5]

He died in 1908. His obituary mentions that he was survived by a
brother who was also a pastor in Eastover, SC. (Is this the Red
Stroy who was one of the founders of the St. Philip African
Methodist Church located just south of the Kensington?) Jacob
Stroyer was eulogized as a selfless giver with a servant heart. The
Boston Herald mentions that attendance at Jacob Stroyer's funeral
was one of the largest in a number of years. More than 400 people
from all walks of life attended his funeral, including the Mayor of
Salem, Massachusetts and from many denominations. [6]

A poem about him accompanied the report of his funeral in the
Salem newspaper.

Cause you and I have skins of white
This doesn't make us great.
I knew a face as black as night
A face which showed the Christian light
In a most happy state.
Men whisper 'Jacob Stroyer's dead,'
Perhaps few eyes are dim.
But o'er that dark and honored head
Are Angel's blessing him.
We elevate our heads with pride.
The dollar is our King.
But Jacob Stroyer worked and died –.
He hadn't anything.
Only a Fortune of Christian love,
Richer than a millionaire.
Oh! He had wealth of the Things Above –
Now he is happy there.
[Signed] Fred G. Walker

Tribute paid to Former Slave, Rev. Jacob Stroyer, Salem Evening
News, February 10, 1908 [7]

**Stroyer headstone in Greenlawn Cemetery
Salem, Massachusetts**

Headstone inscription:
JACOB STROYER
BORN A CHATTEL OF COL M.R. SINGLETON
NEAR COLUMBIA S.C. 1848
WOUNDED BY THE BURSTING OF A SHELL WHILE AT WORK
WITH OTHER SLAVES REPAIRING THE DAMAGE DONE BY
THE UNION GUNS DURING THE THIRD BOMBARDMENT OF
FORT SUMTER IN THE CIVIL WAR
EMANCIPATED BY PROCLAMATION OF PRESIDENT LINCOLN
EDUCATED BY HIS OWN LABOR
ORDAINED TO THE MINISTRY BY THE PASTOR OF THE
COLORED MISSION SALEM TWENTY-FIVE YEARS
DIED FEB 7, 1908
ERECTED BY A FEW FRIENDS WHO MEETING HIM ONLY
LEARNED TO SEE AND ADMIRE THIS SLAVE BORN BLACK
SOUL SPOTLESS IN [word unclear?] SELFLESS SIMPLICITY
[word unclear?] IN MERRIMENT ...TIRELESS IN PATIENCE
[LOFTY?] IN LOYALTY... STEADFAST IN FAITH
SELF SACRIFICED TO HIS PEOPLE AND HIS GOD

To this day, someone periodically puts flowers on his grave.

George Trenholm

George Trenholm (1807-1876) was a financier and bank owner whose company was the exclusive banker for all Confederate government business in England, but it was as a blockade runner that he became wealthy and famous. By war's end he is said to have owned sixty ships and a fortune in excess of a billion dollars or more in today's money, making him one of the richest men in the South. In the summer of 1864 he became the Confederate Secretary of the Treasury. Most of the gold from the Confederate Treasury has never been found and it is thought by many that George Trendholm was involved in hiding it. Treasure seekers still pursue its legendary riches.

He was tall and handsome, full of charm and had the "sweetest smile of any man." He also shared many other characteristics with Rhett Butler of *Gone With The Wind*—some good, some bad. Dr. E. Lee Spence, underwater archaeologist, treasure hunter, and the locator of the Confederate submarine *Hunley*, became interested in the similarities between George Trenholm and the Rhett Butler character, after he made a chance discovery on one of Trenholm's sunken ships. He began to investigate and became convinced that Margaret Mitchell based her Rhett Butler character largely on the real George Trenholm. Dr. Spence's book, *The Treasures of the Confederate Coast: The Real Rhett Butler Revealed & Other Revelations,* established a strong case in this regard. Margaret Mitchell, author of *Gone With the Wind,* always denied that Trenholm was the model for Rhett Butler and that her book was completely fiction, but many of Mitchell's descendants and Dr. Spence believe otherwise.

Places

Washington Race Course-Gone But Not Forgotten: Horseracing ceased at the Washington Race Course with the advent of the Civil War. In the fall of 1864, the infield of the Race Course became a prisoner of war camp for captured Union Officers. By the end of the war in April of 1865, 257 prisoners had died and were buried in unmarked graves, behind what had been the judge's stand.

During the last two weeks of April 1865, freedmen exhumed the bodies and reburied them, names unknown, providing markers for each. The freedman built a fence around the burial ground. An archway entrance to the cemetery was erected and "Martyrs of the Race Course" was inscribed upon it.

Martyrs of the Racecourse graveyard

On May 1, 1865, a procession of thousands, (newspaper reports say ten thousand) mostly African-Americans, including children and a brigade of African-American Union Soldiers, made their way to the site. The soldiers, who included the 54th Massachusetts, marched in solemn military order to the burial ground. A psalm was read, a prayer was said, hymns and songs were sung, speeches were given. People brought flowers to the site. They were strewn on the graves by the children. After the ceremonies, people stayed at the site all day picnicking and as the day ended, drifted away back to their homes.

Decoration of soldier's graves had already begun during the Civil War, but this was the first systematic, intentional gathering of its kind in American history. The first Decoration Day, later to be called Memorial Day, began on the grounds of the Washington Race Course. This story had been largely lost to history until just a few years ago. During the 1870's the soldier's bodies were exhumed and re-interred at the National Cemeteries that had been established in Beaufort and Florence, South Carolina.

After the "Martyrs of the Race Course" soldiers were re-interred in the National Cemeteries, the South Carolina Jockey Club reorganized itself in 1875. Within a few years the club began holding races once again at the Washington Race Course. They continued to do so through the 1882 season. At that time the Jockey Club met and decided to discontinue the racing due to the waning interest of horse owners and spectators alike.

In 1899 the Club disbanded and donated their remaining assets (the Race Course, some adjoining land and $13,500 in cash and securities) to the Charleston Library Society.

The Library Society leased the property to the South Carolina Inter-State and West Indian Exposition that ran from December 1901 to June of 1902. To accommodate the Exposition most of the buildings and fencing that remained were torn down. After it closed, the City of Charleston purchased the property and began development of Hampton Park, named for Wade Hampton III, Confederate General and South Carolina Governor. (Today, the Mary Murray Drive that encircles Hampton Park, is laid almost exactly on the Washington Race Course bed.)

Mary Murray drive

The four entry posts from the race course became surplus property. In 1903, Augustus Belmont Jr., a New Yorker and part-time South Carolina resident, offered to buy them. Belmont and his partners were developing a a new race track in New York and wanted to to install them there. Instead, the City of Charleston donated them. They were shipped, repaired and installed at the new track on Long Island, New York. On opening day at the racetrack, May 4, 1905, 40,000 spectators streamed past the entry gates at Belmont Park that had once graced the Washington Race Course.[8]

In the 1950's and 1960's, the Belmont Race Course grounds were completely renovated Only two features from the old Belmont Park survived. One was the racing motif iron railings that are near the present day walking ring. The other survivors are the four entrance pillars from the Washington Race Course. They can be seen to this day at the Clubhouse Entrance. (see picture on next page)

Belmont Clubhouse Pillars

White Sulphur Springs: After the time of Colonel Singleton, the Springs continued to be a noteworthy place, During the Civil War in August 1863, The two-day Battle of Dry Creek was fought there. The leader of the victorious Confederate forces was Colonel George S. Patton, grandfather of the legendary World War II general of the same name.

After the Civil War Robert E Lee came to the Springs, coming for three successive seasons before his death in 1870. Confederate generals Joseph E. Johnston and P.G.T. Beauregard, as well as former Confederacy President Jefferson Davis, also visited White Sulphur Springs in the postwar years.

Robert E. Lee reputedly made a highly public gesture of reconciliation with Northern generals after the Civil War at White Sulfur Springs. Before the war, the Springs had been primarily a place for the Southern aristocracy. After the war more or more wealthy Northerners, nouveau riches and war profiteers in the eyes of many Southerners, began to frequent the Springs, bringing Union Generals with them. The Southerners shunned the Northerners, refusing to sit on the same side of the dining room with them. Many Southerners considered the Yankees to be interlopers, to say nothing of the lingering enmity that they felt toward the North after the war. When Lee would enter the grand dining room everyone would stand as a mark of respect until he was seated. Noticing how the Northerners were ostracized, he is said to have crossed the dining room, warmly greeted some Union Generals, and sat down to dine with them. This changed the whole tenor of the Springs and made for much more convivial dining.

Another postwar visitor was Edward, the Prince of Wales. As Edward the VII he succeeded his mother, Queen Victoria, to the English throne. The Edwardian Era (1901-1910) of style and fashion was named for him.

In later years, White Sulphur Springs would be known as the Greenbrier Resort. It is still a renowned destination, a National Historic Landmark, and its historic 650 room Grand Hotel overlooks the resort. Twenty-six Presidents have visited the White Sulphur Springs/The Greenbrier. Situated on 6,500 acres, the Greenbrier offers every conceivable activity and amenity. There are multiple restaurants, nightly entertainments, fashion shows and a Casino Club. Championship sporting events, including boxing and a regular stop on the PGA golf tour, are held there. There are three other golf courses, off-road driving adventures, a shooting range and gun club, hunting on the private preserve, fly fishing, indoor and outdoor tennis, indoor and outdoor swimming pools, and horseback riding trails. Falconry and carriage rides are also available. The indigenous natural spring water is still available. The antebellum spring house once renowned for its curative powers still stands, harkening back to the roots of White Sulphur Springs. A modern 40,000 square ft. health spa is another connection to its health resort roots.

During the Cold War, a complete underground facility was built in secret under the Grand Hotel at the Greenbrier. It was begun in 1958 and completed in 1961; its purpose was to house Congress in the event of a nuclear war. It encompassed over 112,000 square feet, about the size of an average WalMart. There were eighteen dormitories (with a sleeping capacity of over 1.100), a complete medical clinic, pharmacy, cafeteria, a power plant, fuel storage, water supply, and meeting rooms for the House and Senate to sit in session. It was known as the "Bunker" and was kept ready and fully supplied for 33 years. It remained a closely guarded secret until a news story in the Washington Post in 1992 revealed its existence, forcing the government to decommission it. It was converted to use as data storage facility for private businesses and today tours of the facility are available to guests and visitors to the Greenbrier.

Things

Angelica's Portrait: During Jackie Kennedy's televised tour of the White House in 1962, she stopped at Angelica's portrait in the Red Room and said in her iconic, quiet, breathless way, "It's one of the best pictures in the White House. It really is terribly good." (On February 14th, 1962, First Lady Jacqueline Kennedy gave a tour of the White House. The full tour of the White House was hosted by CBS's Charles Collingwood and was shown on CBS, NBC and ABC.)

Angelica Singleton Van Buren

John Califf, the Triad architect who did the the historical and architectural survey of the Kensington before restoration, related a story about Angelica's portrait.

> In the 1980s I was doing some work at the Lace house, the official guest house for the Governor of South Carolina at that time. I was walking through the home accompanied by the Governor's wife, Ann "Tunky"

(her nickname since childhood—meaning in Gullah "sweet little baby") Riley. We saw a large portrait, a copy of the original Inman portrait of Angelica Singleton displayed in the White House, and I began telling her about Angelica.

"Some time later I got a call from Mrs. Riley saying, 'John, you saved my LIFE!'. She explained that when Ronald Reagan was in the White House he had hosted a dinner for all the Governors and their wives and the Rileys had attended. She said she felt 'like a fish out of water with all those Republicans,' particularly with the President being a Republican. She was standing in the Red Room waiting for her husband, and 'Here came Ronnie.' She wondered what in the world was she going to talk to him about. She looked up and there was the portrait of Angelica and she started telling him all about her. She said he was very interested, listened attentively and hadn't heard the story. Mrs. Riley told me that I saved her life." [9]

Angelica's Van Buren Pearls: In 1840, the Sultan of Muscat gifted the United States with a number of gifts including Arabian horses and 150 pearls in recognition of the 1833 treaty of friendship signed by the Sultanate of Oman and the United States. President Van Buren accepted these gifts on behalf of the United States, but not as a personal gift. He had the pearls (two drop-shaped pearls of thirty grains each and the remaining 148 individual pearls totaling 700 grains) made into two pendants and a necklace. These would grace Angelica Singleton Van Buren in her famous Red Room portrait. The gown in the portrait is the white satin gown that Angelica is thought to have worn when she was presented to Queen Victoria.

After Van Buren left office in 1841, Angelica had the pearls returned to the United States government and they were deposited in the Treasury Department vault. They stayed there until the dawn of the twentieth century, when they were moved to the National Museum of the Smithsonian Institution.

Angelica's Pearls;. According to family descendants, Angelica had many pieces of jewelry. Some of these are in the possession of present day family members. The pearls pictured below were originally given to Mrs. John Coles "Bonnie" Singleton by Angelica in 1842. They were then passed down through her female descendants to Harriet Dwight Travers Yarbrough, the present owner, and Angelica's third great niece.

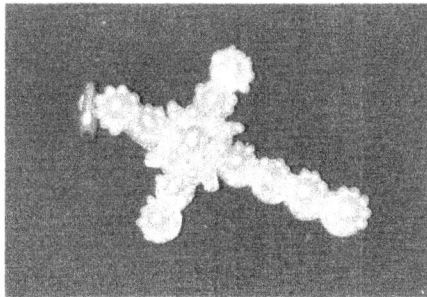

Angelica's Pearl brooch and cross

Events

The Wedding of Charles Henry Barron and Daisy Singleton: It was held at the Kensington Mansion.

The account from *The State* newspaper of April 23, 1907, probably written by Mary Carter Singleton Dwight, goddaughter of Richard Singleton and cousin to the bride.

> Notable among social events of the week throughout the entire state was the marriage at Acton on Tuesday evening of Miss Eliza [Daisy] Singleton, Col. and Mrs. Richard Singleton's youngest daughter, to Mr. Charles Henry Barron, one of the most popular society men of Columbia and one of the most promising young lawyers in South Carolina, junior member with his father, Mr. J.T. Barron, in the firm of Barron, Moore & Barron.
>
> Kensington, the old Singleton home, synonymous with generations of lavish and elegant hospitality, has perhaps, never for any other former social function at any time gathered a larger company nor presented a more brilliant scene than for the wedding on Tuesday, and certainly no where else in South Carolina could be found a more ideal setting for such an affair. The entire place, the handsome old Southern mansion standing at the head of a long avenue of live oaks, the flower garden, where roses run riot and mingle with lilacs and sweet syringas [a Japanese Tree Lilac] in quaint box bordered beds and the fields stretching away on all sides - all breathe of romance and poetry, and the guests of Tuesday evening, seeing it all in a flood of moonlight fell under the influence of the surroundings and of the occasion and felt that the history of proverbial antebellum hospitality was repeating itself in the most idealistic style for the particular occasion.
>
> The special train over the Atlantic Coast Line, carrying a party of 200 or more from Columbia, was met at the

station by carriages and wagonettes and the guests were driven up to the house, where Col. Singleton was waiting on the steps to welcome them. Mr. and Mrs. Matthew R. Singleton, Misses May and Virginia Singleton and the girls and men who were staying in the house - Mmes. Frances and Pauline Dill and Amyrillis Jervy of Charleston; Floride Barron and Jessie McKay of Columbia; Sophie Aldrich of Barnwell, Lucille Wilson of Newberry, and Rhett Sheppard of Edgefield; Messrs. Walter Green, Barnie Heyward, Dick Reed and Douglas McKay of Columbia, and Dr. Allen Jervey and Lee Holmes of Charleston greeted the guests informally in the hall.

The decorations were very elaborate and beautiful. Through the center of the hall the ceiling rises in a lofty rotunda and around the balustrade of the balcony thus formed southern smilax [bright green vine] was festooned, intertwining the friezes around the ceilings and draping the portraits and pictures on the walls. Roses were everywhere in profusion. filling great jars and vases and banking high the broad marble mantels in all the rooms - pale yellow were in one parlor, crimson in the library, and in the pretty little den where the guests all registered in the wedding book, the roses were all a lovely pink. At the extreme end of the hallway, a pretty bower was formed of vines and branches of white syringa blossoms, and there the ceremony was performed.

At the first notes of the wedding march played on piano and violin by Miss Sophie Aldrich and Miss Helen Tillinghast, the two officiating clergymen, the Rt. Rev. Ellison Capers, Bishop of the diocese, and the Rev. Mr. Tillinghast, the bride's rector, took their places and then from the library, through an aisle formed of ribbons held by Mr. Walter Taylor Green and Mr. Nathaniel Barnwell Heyward, Mr. Douglass McKay and Dr. Allen Jervey of Charleston, came the bride's mother with her son, Mr. Matthew R. Singleton. The maid of honor, Miss Lillian Singleton, walked alone, wearing an exquisite gown of pink silk tissue figured in ivy-leaf design and made with a filmy yoke in soft opal tints. She carried an armful of pink roses, tied with streamers of pink maline [a fine netting]. From an opposite corridor came the groom with his best man, Mr. T.J. Goodwyn, and awaited the bride who entered with her father. More stately and beautiful than ever was she in her wedding gown of soft shimmering Diana silk, made princess style en train, and rich in quantities of rare lace. Fresh orange blossoms encircled her dark hair and held in place the wedding veil, and beautiful bride roses formed the bouquet she carried. The Rev. Mr. Tillinghast read the betrothal service and then the bishop, in his sweet impressive manner, performed the marriage ceremony and pronounced the benediction.

To the strains of the "Bridal Chorus" from "Lohengrin" the bride and groom then led the way into the drawing room, where they received with Col. and Mrs. Singleton and the maid of honor and best man. The girls of the house party mingled among the guests in different parts of the house and Miss Jessie McKay and Miss Rhett Sheppard of Edgefield served delicious punch in one of the side corridors. The wide folding doors at the end of the hall were thrown open and the guests were invited into the dining hall. Everything there was lovely white and green. Smilax and sweet syringa entwined the archways and filled the niches and alcoves in the walls and the brides table was exquisite with bride roses and dainty smilax and gauzy maline and burning white tapers.

Supper was served in several courses on small tables about the room and old sherry and champagne punch flowed abundantly. The wedding presents displayed in the library were unusually elegant and numerous. evidencing the prominence of both families and the widespread popularity of both the young people. The special train returned to Columbia at midnight and the house party of girls and men broke up the next day, most of the bride's former school friends from Converse going to their alma mater to the Spring Music Festival.[10]

The 1840 Presidential Election Campaign: The campaign slogan "Tippecanoe and Tyler Too" was the chief campaign slogan for William Henry Harrison (hero of the battle of Tippecanoe in the War of 1812) and his Vice-Presidential running mate, William Tyler. Martin Van Buren's political opponents chanted, "Van, Van, he's a used-up man" or taunted, "Van, Van, you're a washed-up man." He was also referred to as "Martin Van Ruin" by the opposition and "Little Van." Van Buren was actually average in height for the time—5'6", but he was portly with huge sideburns and a bald head which made him appear more squat and unattractive. He also was a fancy dresser, given to silks and satins.

Martin Van Buren

Van Buren's personal appearance and manner had been attacked before by his political opponents. Five years before, David Crockett, of frontier and Alamo fame and a Congressman, had written a book entitled *The Life of Martin Van Buren*. Crockett had done so after his own defeat in the Congressional election of 1834.

The book was a scurrilous personal attack against Van Buren being chosen as Andrew Jackson's successor for nomination of President in 1836, instead of a friend of Davy Crockett's. Crockett even accused Van Buren of wearing a corset:

> He is laced up in corsets, such as women in a town wear, and, if possible, tighter than the best of them. It would be difficult to say, from his personal appearance, whether he was a man or woman, but for his large red and gray whiskers.[11]

During the 1840 election campaign Van Buren was portrayed as an aristocrat and a dandy as opposed to the homespun man of the people, William Henry Harrison. It wasn't true. William Henry Harrison was from a FFV (First Family of Virginia) and came from an even more aristocratic and wealthy background than did Van Buren.

Short simple songs called ditties were also a big part of the campaign.

The lyrics to one ditty sung by Van Buren's opponents were:

> "Old Tip he wears a homespun coat,
> He has no ruffled shirt-wirt-wirt,
> But Mat he has the golden plate,
> And he's a little squirt-wirt-wirt."

As part of the marketing of William Henry Harrison, his supporters portrayed him as being born in a log cabin and that he was fond of hard cider, so he would be seen as a man of the people. The campaign produced many products, common today, portraying the candidate himself or a characteristic of his. One of these products was "Old Cabin Whiskey," packaged in bottles shaped like log cabins to make a connection with Harrison's supposed log cabin birth. The product was produced by the E. C. Booz Distillery in Philadelphia. Though the origin of the word *booze*, referring to alcoholic beverages, predates the campaign by hundreds of years, the campaign certainly popularized the term.

In an effort to market their candidate, Martin Van Buren's supporters adopted the phrase "OK". The expression had become popular in Boston, as a way of saying that everything was all right. Because Van Buren was from Kinderhook, New York, they began calling him "Old Kinderhook", possibly also to link him to Andrew Jackson's moniker "Old Hickory" and to demonstrate that he was a regular guy and man of the people. Van Buren even began to write *OK* next to his signature. The phrase became wildly popular and has remained so to this day. It is said to be uttered by Americans on the average of seven times a day and is known and used worldwide. There's something quintessentially American about it, denoting optimism and can-do.

Lifestyle

Etiquette: The Sumter Banner newspaper (1846-1855) dispensed some advice for gentlemen:

"No perfect gentleman will pick his teeth at the table…Nor will he use his nose in company, as if playing second to a bugle…A perfect gentleman does not wipe his mouth upon the table cloth, nor spit upon the carpet…."

In church it is suggested:

The perfect gentleman "if he must yawn, whether in or out of Church, will be very shy about it—Nor will he lie down in his pew."

Hunting: A news article in 1825 mentions a squirrel hunt in the Sumterville (Sumter) area that was conducted as a contest for a barbecue. Two teams of twenty men each were organized. After three days of hunting, the winning team had killed 2,844 squirrels and the losers, 2.726, for a total of 5,570. (It was estimated that 174 bushels of corn had been saved by their efforts.)[12]

Robert W. Andrews, a resident of Stateburg, wrote about another early nineteenth century experience he had.

> Aside from acting as landlord of this hotel [in Stateburg], I was also provision dealer for all that section of the country, killing and quartering my own beef and other meats. There was at this time a man named Joseph Cox, who owned a herd of wild cattle in the Wateree Swamp, which I bought from him at the rate of one dollar per head, up to the number of 50; all over that number which I had shot would be clear gain for me. The Wateree Swamp was a tract of land, 10 miles wide and extending some 30 miles long, or to the junction of the Wateree and Santee rivers. Here was great sport. The wild cattle were hunted in exactly the same manner as the deer, which latter was also very plentiful in the swamp as well as turkeys, coons,

pigeons, etc…When a fat beeve [beef] was required, either for the hotel or market, or if a guest wished a day's good sport, I could take them into the swamp, and unleashing our dogs, give them a shot at some large game before they had been half an hour in the stand. And here it might as well be stated, I retained the exclusive right over these wild cattle for eight years, and then sold it for one hundred and fifty dollars, having in the meantime killed off somewhere in the neighborhood of two hundred head.[13]

Politics: The *bull pen* system: was used in "closely contested" elections in antebellum Columbia. Opposing factions would "corral" qualified voters in enclosures, "plying them with food, liquor" and other blandishments, possibly including women—and then at the appropriate time, faction leaders "marched them off to the polls" to vote. At that time, votes were cast by declaring them out loud. "Many of these individuals were Sandhillers" (a disparaging term attached to poor whites living in the piney-wood sandy hills in South Carolina and Georgia), who picked up some ready cash by this practice.[14]

Dr. Samuel Leland, a resident of lower Richland District (County), recorded in his diary his thoughts about Richland District voting corruption:

I suppose Richland District [County], without any exception is the most thoroughly corrupt place in the United States. The inhabitants, for the most part…sell their votes with such unblushing affrontery. The candidates do not even trust those they bribe, but only pay after they are seen to vote by some responsible person.[15]

South Carolina Code: According to Mary Boykin Chesnut, Civil War diarist and native South Carolinian:

> ...Now Listen! Here it all is in a nutshell. Man may be dishonest, immoral, cruel, black with every crime. But take care how you say so, unless you are a crack shot and willing to risk your life in defense of your words. For as soon as one defamatory word is spoken, pistols come at once to the fore. That is South Carolina ethics. If you have stout hearts – and good family connections—you can pretty much as you please.

> Diary entry, June 12, 1862 [16]

Glossary

Civil War Names: These names reflect the historical, political, and cultural sensitivities of different groups and regions for what is widely known as the Civil War.

The Civil War

War Between the States

The Confederate War

War for the Southern Confederacy

War of the Rebellion

War For Southern Independence

War Of Southern Independence

The War for States' Rights

The *Wah*

The Great Rebellion

Mr. Lincoln's War

Mr. Davis's War

War of Northern Aggression

War of Southern Aggression

War for the Union

The Freedom War

War of Separation

War of Secession

Second American Revolution

War of the Sections

The Brothers War

The Late Unpleasantness

The Recent Unpleasantness

Cross-writing: Technique used in the nineteenth century to economize on stationary and postage, which were expensive. When the writer finished writing on a page, he would turn the paper ninety degrees and continue writing, creating another level of writing over the first one. Henry James, Jane Austen, and Charles Darwin, as well as Marion and Angelica Singleton employed this technique. (Angelica's handwriting is extremely difficult to read, especially when she was in a hurry and cross-writing.) For an example of cross writing, see next page.

Example of cross-writing

Heart pine: Building material used in many area plantation homes. It is very hard and insect-resistant, but also highly flammable. It consists of the heartwood of long-leaf pines. The trees had to grow large enough to develop heartwood. The heart pine available now is almost entirely recycled timber, highly prized, and it can cost more than mahogany.

It is said that when the Fork Plantation house burned down, the fire could be *heard* two miles away in Eastover. I believe Home Place was built using heart pine. A torch made of heart pine (known as a fat lighter) is what started the fire that burned down Home Place. Most of the Singleton family plantations burned down. Heart pine was probably a major contributing factor.

Osnaburg: Medium to heavy cotton fabric, currently used for drapes, used at Kensington for slave garments. (Jacob Stroyer refers to this material being used for slave garments on the Kensington.)

Paling fences: Picket fences used to corral livestock. The design was brought from West Africa by slaves.

Sandhillers: Refers to poor whites living in the pine wood sandhills of South Carolina and Georgia, from the 1913 Webster's Dictionary. It is a pejorative term.

Sandlapper: Upon visiting Columbia and Lancaster, South Carolina in 1791, George Washington dubbed the people living on the sands near the river shores as "sandlappers." It's a term used by many as a general term for South Carolinians, while others associate it more with the Atlantic coast. Others use the term to refer to the sand hills of the Midlands, home of the Singletons. *The Sandlapper* is the name of the state's official magazine.

"Sick Season"-(the summer and early fall): White South Carolina Lowcountry and Midlands planters and their families sought refuge from the heat and mosquito borne diseases such as malaria and yellow fever of the "sick season" by journeying north to higher elevations.

In 1836, Tyrone Power (great-grandfather of Tyrone Power, the actor), commented in his book, *Impressions of America,* about the sick season.

> After the February Race Meeting in Charleston "… the country families once more return to their plantations, where they can remain with safety until about the second week in April: after which date the choice between country and city may be summed up in the words of Shakespeare, to 'go and live, or stay and die;' since to stay is assuredly to die, after once the malaria is fairly in movement. Formerly, the winter campaign used to be prolonged until the middle of June; but of late years the time is been from some cause or other, gradually abridged by common consent, until now 15 April is considered the last day of security." [17]

Notable Singleton/Kinloch August and September "Sick Season" deaths in the eighteenth and nineteenth century:

-Matthew Singleton (1730-1787) September 20

-Mary Rebecca Singleton McDuffie (1805-1830) September 14

-Richard Singleton (1817-1833) August 14

-John Coles Singleton (1813-1852) September 20

-Matthew Richard Singleton (1817-1854) August 18

-Frederick Kinloch (1791 – 1856) August 7

-Mary I'on Lowndes Kinloch (1800-1865) September 27

Swept yards: Yards are swept down to the dirt creating a rock-like surface, presenting a clean appearance and cutting down on insects. The practice was brought from West Africa by slaves and adapted by plantation owners. It is still seen in certain places in the South, most often today in African-American yards. During antebellum times, it is believed the Kensington had a swept yard on the river side of the mansion.

Horseracing

Colonel Singleton's Horseracing Triumph: He won every race during Race Week at the Washington Race Course in 1827.

-Monday, February 26—His three-year old chestnut colt, Red Gauntlet, sired by Sir Archie, won in a Colt Stake with four nominations of $200 each. The race consisted of two mile heats.

-Wednesday, February 28—His three-year-old chestnut colt, Red Gauntlet, sired by Sir Archie, won the Jockey Club Purse of $754, walked over—no competitor started against him. The race consisted of four mile heats.

-Thursday, March 1—His four-year-old gray filly, Ariel, sired by Eclipse, won the Jockey Club Purse of $565. The race consisted of three mile heats.

-Friday, March 2—His four-year-old bay filly, Nondescript, sired by Kosciusko, son of Sir Archie, won the Jockey Club Purse of $377. The race consisted of two mile heats.

-Saturday, March 3—His four-year-old gray filly, Ariel, sired by Eclipse, won a Handicap Race of $354. The race consisted of three mile heats.[18]

Sir Archie

Sir Archie (1805-1833): He was a charter member and second horse inducted into the National Museum of Racing and Hall of

Fame in 1955. He was chestnut, with a small patch of white on his right rear pastern (bone between the fetlock and the hoof). At the shoulder he was more than five feet tall and at over sixteen hands high, as big as Secretariat. As a racer, no horses could be found to challenge him, but it is his greatness as a stud that is unrivaled in American racing history. He stood at stud at Mowfield plantation, in North Carolina for 17 years. Even at the advanced horse age of 24 years old, he still commanded a stud fee of $100. It is estimated that during his lifetime he earned over $76,000 in stud fees.

All twelve Triple Crown winners, including the 2015 winner, American Pharoah, are descendants of Sir Archie, with the single exception of Citation in 1948. Every horse entered in the 2012 Kentucky Derby was a direct descendent of Sir Archie. Some of his champion descendants were Man of War, War Admiral, Sea Biscuit, Native Dancer, Bold Ruler, Secretariat, Seattle Slew, Affirmed, Cigar, Barbaro and I'll Have Another.

He is buried somewhere on the Mowfield plantation. His exact burial site is unknown. It is said that he was buried with silver horseshoes on. Who knows! If anyone earned them, he did.

Genealogies

Matthew Richard Singleton (1817-1854) Relatives:

Great Grandfather-Matthew Singleton (1730-1787) Colonel in American Revolution serving under General Frances Marion, "The Swamp Fox."

Grandfather-John Singleton (1754-1820) Captain in American Revolution, served under General Frances Marion, "The Swamp Fox."

Grandfather-General Richard Richardson (1704-1780) Revolutionary War general, six of his lineal descendants became South Carolina Governors.

Uncle-John Rutherfoord (1792-1866) Governor of Virginia.

Uncle-Edward Coles (1786-1868) Governor of Illinois, Abolitionist.

Uncle-Andrew Stevenson (1784-1857) Congressman, Speaker of the House of Representatives, United States Minister (Ambassador) to England.

First Cousin-John White Stevenson (1812-1886) Lieutenant Governor, Governor of Kentucky, Kentucky Congressman, Senator.

Third Cousin-"Dolley" Madison (1768-1849) Hostess (First Lady) of the White House, wife of President James Madison.

Third Cousin – John Peter Richardson (1801-1864) Governor of South Carolina (1840-1842), Founder of the Citadel.

Fourth Cousin-Patrick Henry (1736-1799) Five-term Governor of Virginia, Revolutionary War firebrand, best known for "Give me liberty or give me death" speech.

Sixth Cousin-William Campbell Preston (1794-1860) South Carolina Senator (1833-1842).

Sister-Angelica Singleton Van Buren (1816-1877) Married Abraham Van Buren, son of President Martin Van Buren, served as the Hostess of the White House (First Lady).

Half-Sister-Mary Rebecca Singleton(1805-1830) Married to George McDuffie (1790-1851) S. C. Governor (1834-1836), (Seven-term South Carolina Congressman, United States Senator).

Niece-Rebecca Coles Singleton (1838-1862) Married to Alexander Cheves Haskell (Confederate Colonel, Associate Supreme Court

Justice for South Carolina).

Half-Niece-Mary Singleton McDuffie (1830-1874) Married to Wade Hampton III (1818-1902) (Confederate General, South Carolina Senator, and Governor).

Complied by Carl DuBose

Martha Rutledge Kinloch Singleton (1818-1892) Relatives:

Great-great Grandfather-John Cleland Member of ten-man Grand Council of South Carolina who managed the colony's affairs from 1664-1719. Member of Council of East Florida, President of the St. Andrews Society.

Great Grandfather-Francis Kinloch (1720-1767) Member of twelve-man His Majesty's Council which succeeded the Grand Council in managing South Carolina's affairs.

Great Grandfather-Rawlins Lowndes (1721-1800) Second Governor of South Carolina.

Great Grandfather-John Rutledge (1739-1800) Member of First Continental Congress, Member United States Constitutional Convention, Signer of the Declaration of Independence, First Governor of South Carolina, Justice of the U.S. Supreme Court and second Chief Justice.

Great-great Uncle-Edward Rutledge (1749-1800) Member of First Continental Congress, signer of the Declaration of Independence, seventh Governor of South Carolina.

Great-Uncle-William Jones Lowndes (1782-1822) U. S. Congressman for South Carolina. Lowndes County Alabama was named for him.

Uncle-William Aiken (1806-1887) Governor of South Carolina.

Grandfather-Thomas Lowndes (1766-1843) United States Congressman for South Carolina

Grandfather-Francis Kinloch (1755-1826) Served as Captain in Revolutionary War, Member of the South Carolina House of Representatives, Served in Second Continental Congress

Grandfather-Francis K. Huger, Jr (1755-1826?) Member of Continental Congress, Minister to Russia, owned Kensington Plantation in Georgetown, South Carolina.

Second Cousin-Colonel Francis K Huger, MD (1773-1855)

Involved in effort to free LaFayette (Revolutionary War hero), from imprisonment in Austria. He was imprisoned for his action. Married to Harriett Pinckney, daughter of General Thomas Pickney (Veteran of the Revolutionary War and War of 1812, SC Governor, United States. Congressman, and United States Minister to Great Britain).

Step-cousin-Elizabeth Kinloch (1784-?) Married Hugh Nelson (1768-1836) (Congressman and Minister (Ambassador) to Spain in 1823).

Third Cousin-Harriett Horry Rutledge Married Dr. St. Julian Ravenel (1819-1882). (A developer of the Civil War semi-submersible "The David").

Third-Cousin-John Facheraud Grimke (1752-1819) Senior Associate Justice of South Carolina Court of Commons Pleas (1783-?).

Third Cousin-Rev. Francis Rutledge (1799-1866) The First Episcopal Bishop of Florida.

Fifth Cousins-Sarah (1792-1873) and Angelina (1805-1879) Grimke were Abolitionists, began world peace movement, feminists. Frederick Grimke (1791-1863) Ohio Supreme Court Judge.

Sixth Cousins-Archibald Grimke (1849-1930) and Francis Grimke (1850-1937) Founding members of the NAACP.

Distant Cousin-Archibald Hamilton Rutledge (1883-1973), educator and first Poet Laureate of South Carolina (1934-1973).

Eighth Cousin-Sophonisba Preston Breckinridge (1866-1948) led social work education movement in the United States. First woman to be admitted to Kentucky Bar. First woman to receive Ph.D from the University of Chicago in political science in 1901. She helped organize Women's Peace Party and Women's International League for Peace and Freedom. She was active in Women's Suffrage and the NAACP. Was Vice President of the National American Women's Suffrage Association.

Compiled by Carl DuBose

Selected In-Depth Genealogy
of the Builder of the Kensington
Matthew Richard Singleton (1817-1854)
(but NOT complete):

|MATTHEW SINGLETON (1730-1787) - **Builder of Kensington's Great Grandfather**
| Wife-Mary "Nancy" James (1735-1784) m. 1750
| *Their (7) Children*
| **1** Nancy Ann Singleton (1750-1798)
| **2** Mary Singleton (1761-1783)
| **3** Robert Singleton (1763-1800)
| **4** Alice Singleton (1765-1765
| **5** Sherwood James Singleton (1770-1800)
| **6** Rebecca Singleton (1774-1774)
| **7 John Singleton** (1754-1820) - **Builder of Kensington's Grandfather**
| |Wife- Rebecca Richardson Cooper (1752-1834) m. 1774
| |*Their(6) Children*
| | **1** John Peter Singleton (1775-1800) Unmarried
| | **2** Matthew Richardson Singleton (1783-1793)
| | **3** Rebecca Singleton (1788-1810)
| | **4** Harriet Richardson Singleton (1779-1817)
| | ¹ˢᵗ Husband-Robert Broün (1781-1809) m. 1801
| | *Children of Harriet and Robert (3•)*
| | •¹Charles Dundas Deas Broün (1807-1839) unmarried
| | •²Robert Henry Broün (1809-1835) unmarried
| | •³John Peter Broün (1806-1895)
| | Wife-Abigail "Abby" Hinman Day Broün (1813-1889) m. 1837
| | *Children of John & Abigail (8)*
| | ¹Harriet Singleton Broün (1838-1914)
| | Husband-John Coles Singleton Jr. (1844-1919) m. 1868
| | *Children of Harriet and John (5)*
| | ¹John Singleton (1869-1897)
| | ²Mary Carter Singleton (1871-1958)
| | Husband-Francis Marion Dwight, M.D. (1860-1943) m. 1892
| | ³Harriet "Hallie"/ "Hattie" Broün Singleton (1874-1958)
| | ⁴Lucy "Lessie" Everett Singleton (Rodes) (1877-1966)
| | ⁵Cleland Matthew Singleton (1879-1879)
| | ²Mary Singleton Broün (1840-1895)
| | ³John Singleton Broün (1842-1859)
| | ⁴Robert Broün (1844-1904)
| | ⁵Elise Hinman Broün (1846-1935?)
| | ⁶Annie Hinman Broün (1848-1889)
| | Husband-Richard Richardson Singleton (1840-1900) m. 1868

```
|   |        ⁷Hannah Hinman Broün (1850-1852)
|   |        ⁸Kate Sherwood Broün (1851-1861)
|   | 2ⁿᵈ Husband-(of Harriet) John Russell Spann (1783-1841) m. 1813, no children
|   | 5-Mary Martha Singleton (1785-1863)
|   |    Husband-Powell McRae Sr. (1786?-?) m. 1812
|   |    Children (2)
|   |    •¹Arabella Oldys McRae (1815-1822), unmarried
|   |    •²Powell McRae, Jr. (1814-1844)
|   |       Wife-Julia Matilda May (1819-1879) m. 1839
|   |       2ⁿᵈ Husband Herman Oelrich of Julia McRae Children (5), None listed
|   |          Children from Powell McRae, Jr. (2)
|   |          ¹Mary Singleton McRae (1840-1928)
|   |            1ˢᵗ Husband Robert L. Livingston
|   |            2ⁿᵈ Husband Henry Livingston, brother of Robert L. Livingston
|   |          ²Julia May McRae (1841-1906) (died in Dresden, Germany),
|   |            Husband-Jan Adrian Mazel, m. 1868
|   | 6 Richard Singleton (1776-1852) Father of Builder of Kensington
|   | 1ˢᵗ Wife- Charlotte Videau Marion Ashby (1784-1805) m. 1802
|   |    Child (1of 8)
|   |    •¹Mary Rebecca Singleton (1805-1830)
|   |       Husband-George McDuffie (1790-1851) m. 1829
|   |       Child (1)
|   |       Mary Singleton McDuffie (1830-1877)
|   |         Husband-Wade Hampton III (1818-1902) m. 1858 (no children listed)
|   | 2ⁿᵈ Wife of Richard, Rebecca Travis Coles (1782-1849) m. 1812
|   |    Children (2 through 8)
|   |    •²Elizabeth Isaetta Singleton (1812-1812) (lived only 2 weeks)
|   |    •³Tucker Coles Singleton (1819-1820)
|   |    •⁴John Coles Singleton (1813-1852)  Brother to Builder of Kensington
|   |       Wife-Mary "Bonnie" Lewis Carter (1817-1889) m. 1836
|   |       Children (9)
|   |       ¹Mary Carter Singleton (1837-1863)
|   |          Husband-Reverend Robert Barnwell (1831-1863) m. 1858
|   |       ²Rebecca "Decca" Coles Singleton (1838-1862)
|   |          Husband-Alexander Cheves Haskell (1839-1910) m. 1861
|   |          Child (1)
|   |          Rebecca Singleton Haskell (1862-1946)
|   |       ³Amey C. Singleton (1838?-?)
|   |       ⁴Richard Richardson Singleton (1840-1900)
|   |          Wife-Annie Hinman Day Broün (1848-1889) m. 1868
|   |       ⁵Charles Carter Singleton (1842-1899)
|   |       ⁶John Coles Singleton Jr. (1844-1919)
|   |          Wife- Harriet Singleton Day Broün (1838-1914) m. 1868
|   |       ⁷Marion Deveaux Singleton (1845-1846)
```

|　　| ⁸Lucy Everett Singleton (1848-1890)
|　　| ⁹Martha Southall Singleton (1850-1851)
|　　| •⁵**Videau Marion Singleton**(1815-1867) **Sister to builder of Kensington**
|　　| 1ˢᵗ Husband- Robert Marion Deveaux (1813-1843) m. 1835
|　　| *Children (5)*
|　　| ¹Anne Peyre Deveaux (1836-1907)
|　　|　　　1ˢᵗ Husband-John Burchell Moore (1830-1875) m. 1855
|　　|　　　2ⁿᵈHusband- Richard Irwin Manning (1839-1887) m. 1881
|　　| ²Richard Singleton Deveaux (1837-1847)
|　　| ³Robert Marion Deveaux (1840-1840)
|　　| ⁴Robert Marion Deveaux (1841-1852)
|　　| ⁵Marion Videau Singleton Deveaux (Pinckney) (1843-1927)
|　　|　　　Husband-James S. Pinckney (??-??) m.1885
|　　| 2ⁿᵈ Husband- Reverend Augustus I. Converse (1798-1860) m. 1849, no issue
|　　| •⁶**Sarah Angelica Singleton** (1816-1877) **Sister to builder of Kensington**
|　　| Husband-Abraham Van Buren (1807-1873) m. 1838
|　　| *Children (4)*
|　　| ¹Rebecca Singleton Van Buren (1840-1840)
|　　| ²Singleton Van Buren (1841-1879)
|　　| ³Martin Van Buren (1844-1885)
|　　| ⁴Travis Coles Van Buren (1848-1889)
|　　| •⁷**Richard Singleton** (1817-1833) **Twin to builder of Kensington**
|　　| •⁸**Matthew Richard Singleton** (1817-1854) **BUILDER OF KENSINGTON**
|　　| | (Matthew took his dead twin's name for his middle name after Richard died)
|　　| | Wife-Martha "Mattie" Rutledge Kinloch (1818-1892) m. 1844
|　　| | *Children (3)*
|　　| | ¹**Cleland Kinloch Singleton** (1844-1920) Unmarried
|　　| | ²**Helen Coles Singleton (Green)** (1846-1924)
|　　| |　　　Husband-Allen Jones Green (1848-1910) m. 1868
|　　| |　　　Children (3) **Grandchildren of builder of Kensington**
|　　| |　　　¹Cleland Singleton Green (1872-1951)
|　　| |　　　²Walter Taylor Green (1874-1927)
|　　| |　　　³Helen Singleton Green (Brown) (1881-1957)
|　　| | ³**Richard Singleton** (1851-1921)
|　　| |　　　Wife-Virginia Elizabeth "Eliza" Taylor Green (1852-1933) m. 1870
|　　| |　　　*Children (7) Grandchildren of builder of Kensington*
|　　| |　　　¹Mary "May" Lowndes Singleton (King) (1875-1962)
|　　| |　　　²Matthew Richard Singleton (1877-1910)
|　　| |　　　　Wife-Charlotte Cantey Johnson (1879-1963) m. 1900
|　　| |　　　　*Children (3) Great Grandchildren of builder of Kensington*
|　　| |　　　　¹Richard Singleton (1901-1978)
|　　| |　　　　²Robert Johnson Singleton (1904-1906)
|　　| |　　　　³Martha Rutledge "Dolly" Singleton (1907-1977)
|　　| |　　　³Virginia Taylor Singleton (1879-1924)

| | | ⁴Lillian Singleton (Coker) (1880-1937)
| | | ⁵Lucy Pride Singleton (1883-1919)
| | | ⁶Elizabeth (Eliza) "Daisy" Singleton (Barron) (1886-1968)
| | | Husband-Charles Henry Barron (1880-1922) m. 1907
| | | *Children (4) **Great Grandchildren of builder of Kensington***
| | | ¹Eliza Barron (Macaulay) (1908 - 2003)
| | | ²Charles Henry Barron (1909 - 1991)
| | | ³Mary Lowndes Barron (Smith) (1912 - 2012)
| | | ⁴Jacob Thomas Barron (1918 - 1920)
| | | ⁷Martha Rutledge Singleton (1887-1889)

Obituaries

Matthew Richard Singleton Obituary:

Died, on Friday, 18 August, at his summer residence near Flat Rock, N. C., MATTHEW R. SINGLETON, of Richland District, South-Carolina, aged 37[actually 36] years.

Modest and retiring in his temper and simple in his habits, his tastes led him to be chiefly occupied with agricultural pursuits, but in the sphere to which it was his pleasure to confine himself, few men have commanded more cordial respect and affection. Sincere, humane and generous , with a mind endued with a strong sense of justice and a disposition which rendered him singularly considerate of the feelings and interests of others, he called out strong attachments wherever he was known. His friends, his own family, his servants and the poor will long feel the loss they have sustained by his removal. Though born to wealth, he felt deeply on a review of life, the vanity of everything not bearing on eternal interests. Acknowledging his sinfulness, he had been for many months anxious to learn the truth as it is in Jesus, and desired to die in the communion of the church of Christ.

"Be ye also ready for in such an hour as ye think not, the son of man cometh."

Charleston Courier,
August 28, 1854[19]

Martha Rutledge Singleton Obituary:

Death of Mrs. Singleton
A Christian gentlewoman passes away

After a long illness, beginning with an attack of typhoid pneumonia and lasting through two months, Mrs. Martha Rutledge Singleton, the widow of the late Col. Matthew R. Singleton, one of the most prominent men of this county in ante-bellum days, died at 9:15 o'clock last night at the residence of her daughter, Mrs. Allan J. Green, in this city.

The deceased was a daughter of the late Francis Kinloch, of Charleston, and was a great granddaughter of Governor John

Rutledge and of Rawlins Lowndes. She was in the seventy-fourth year of her age.

She has always lived at her home in this county, near Acton, but had a winter home in Charleston and a summer residence at Flat Rock, which she occupied during her husband's lifetime, but for the past thirteen years she has made her home in this city with her daughter.

She leaves, besides Mrs. Green, two sons, Col. Richard and Mr. Cleland Singleton, who reside on the home place at Acton.

The deceased lived a life that was beautiful in the extreme. She was a brilliant, sympathetic and attractive woman, who endeared herself to all with whom she came in contact. Her death will be mourned by many.

The funeral services will be held at her daughter's residence, corner of Sumter and Pendleton streets at 6 o'clock this afternoon, and the remains will be taken to Flat Rock for interment by the side of her late husband.

The remains will be accompanied on their last sad journey by the sons of the deceased and her grandson, Mr. Singleton Green.

The State, June 14 1892 [20]

Notes

These Notes serve two purposes; one is to cite sources and the other is to give additional information. They are arranged by parts, not chapters.

Repositories and Collections Abbreviations

DUKE   David M. Rubenstein Rare Book & Manuscript Library, Duke University.

SCL   South Caroliniana Library, University of South Carolina.

UNC   Louis Round Wilson Special Collections Library, The University of North Carolina at Chapel Hill.

PART ONE-SETTING THE STAGE

1. Lawson left on his trip of exploration on the day after his 26th birthday in 1701, published a book, "A New Voyage to Carolina", about his journey in 1709 and was killed by the Tuscarora Indians in North Carolina two years later. He was an astute observer and record-keeper and he detailed in his book what he found about the land, Native Americans and the local flora and fauna. His book is still available and can be read free online.

PART TWO-MATTHEW SINGLETON'S TIME (1752-1787)

1. In the 1740's, a few years before Matthew Singleton settled on the east side of the Wateree River, settlers began arriving on the west side of the Wateree River in what would become Richland County, the future location of the Kensington. According to several sources this included other members of the Singleton family. They settled along several creeks in lower Richland County, attracted by the rich bottom lands of the Congaree whose frequent flooding created rich soil.

Robert Mills claimed that Benjamin Singleton was the first settler in Richland County, circa 1740, at the junction of Cane Creek and Broad River at a place called Cowpeas. Robert Mills, *Statistics of South Carolina: Including a View of Its Natural, Civil, and Military History, General and Particular* (Charleston, South Carolina: Hurlbut and Lloyd, 1826), 692.

Another source says that Thomas Brown, an Indian trader with the Catawba Indians, purchased land from them, but that the agreement was disallowed by the Colonial government in 1739. "In 1738, John Cartwright, an agent for one John Selwyn" applied to the crown for 200,000 acres to be settled by a thousand Protestants in ten years. Nothing came of it.

There is a mention of a Richard Singleton, possibly a brother of Matthew (disputed by some), settling on the Richland County side of the Wateree River, in the same vicinity as the Kensington, as early as the 1740's. There are land records indicating two colonial land grants-one for 700 acres in 1749 and another for 300 acres in 1767 to a Richard Singleton.

2. Matthew Singleton's holdings included 2,150 acres in the High Hills area, 300 acres on Shanks Creek in Sumter District, 250 acres on Beech Creek in Craven County, 200 acres on the Santee River, 200 acres in Berkeley County—a total of 3100 acres.

3. The site selected for the second Melrose house was on a high hill with a beautiful view. The site is located within Poinsett Park near Picnic Shelter #5. The hill is terraced down to the west, indicating that the land was worked. Also to the west further on toward the river is a pond and the location of the Singleton Mill. The area around the Mill was a battleground during the Revolutionary War. To the east of the home site are the remains of a basement, probably an outbuilding.

A house called Melrose survived into the 1960's when it burned down, leaving only a chimney. Even that is gone now.

4. J. Nelson Frierson, "Matthew Singleton, Early and Useful Settler in Stateburg," The State, September 24, 1916.

5 .Virginia Eliza (Green) Singleton, Genealogy of the Singletons After Their Emigration to America (Columbia SC: Publisher not identified, 1914),12. (Henceforth-GOTS)

6. Ibid., 12, 13.

7. Ibid., 1-2.

8. Edward McCrady, a local historian, recorded 137 clashes between the forces and 103 of them had South Carolinians fighting on both sides. Kevin Phillips, The Cousins Wars: Religion , Politics, and the Triumph of Anglo-America (NY: Basic Books,1999), 638.

9. J. Nelson Frierson, "Matthew Singleton, Early and Useful Settler in Stateburg," The State, September 24, 1916

10. Singleton, Genealogy of the Singletons, 11.

11. John C. Parker Jr., Parker's Guide to the Revolutionary War in South Carolina : Battles, Skirmishes and Murders (Patrick SC: Hem Branch Publishing,2009), 346,350.

12. The Cane Savannah plantation passed to Matthew's daughter, Nancy, and her husband, Isham Moore, and onto the Moore descendants. It stayed in the Moore family into the 20th Century. The main house at Cane Savannah burned down around 1920. The property was sold off in 1930 and was later broken up into individual tracts. An historical marker erected by the Sumter County Historical Commission remembers it.

The Singleton Family Cemetery was established by John Singleton, Matthew's son, in 1796, on the grounds of what was once Melrose plantation. It is believed by some that Matthew Singleton's remains were re-interred there. A modern grave marker in his memory has been placed in the cemetery. The Singleton Family Cemetery exists to this day under the auspices of Sumter County Historical Commission. There are forty-three known graves dating from 1796 to 1944. The Singleton Family Cemetery was placed on The National Register of Historic Places in 1976.

PART THREE-THE JOHN SINGLETON ERA (1787-1820)

1. Letter, John Singleton to Richard Singleton, 8 October 1807, Singleton Family Papers, #3, Southern Historical Collection, Louis Round Wilson Library, The University of North Carolina at Chapel Hill. (Henceforth-UNC)

2. *City Gazette*, Charleston, March 31, 1821; The Singleton loads of cotton were usually 100 bale quantities. South Carolina cotton bales were typically around 320 pounds. In the deep South-Louisiana, Mississippi, Alabama etc. bales were larger, exceeding 400 pounds.

3. Broadwell, *The Singleton Family of Sumter County* ,23.

4. Charles Broadwell, *Sketches of Planters, Plantations, and Living Along the Great Road, Saint Marks's Parish 1700-2000* (Sumter SC, Sumter County Genealogy Society,2010),61-62.

5. Agreement between John Singleton and Isham Moore, 27 June 1796, Singleton Family Papers, UNC.

6. Broadwell, *Sketches of Planters, Plantations, and Living Along the Great Road,* 62.

7. Today's Highway 261 roughly follows the original King's Highway roadway at this location. A marker alongside the highway indicates the location of Midway.

8. Singleton, *Genealogy of the Singletons*, 11.

9. Mrs. LeRoy Halsey, compiler, *Sketches of the Singleton Family* (Sumter County Genealogical Society), 5.

10. Mills, Statistics of South Carolina, 749.

11. Edwin J. Scott, *Random Recollections of a Long Life:1806-1876* (Columbia, S.C.: C.A. Calvo, Jr., 1884),13.

12. When the wagons got just south of Manchester, the road forked and the wagons turned onto the hard clay road that went east from there, which provided better road surface than staying on the sandy Great Road, After utilizing the better road surface, the travelers got back onto the Great Road

south of Manchester at a little town called Fulton (where Richard Singleton would later own a factory plantation) and journeyed onto Charleston. Fulton was a fairly good sized town. Now all that remains is an historical marker at the location. (From a conversation with local historian, Charles Broadwell.)

13. Scott, *Random Recollections of a Long Life,* 13-14,

14. It is believed by some that the vacation home was later inherited by Capt. John's daughter, Mary Martha McRae, upon his death. The original will does not exist, only a partial transcript. The part that exists does not mention this property.

15. Halsey, *Sketches of Singleton Family,*3-4.

16. Ibid., 5. This version was originally from John Peter Broün, grandson of Capt. John and Mrs. John Singleton. He said that his grandmother, Mrs. John Singleton, had told him the story over and over again. He then told the story to his grandchildren, continuing the storytelling cycle.

17. Singleton, *Genealogy of the Singletons,* 13-14.

18. Ibid., 11.

19. A partial list of annual South Carolina race event locations would include: St. Mathews, Pendleton, Greenville, Barnwell, Newberry, Pineville, Laurensville, Union, Deadfall, Beaufort, Strawberry, Georgetown, Fulton, Camden, Columbia, Orangeburg, Cherokee Ponds, Limestone Springs, Yorkville and Charleston. John Beaufrain Irving, *The South Carolina Jockey Club* (Charleston, SC: Russell and Jones,1857), 157. (Also known as *The History of the Turf in South Carolina*)

20. John Russell Spann, a famous horse racer and breeder of Bertrand, considered by many as the greatest horse in South Carolina history, married a second time circa 1825 to Margaret Harriet Richardson. She was the cousin of his first wife, Harriet Richardson Singleton Broün Spann. Margaret Harriet Richardson was a daughter of Gov. James B. Richardson and his wife Anne Cantey Sinkler. Her grandparents were General Richard Richardson and his second wife, Dorothy Sinkler.

21. Virginia G. Meynard, *History of Lower Richland County and Its Early Planters* (Columbia SC: VGM Books, 2010), 330.

22. Will of John Singleton, 30 July 1817, Singleton Family Legal Papers, South Caroliniana Library, University of South Carolina. (Henceforth-SCL); See Samuel H. Williamson, "Seven Ways to Compute the Relative Value of a U.S. Dollar Amount, 1774 to present," Measuring Worth, 2015, URL: www.measuringworth.com/uscompare/."

PART FOUR-COLONEL SINGLETON REIGNS (1820-1852)

1. Mary Carter Singleton Dwight, *A History of My Long Life to Leave My Children and Other Descendants* (Privately printed, 1960), 12.

2. Singleton, *Genealogy of the Singletons*, 14.

3. Cassie Nicholes, *Historical Sketches of Sumter County: Its Birth and Growth* (Sumter, SC: Sumter County Historical Commission, 1975), 362.

4. Singleton, *Genealogy of the Singletons*, 14.

5. Nicholes, *Historical Sketches of Sumter County*, 363.

6. Letter, Henry Watson, Jr. to Julia Watson, 18 May 1834, Henry Watson Jr. Papers, David M. Rubenstein Rare Book & Manuscript Library, Duke University. (Henceforth-DUKE)

7. Singleton, *Genealogy of the Singletons,* 14.

8. Number of slaves, not acreage, determined whether or not a property was given the designation of being a plantation. Scholars differ as to how many slaves constituted a plantation; anywhere from fewer than twenty to fifty. Kenneth Stampf, one of the best-known scholars on slavery defined a planter as an owner of at least twenty slaves, but he divided them into three groups. Fewer than ten was considered substantial. He defined small planters as owning between ten and thirty slaves and those who owned thirty or more were considered large planters.

Kenneth Stampf, *The Peculiar Institution: Slavery in the Antebellum South* (New York, NY: Vintage Books, a division of Random House, Inc, 1989, originally published by Alfred A. Knopf, Inc,1956), 30-31,36,38.

9. James W. Watts wrote a letter to the editor of *The South Countryman* dated Oct.14,1858, later reprinted in *The American Farmer*. In his letter Mr. Watts said that he had obtained his African Broad Tail sheep from a flock, formerly owned by the late Col. Richard Singleton, who had cross-bred them with the common sheep to produce a hardier breed well-suited to Southern climes. *The American Farmer*, "The American Farmer: Devoted to Agriculture, Horticulture and Rural Life", February, 1859, 268.

10. Letter, Richard Singleton to Mr. McBee, 10 January 1840, Singleton Family Papers, #124; Letter, Mr. McBee to Richard Singleton, 22 January 1840, Singleton Family Papers, #124, UNC.

11. One hundred shares of South Carolina Railroad stock were a part of Colonel Singleton's estate. Will of Richard Singleton, 22 July 1848, Singleton Family Legal Papers, South Caroliniana Library, University of South Carolina. The South Carolina Rail Road Company was formed in 1844 by the merger of the South Carolina Canal and Rail Road Company (SCC&RR) into the Louisville,

Cincinnati and Charleston Railroad Company.

12. Halsey, *Sketches of Singleton Family*, 7.

13. Ibid., 8.

14 William T. Porter, ed., "Phenomena, The Property of Col. Richard Singleton, Singleton Hall, SC With Incidental Notices of His Stud," *American Turf Register and Sporting Magazine* (March 1840): 144.

15 Dwight, *My Long Life*, 7.

16 Helen Von Kolnitz Hyer, "Relics From Home Place," *International Studio*, Vol. 80, # 330 (November,1924), 140.

17. Ibid., 141

18. Nicholes, *Historical Sketches of Sumter County*, 352.

19 The pottery was founded in the 1790's at Longport Staffordshire by John Davenport, Eliza Barron Macaulay, *Kensington* (Typescript, unpublished), 2.

20. Hyer, "Relics From Home Place," *International Studio*, 141-142.

21. *Eliza Barron Macaulay, Kensington unpublished typescript*, 3.

22. Receipt, Payment from James A . Miller Jr. to John Dunbar Paul, on behalf of Richard Singleton's bill, 22 May 1826, Singleton Family Papers, #252-254, UNC.

23. Halsey, *Sketches of Singleton Family*, 10-11.

24. Porter, *"Phenomena,"* 144.

25. Mrs. Anne Royall, *Southern Tour or Second Series of the Black Book*, Volume 2 (Washington: 1831), 39.

26. Perceval Reniers, *The Springs of Virginia: Life, Love and Death at the Waters 1775-1900* (Chapel Hill, NC: The University of North Carolina Press,1941), 49.

27. Ibid., 57-58.

28. Ibid.,56-58.

29. Halsey, *Sketches of Singleton Family*, 7.

30. Mrs. Mary Rebecca Singleton McDuffie died September 14, 1830, at her father's home. *Charleston Courier*, September 21, 1830.

31. Reniers, *Springs of Virginia*, 121.

32. Mark Pencil [pseud.] , (Mary M. Hagner),*White Sulphur Papers, or Life*

at the Springs of Western Virginia (New York: Samuel Colman,1839), 86.

33. Ibid., 25.

34. William Alexander MacCorkle, *The White Sulphur Springs: the traditions, history, and social life of the Greenbrier White Sulphur Springs* (New York, NY: The Neale Publishing Company, 1916), 175-176.

35. Jerome Napoleon Bonaparte's father, Jerome Bonaparte, brother of Napoleon, had been married to Betty Patterson, an American, until Napoleon had the marriage annulled to make a more advantageous political match for his brother and himself. Betty Patterson Bonaparte and her son, Jerome Napoleon Bonaparte, remained in America and lived in Baltimore. It is believed that, Jerome Napoleon Bonaparte, a friend of Matthew Richard and Martha Singleton, also paid visits to the Kensington in later years.

36. Editor unknown, *Poems of the Late Francis S. Key, Esq., Author of "The Star Spangled Banner"*, with an introductory letter by Chief Justice Taney(New York : Robert Carter & Bros, 1857), 121-122. Roger B. Taney, Chief Justice of the United States Supreme Court, was Francis Scott Key's brother-in-law. Taney is most known for his involvement in the Dred Scott decision in 1857, the same year he wrote the book introduction. It declared that African Americans, whether enslaved or free, could not be American citizens and therefore had no standing to sue in federal court, and that the federal government had no power to regulate slavery in the federal territories acquired after the creation of the United States. The decision inflamed regional tensions and was another factor in bringing on the Civil War four years later.

37. An historical marker in Columbia, S .C. at the corner of Devine St. and Sims Ave., Columbia, SC commemorates the founding of the Columbia Jockey Club and the location of the racetrack nearby.

38. The Godolphin stud fees of $853.50 for 1834 were owed by 19 individuals including B.F. Taylor, Wade Hampton II-two of his closest friends. Accounts due stud fee list , Richard Singleton, 1834, Singleton Family Papers, SCL.

39. Irving, *South Carolina Jockey Club* ,188.

40. Ibid., 173.

41. Ibid., 173.

42. Porter, *"Phenomena,"* 144.

43. Irving, *South Carolina Jockey Club*, 174.

44. Ibid., 172-173.

45. Porter, *"Phenomena,"* 145.

46. Irving, *The South Carolina Jockey Club*, 173.

47. In the 1830's and 1840's, improvements were made to the Washington Race Course "The entrance to the Ladies Stand is from the rear of the edifice, the ladies alighting from their carriages, protected by an arched way from the weather, and ascend a flight of stairs, which conducts to a handsome saloon, communicating by large windows, (the whole height of the building, from the ceiling to the floor) with a wide balcony, calculated to accommodate many hundred spectators, and commanding a full view of the Course. On either side of the saloon are retiring and refreshment rooms. These different compartments are carpeted, and furnished in good taste, and reserved for the ladies that may honor the club with their attendance. The balcony of the grandstand descends gradually by easy steps to the course, but without any egress in that direction;.."

"We must not omit to mention, that, at considerable expense, the Club put up a Citizens Stand, open to all, gratis—the second story arranged with rows of seats, one above the other; the lower floor divided off into different compartments, some commodiously and conveniently arranged for the accommodation of small or large parties, and fitted up in good taste. Many of these refreshment rooms are superintended by well-known habitués of the locals, well experienced in such undertakings, and to cater to the tastes and appetites of the most fastidious." Ibid., 148-150.

48. Ibid., 52.

49. Ibid., 149.

50. Ibid., 89.

51. Inventory and Appraisement of the Home Place Estate of Richard Singleton, Singleton Legal Papers, SCL.

52. Tyrone Power, Esq., *Impressions of America During the Years 1833, 1834 and 1835*, Volume 2 (Philadelphia PA: Carey, Lea and Blanchard, 1836),56.

53. From *The South Carolina Jockey Club*, on the occasion of one of the balls, circa 1850:

"It is the opinion of many that the annual ball was fully equal, if it did not exceed attraction and brilliancy any that preceded it. The rooms were well lighted, and the company was seen to the best advantage. Every shade and color of dress, blending harmoniously, heightened by tout ensemble [individual parts forming a whole] and produced an exhilarating effect..."

"The younger portion of the company entered into the pastime of dancing con amore [with zeal], particularly the modern Polka, which is now been regularly established in our society is a very favorite dance, superseding entirely the Waltz of former years..."

"In New York they are not going to stop at the Polka, but are about to introduce a new style of Cotillion, called the Kiss Cotillion's – the peculiar feature of which is, that you kiss the lady as you swing corners. The writer from whom I derive my information, announces that he is as bachelor, and, like myself, a crusty sort of person, never dances the polka, and does not approve of it, but yet would not mind waving his objections to the amusement, so far as to "swing corners now and then in Cotillion!" Irving, *The South Carolina Jockey Club*, 128.

54. Ibid., 150.

55. Wikipedia, *Learned Pig*, last modified 28 September 2015, https://en.wikipedia.org/w/index.php?title=Learned_pig&oldid=683220362

56. Letter, John Coles Singleton to Richard Singleton, 11 March 1827, Singleton Family Papers, #74-81, UNC.

57. Letter, Richard Singleton to Alan Bradford, 23 December 1833,Singleton Family Papers, SCL.

58. From a Diary entry of Mrs. William Campbell Preston, wife of Senator Preston, a cousin, June 17,1834?, from Washington, D.C. Diary of Mrs. William Campbell Preston (Louisa Penelope Davis, the daughter of Dr. James Davis, of Columbia South Carolina) (1834-1838) (Typescript 1930) pg.4, SCL.

59. Letter, Rebecca Singleton to Marion and Angelica Singleton, 16 May 1830, Singleton Deveaux Collection, SCL.

60. Reniers, *Springs of Virginia* , 76-77.

61. Letter, Marion Singleton to Angelica Singleton, 20 November 1832, [Singleton Deveaux Collection?], SCL.

62. Eldest daughter, Anne Peyre Singleton Deveaux(1836-1907), would marry John Burchill Moore, grandson of Isham Moore, who had married Anne Peyre's great, great grandfather's sister and who had inherited Cane Savannah Plantation. John Burchill Moore was of great assistance to Marion during her troubles with her second husband, Reverend Augustus Converse. The Moores' three children would be born at Cane Savannah and Mr. Moore would die there. Anne Peyre married a 2nd time to Richard Irvine Manning. Marion's youngest daughter Marion Singleton (1843-1927) would marry a Pinckney, James S., but there would be no children, (or issue, in the language of the day), from that marriage.

63. Elizabeth Allen Coxe, *Memories of a South Carolina Plantation During the War* (Philadelphia: Privately printed, 1912), 75-77.

64. Singleton, *Genealogy of the Singletons,* 18;

Raiford's Creek Plantation, located approximately twelve miles from Columbia, is the plantation the John Coles found after his dispute with his father. Richard Singleton's will of 1848, item 6, states "purchased from William M Myers by John C Singleton but paid by me, R. Singleton." Will of Richard Singleton, 22 July 1848, Singleton Legal Papers, SCL.

65. Queen Elizabeth II is second cousin six times removed to Washington. The common ancestor of the Queen and Robert E Lee is Col. Augustine Warriner the elder, the first of that family to settle in Virginia. Through this connection, her Majesty Queen Elizabeth II is fifth cousin four times removed to Lee. (Through the research of Lynn Landreth, a direct descendant of John Coles and Mary "Bonnie" Lewis Carter Singleton)

66. Singleton, *Genealogy of the Singletons,* 18-19.

67. John Hammond Moore, *Columbia and Richland County: A South Carolina Community, 1740-1990* (Columbia : University of South Carolina Press, 1993), 149-150.

68. Macaulay, *Kensington*, 1; Singleton, *Genealogy of the Singletons,* 22-23.

69. After Henderson's death, five U.S. presidents- Martin Van Buren, John Tyler, Millard Fillmore, Franklin Pierce and James Buchanan stayed in his cottage (the present-day "President's Cottage Museum") between 1838 and 1860.

70. "To the beauty of fair Greece, And the grandeur of old Rome." Edgar Allen Poe, "To Helen", *Poems by Edgar A. Poe* (NYC: Elam Bliss,1831), 39. It was later reprinted in 1836 in the *Southern Literary Messenger*; Reniers, *The Springs of Virginia*, 114-115.

71. To get a sense of the social whirl that Angelica was a part of in Washington, see Diary of Mrs. William Campbell Preston, wife of Senator Preston, a cousin, (Louisa Penelope Davis, the daughter of Dr. James Davis, of Columbia South Carolina) (1834-1838) (Typescript 1930) South Caroliniana Library, University of South Carolina.

72. Letter, Marion Singleton to Dear Mother, 23 March 1838, Angelica Singleton Van Buren Papers, Library of Congress.

73 Broadwell, *Sketches of Planters, Plantations, and Living Along the Great Road,* 55.

74. Reniers, *Springs of Virginia*, 132,134-136.

75. Letter, John Coles Singleton to Richard Singleton, 10 February 1837,Singleton Family Papers, Folder #115, UNC.

76. Letter, Matthew R. Singleton to Richard Singleton, 31 December 1836,

Singleton Family Papers, Folder #111, UNC.

77. Macaulay, *Kensington*, 5; Letter, Richard Singleton to William Ford, Esq., 2 April 1839, Singleton Family Papers, Folder #122, UNC.

PART FIVE-ANGELICA TAKES CENTER STAGE

1. Halsey, *Sketches of Singleton Family*, 11.

2. *Boston Post*, January 2, 1839.

3. Edward L. Widmer, Martin Van Buren (NYC : Times Books, Henry Holt and Company, 2005), 112.

4. Letter, Your Sister SCS [Sarah Coles Stevenson] to my precious sisters, 15 May 1839, Sarah Coles Stevenson Papers, DUKE.

5. Letter, Your Sister SCS to My beloved sisters, May 1839, Sarah Coles Stevenson Papers, DUKE.

6. Letter, Your Sister SCS to My beloved sisters, May 1839, Sarah Coles Stevenson Papers, DUKE.

7. Letter, Matthew Singleton to Richard Singleton, addressed My Dear Friends, 16 May 1839, Singleton Family Papers, SCL. According to the *History of the Oxford Bodleian Library* online: in 1849, ten years after Matthew's visit and six years after the publication of a new catalogue in three folio volumes, there were estimated to be 220,000 books and some 21,000 manuscripts in the library's collection,

8. Letter, Your Sister SCS to My beloved sisters, May 1839, Sarah Coles Stevenson Papers, DUKE.

9. Letter, Your Sister SCS to her sisters, 17 May 1839, Sarah Coles Stevenson Papers, DUKE.

10. Letter, Your Sister SCS to her sisters, 17 May 1839, Sarah Coles Stevenson Papers, DUKE.

11. *Charleston Courier*, July 29, 1839.

12. Letter, Your Sister SCS to My beloved sisters, and My dear and precious Edward & dear name sake, 29 July 1839, Sarah Coles Stevenson Papers, DUKE.

13. Letter, Your Sister S.C. Stevenson to sisters and brother, 18 August 1839, Sarah Coles Stevenson Papers, DUKE.

14. Ibid.

1.5 Letter, SCS to My beloved sisters, 25 December 1839, Sarah Coles Stevenson Papers, DUKE.

16. Letter, Matthew Singleton to Richard Singleton, 19 April 1840, Singleton Family Papers, Folder #124, UNC.

17. The Gold Spoon Oration, also known as "The Regal Splendor of the President's Palace", was given by Representative Charles Ogle in the United States House of Representatives April 14-16, 1840

18. Laura C. Holloway, *The Ladies of the White House* (Cincinnati: Forshee & McMakin, 1882), 344.

19. A copy of the portrait of Angelica that hangs in the Red Room in the White House, decorates a wall at Lindenwald. Mary Singleton McDuffie Hampton, a niece of Angelica's and frequent visitor to Lindenwald, traveled to Europe with the Van Burens in the 1850's. Mary was a particular favorite of former President Martin Van Buren and her portrait hangs in the breakfast room of Lindenwald.

20. Letter, Abraham Van Buren to [?] Van Buren, 23 April 1841, Van Buren Papers, Library of Congress.

PART SIX-TROUBLING TIMES

1. "Horrid Murder", *Charleston Courier*, July 28, 1842

2. Jacob Stroyer, *My Life in the South* (Salem, Massachusetts: Newcomb and Gauss, 1898), 55-56.

3. Ibid.,15.

4. Letter, Richard Singleton to Robert Deveaux, 6 August 1842, Singleton Family Papers, Library of Congress.

5. "Wm. C. Preston," *Charleston Courier*, January 10, 1843.

6. Letter, John P. Richardson to Richard Singleton, 10 November 1842, Singleton Family Papers, UNC; Letter, James D. Treadwell to Richard Singleton, 31 December 1842, Singleton Family Papers, UNC.

7. Julian A. Selby, *Memorabilia and Anecdotal Reminiscences of Columbia, S. C., and Incidents Connected Therewith* (Columbia, S. C. : R.L. Bryan Company,1905), 63.

8. Letter, Gabriella Huger to Mrs. Marion Singleton Deveaux, 12 June 1844, Singleton Deveaux Collection, SCL.

PART SEVEN-MATTHEW AND MARTHA

1. Lindsay Berit Crawford, "Martha Rutledge Kinloch Singleton of Kensington Plantation: Portrait of a South Carolina Widow" (Master's Thesis, University of South Carolina, 2007)18-19; Invitation, 23 February 1845, Folder 11/544/1, St. Cecilia Society Collection, 1830-2005. (1146.00) South Carolina

Historical Society , Charleston.

2. Reprint from the Baltimore Sun in the New York Times, February 14, 1896; The St. Cecilia Society is still active today and remains exclusive. For the last hundred-plus years, membership has been restricted to male descendants of previous members of the society, effectively limiting members to those whose families have lived in Charleston for many generations. Instead of the three or four annual balls that were once held, it has been reduced to one, held annually in January.

3. Education did not stop with the male side of the family. Martha's maternal aunt, Harriet Lowndes Aiken, was well educated and was said to have spoken four languages. Mary I'on Lowndes Kinloch, Martha's mother, would have most likely received the same type of education. Crawford, "Martha Singleton," 12-13.

4. Eliza Cope Harrison, ed., *Best Companions: Letters of Eliza Middleton Fisher and Her Mother, Mary Hering Middleton, from Charleston, Philadelphia and Newport, 1839-1846* (Columbia , SC: University of South Carolina Press, 2001), 258.

5. Letter, J.L. Petigru to Col. A. Van Buren, 13 February 1859, Singleton Family Papers, SCL; Jacob Stroyer, mentions that his mother, Chloe, lived on the Headquarters Plantation when it was owned by a Mr. Crough before it was sold to Colonel Richard Singleton. Stroyer, My Life in the South (1898 Edition), 14.

6. Richland County Landmarks Designation Application, Kensington Slave/Tenant Dwelling Application, Appendix A, submitted by Mary Sherrer, April 2007.

7. Letter, Matthew Singleton to Wright and Hawks, [9?] February 1844, Singleton Family Papers, SCL.

8. Letter, Matthew Singleton to Wright and Hawks, 19 July 1844, Singleton Family Papers, SCL.

9. Matthew R. Singleton Estate Inventory, 12 January 1855, Richland District Probate Court Estate Papers, Matthew R. Singleton, South Carolina Department of Archives and History, Columbia, South Carolina.

10. Letter, Martha Singleton to Cleland Singleton, addressed to my dear son, 17 December [1858?], Singleton Family Papers, SCL; Among the books in the present Kensington collection are two inscribed with Martha Singleton's name. One is "Adam Bede", written under the pen name of George Eliot, published in 1859. The author was in reality a woman, Mary Ann Evans. I think Martha would have appreciated Mary Evans's need for a pseudonym, for as a widow, she had to act in what was truly a man's world. The second book inscribed by Martha was, "It Is Never Too Late To Mend: A Matter of Fact

Romance", in two volumes, by Charles Reade, copyrighted in 1856.The story is about a ruthless squire who becomes obsessed with a younger woman and conspires to have her lover framed and sent to jail. In 19th Century England, both George Eliot and Charles Reade were mentioned in the same breath with Charles Dickens.

11. Letter, Rebecca Singleton to Martha Singleton, 18 June 1846, Singleton Family Papers, SCL.

12. Letter, Mary Singleton McDuffie to Col. Richard Singleton, 26 June 1851, Singleton Family Papers, SCL.

13. The United States Census of 1850 lists a governess, W. Pritchard, age twenty-seven, born in England, living at the Kensington. Cleland was six and Helen was three.

14. Letter, Martha Singleton to Cleland Singleton, addressed to my dear son, 17 December [1858?], Singleton Family Papers, SCL.

15. Macaulay, *Kensington*, 9.

16. Stroyer, *My Life in the South* (1898 Edition)10; Crawford, "Martha Singleton", 23.

17. Matthew subscribed to many farm magazines: *The Cultivator, New York Albion, Palmetto State Banner, The New York Spirit of the Times, The Horticulturist, New England Farmer, American Farmer*. Subscription receipts, Kenneth Stampp, ed., *Records of Ante-bellum Southern Plantations from the Revolution through the Civil War, Series J*, Bethesda, Maryland: University Publications of America,1990, Microfilm of the Singleton Family Papers, UNC.

18. Singleton, *Genealogy of the Singletons,* 23.

19. Ibid., 23.

20. Kensington Plantation (Main house), Historic American Building Survey, HABS # SC – 129, Data files, 8, *Library of Congress*. http://www.loc.gov.

21. Irving, *South Carolina Jockey Club*, 123.

22. Letter, John Peter Broün to his wife, Abby, 19 April 1846, Family collection of Lynn Landreth.

PART EIGHT-MORE CHANGES

1. The passenger list of the steamship Southerner bound for New York shows Mrs. Van Buren two children and a nurse on board. *Southern Patriot*, Charleston, S.C., June 14 1847; The passenger list of the steamship Northerner from New York shows Col. Van Buren, lady [Angelica], two children and servant. *Charleston Courier*, S.C, November 28, 1849.

2. Accessed 2.1.2015. https://kihm3.wordpress.com/2011/12/11/when-rectors-attack/

3. Reniers, *Springs of Virginia*,168-169.

4. Ibid., 173.

5. Ibid., 172.

6. Letter, Richard Singleton to Matthew Singleton, 10 September 1852, Singleton Family Papers, SCL; The *Charleston Courier* reported on September 2nd "crops on the Wateree are utterly destroyed" and the trestle and railroad bridge over the Wateree are still holding upriver in Camden; On September 6th, the *Charleston Courier*, reported that "the trestle work and bridge over the Wateree on the railroad line was carried off yesterday morning, September 5th."

7. Singleton, *Genealogy of the Singletons,*18; The passenger list from the steamer C. Vanderbilt from Wilmington, says JC Singleton, listed next to Mary Chesnut who was a close friend of Mrs. J.C. Singleton. *Charleston Courier*, September 13, 1852. Was it John Coles or Mrs. John Coles? If it was John Coles, he would be die one week later.

8. Reniers, *Springs of Virginia*,173.

9. Singleton, *Genealogy of the Singletons,* 18; *Charleston Courier*, September 22, 1852.

10. Stroyer, *My Life in the South* (1898 edition), 39-42.

11. Singleton, *Genealogy of the Singletons,*15.

12. Broadwell, *Sketches of Planters, Plantations, and Living Along the Great Road,*, 58.

13. Singleton, *Genealogy of the Singletons,* 15.

14 Newspaper accounts of the railroad accident:

According to the Charleston Courier as to the cause of the accident:
"As rumors have existed that there was decayed timber on the culvert which had yielded to the weight of the train, we have taken some pains to inquire into the fact. The road had been rebuilt from the junction to the river, and the timbers are stated by authority, to have been perfectly sound. The heavy rains inundating the bank caused the accident. A half hour before the accident a heavy train, with a twenty ton engine had passed over it – and had passed daily for three weeks – the Antelope engine, connected with the passenger train to which the accident occurred is one of the lightest in the Company's service, being only of thirteen or fourteen ton weight. It had been placed on that road in consequence of being lighter than any other. If there had been rotting

timber present, the Charlotte engine of 20 tons, which passed over half an hour before, would have more certainly crushed it than an engine of six tons less weight." *Charleston Courier*, December 1,1852 ;

The *Darlington Flag* newspaper account as to where Colonel Singleton and his grandson were riding in the train: All the people killed and injured were in what was known as the "blue car", usually used for servants. It had seat cushions and stuffed benches for the accommodation of passengers and was used for that purpose from time to time. Three cars were plunged into the water – the tender behind the engine, the baggage car and the blue car. The blue car is where Col. Singleton and his grandson were sitting. *Darlington Flag* newspaper account, published in the *Charleston Courier*, December 24, 1852

15. Samuel Leland Journal, 26 November 1852, Samuel Wells Leland Papers, 1845-1876, SCL.

PART NINE-HIGHS AND LOWS

1. The figures for plantation acres and slaves were compiled from a variety of sources including the Wills of John and Richard Singleton, slave schedules, and miscellaneous other sources. It is an estimate.

2. Richard Singleton Estate Inventory and Appraisement, Singleton Legal Papers, SCL; See Samuel H. Williamson, "Seven Ways to Compute the Relative Value of a U.S. Dollar Amount, 1774 to present," Measuring Worth, 2015, URL: www.measuringworth.com/uscompare/. See also Professors Williamson and Cain's essay on the same site, "Measuring Slavery in 2011 Dollars."

3. Raiford's Creek is the plantation that John Coles purchased after his dispute with his father that Colonel Singleton's friends had enabled him to buy. The Plantation was located approximately twelve miles southeast from Columbia. Richard Singleton's will of 1848, item 6 affirms the ownership: "purchased from William M Myers by John C Singleton but paid by me, R. Singleton." Will of Richard Singleton, 22 July 1848, Singleton Legal Papers, SCL.

4. Letters Testamentary, (Sumter District Court document laying out requirements of probating Richard Singleton's Will), 3 December 1852, Singleton Legal Papers, SCL.

5. Return of Matthew R. Singleton, executor of Richard Singleton,(Statement of bonds, notes, cash and cotton assets of Richard Singleton Estate), 26 April 1853, Singleton Legal Papers, SCL.

6. Richard Singleton Estate, Inventory and Appraisement, Singleton Legal Papers, SCL.

7. Richard Singleton Estate, Inventory and Appraisement, Singleton Legal Papers, SCL; John Singleton(Richard Singleton's father) had put part of his estate into trusts for his daughter Mary McRae and his Broün grandsons. John

Peter Broün was the only surviving Broün grandson. In 1853, $1018.48 was dispersed to both Mary McRae and John P. Broün from the John Singleton trust estate. The largest amount of cash in Richard Singleton's estate was from the trust estate of John Singleton in the amount of $39,371.51. Return of Matthew R. Singleton, executor of Richard Singleton, 26 April 1853, Singleton Legal Papers, SCL.

8.Letter, Andrew Stevenson to Colonel M.R. Singleton, 2 December 1852, Singleton Family Papers, SCL.

9. For a in-depth treatment of the Converse and other Singleton family lawsuits, see *The Singleton Family of South Carolina: Story of Divorce , Mayhem ,Greed ,Destruction, (The Real Story of the Singleton Lawsuits)* by Charles Broadwell, available through the Sumter County Genealogical Society, Sumter, South Carolina

PART TEN-THE KENSINGTON

1. Ralph M. Boyd , Project Director for the Kensington restoration in the 1980's, believes that the original existing building was a T-shaped office building with the crossbar of the T on the west side and "not a home". He also believed that the Singleton family plantation business was directed from there, hence its name: Headquarters. Ralph Boyd interview, October 29, 2012.

2. Boyd believes that Matthew may have also been influenced by what he saw at the Kensington Palace in London. Ibid.

3. Two well known examples of the work of Jones and Lee are The Farmers and Exchange Bank in Charleston, a National Historic Landmark, and Richard Furman Hall at Furman University. Both buildings reflect an Italianate influence that was also in evidenced in the Kensington Mansion design. All three buildings were completed in 1854.

Edward C. Jones designed the St. John in the Wilderness church in Flat Rock, North Carolina. Matthew and Martha Singleton are both buried in that church cemetery. Mr. Jones also designed the Magnolia Cemetery in Charleston where Matthew and Martha's son, Cleland Singleton, chose to be buried.

Francis D. Lee, engineer and architect, also designed the *David*, a class of semi-submersible ships that was used to attack Union blockading ships during the Civil War. Part of his design was the spar torpedo which in addition to the ram was the offensive weapon of the *Davids* . His spar torpedo design was also used by the Hunley in the first successful attack and sinking of a warship by a submarine—*USS Housatonic* on February 17, 1864. Additionally, Lee designed and supervised construction of many of the Confederate defenses of Charleston Harbor, including Battery Wagner, the fort charged by the 54th Massachusetts Infantry.

After the war, Napoleon III tried to lure Francis Lee to France to design engines of war for France, but Francis Lee chose to stay in America. He moved to St. Louis in 1866 where he continued his architectural practice.

4. "At home it was known as the Old World. To them it was all new." David McCullough, *The Greater Journey: Americans in Paris* (New York, London, Toronto, Sydney: Simon & Shuster, 2011), 19. David McCullough's view of 19th Century Paris captures the wonder and fascination that Americans, like Matthew and Angelica felt on journeying there.

5. Twenty-five letters sent to Matthew Singleton reflect the contractor and subcontractor side of the renovation and construction of the mansion. Twenty-five Letters from Jones and Lee and various subcontractors to Col. M.R. Singleton, 7 May 1852-16 March 1854, Singleton Family Papers, Folder 157-162, UNC.

6. John Califf, architect for Triad Architectural Associates, did an analysis with drawings for an ad-hoc historical preservation committee for the Kensington in 1980. It was done before Union Camp purchased the property and restored it. Mr. Califf believes that one section was moved, not both and that the center section was then built. An indicator of the joining of the new and the old is a small elevation distance between the upstairs bedroom wings and the central hall that connects them. John Califf interview, August 2011.

7. The Kensington also featured ram's head capitals similar to ones seen at the Fontainebleau Palace as well as heavy arcades and balustrades used at the Louvre and the Palace of Versailles. The cross-shaped house plan, the vaulted ceiling in the dining room and the plaster decorations used in the interior are all found in French buildings and palaces of the time. Many of the ornate interior plaster decorations used in the Kensington can be found in the Benault's catalogue printed in France in 1813. The narrow, hidden staircase to the upper story in the Kensington is also a decidedly French design. Ibid.

8. Ibid.

9. Ibid.

10. Triad Architectural Associates, *The Kensington House: An Architectural and Historical Survey* (Columbia, S.C.: 1980), 13.

11. Ibid., 12.

12. Califf interview, August 2011.

13. In 1980 John Califf, the architect who directed the preparation of *The Kensington House: An Architectural and Historical Survey* report, believed that this was the original color scheme. *Triad, The Kensington House, 6;* Mr. Califf seems to have changed his mind. In an interview in August of 2011, he indicated that he believed the original exterior paint scheme was a stone gray

or drab warm gray, in order to look like a French Chateau.

14. Califf interview, August 2011.

15. "The interior walls and plaster details, including door and window frames were to be painted in lead white zinc or white French zinc." Ibid.

16. Triad, *The Kensington House*, 6; Several painting proposals and estimates were done for the Mansion:

W. L. Johnson proposed the following:

Outside Paint Specifications
-All the outside of the Building, including the Columns, Balustrades & Columns Gray Stone color-3 coats
-All blinds & shutters, Gray Stone-3 coats
-Outside of sash white lead.
-Outside doors grained Oak.
-Tin roofing on porch and dome-3 coats Brown [...?...] Paint
-Back & front steps & pedestals of large front columns Brown Stone,
-Overhead ceiling of all piazzas & colonnades-3 coats lead

Inside Paint Specifications
-No Mantels
-All rooms and frames-3 coats Lead 1 coat White Zinc
-All window frames and sash-3 coats lead, 1 coat white zinc
-All washboards-3 coats lead, 1 coat zinc
-All staircases-Varnished
-Iron balustrade-bronze green and bronze
-Skylights in dome-plain colour

Mr. Johnson's estimate, including lodging and board for him and his hands, was $945. Letter, W.L. Johnson to Col. M.R. Singleton, 2 January 1854, Singleton Family Papers, Folder 161-162, UNC;

Another estimate was from William Barney. His estimate for painting the entire place was $1500. It would have been $1350, but using sanded paint on the exterior to give a textured look was $150 more. Letter from William Barney to Col. M.R. Singleton, December 1853, Singleton Family Papers, Folder 159-160, UNC;

Which contractor Matthew Singleton selected is unclear.

PART ELEVEN-MATTHEW PASSES THE TORCH

1. Reniers, *The Springs of Virginia*, 169.

2. One small example is a letter from a carriage manufacturer in Charleston in 1852 asking for payment on a long overdue debt. Letter, Reynolds and Co. to M.R. Singleton, 3 April 1852, Singleton Family Papers, SCL.

3. Stroyer, *My Life in the South* (1898 edition), 28-29.

4. Deed of Assignment conveyed to Thomas S. Magg of Charleston, on July 3, 1854, Inventory and Appraisement of the Personal Estate, Goods and Chattel of Matthew R. Singleton, Richland District Probate Court Estate Papers, Matthew R. Singleton, South Carolina Department of Archives and History, Columbia, South Carolina; Matthew entered three races during the 1854 February Race Week in Charleston, taking two seconds and a first. Matthew raced the last Race Week season of his life in February of 1854. John Hopkins, a three year old gelding, won the last race he entered, winning a purse of $300. Irving, *South Carolina Jockey Club*, 136.

5. Richard Singleton, Matthew's twin brother, had died on August 14, 1833, almost 21 years to the day before Matthew's death on August 18, 1854 according to the Singleton genealogy. Singleton, *Genealogy of the Singletons*, 22; In the Singleton Cemetery a death date on Richard's headstone is given as August 18, making it exactly 21 years. There is a letter sent to Mattie from "Your Sister" (sister-in-law, Bonnie Singleton?) in Columbia on August 26, 1854 saying, "How strange, how very strange that the 18 August should have been the fatal day to the twin brothers!" Letter, Your sister to Mattie Singleton, 26 August 1854, Singleton Family Papers, Folder #162, UNC; A newspaper obituary gives the date of death as August 18th. *Charleston Courier*, August 28, 1854.

6. Samuel Leland Journal, 19 August 1854, Samuel Wells Leland Papers, 1845-1876, SCL.

7. Letter, Mary Singleton McDuffie to Mrs. Singleton, 1 September 1854, Singleton Family Papers, SCL.

8. *Charleston Courier*, August 2,1854.

9. L. Mary [last name?] to Mrs. Mattie R. Singleton, Singleton Family Papers, 11 September 1854, Singleton Family Papers, SCL.

10. *Charleston Courier*, August 28, 1854.

11. Letter, Judie [?] to Mattie (Singleton), 10 October 1854, Singleton Family Papers, SCL.

12. Stroyer, *My Life in the South* (1898 edition), 29.

13. Keziah Brevard Journal, 28 November 1860, SCL.

14. Matthew R. Singleton last will and testament, dated April 3,1853. South Carolina Will Transcripts, Richland District, Matthew R. Singleton, Volume 3, Book L, 322-323. South Carolina Department of Archives and History.

15. Letter, Mr. Clark to Mr. King, 20 September 1854, Singleton Family Papers, SCL.

16. Letter, Mrs. MR Singleton to Mr. Clark, 27 September 1854, Singleton Family Papers, SCL.

17. The original diary published in 1905 contains no mention of these observations and comments. Mary Boykin Chesnut, *A Diary From Dixie,* edited by Isabella D. Martin and Myrta Lockett Avary (New York: D. Appleton and Company, 1905)

A second version was published in 1949 and ascribes this quote to Martha Singleton.

"Mrs. Mat Singleton uses English as pure as that of Victoria Regina; such clean-cut sentences, every word distinctly enunciated. She is the delight of her friends, the terror of her enemies. Sometime those words dropped one by one with such infinite precision are drops of vitriol!"

Ben Ames Williams, ed., *A Diary From Dixie by Mary Boykin Chesnut* (Boston: Houghton Mifflin Company, 1949), 494.

In a third version and considered by most scholars the most accurate, Mary Chesnut's Civil War , the quote is ascribed to Mrs. Mat Singleton and Mrs. John [Coles] Singleton:

"...Mrs. Mat Singleton used English as pure as that of Victoria Regina. How I like to hear Mrs. John Singleton's clear-cut sentences, every word distinctly enunciated. I should say she was the delight of her friends, the terror of her foes. I am afraid of those words dropped one by one with such infinite precision – drops of vitriol, sometimes." C. Vann Woodward, ed., *Mary Chesnut's Civil War* (New Haven and London: Yale University Press, 1981), 743. The diary entries were written sometime between February 29, 1865 and March 4,1865.

18. Richland District Probate Court Estate Papers, Matthew R. Singleton, Box 58,package 1432,Microfilm Reel RI74, South Carolina Department of Archives and History, Columbia, South Carolina; Richard Singleton Will, 22 July 1848,Singleton Legal Papers, SCL; Stroyer, My Life(1898 Edition) , 29-30.

19. Will of Richard Singleton, 22 July 1848, Singleton Legal Papers, SCL.

20. In 1858, six years after Col. Singleton's death, Martha had to deal with a note and mortgage for $5,000 against the estate of Colonel Singleton by his nephew, John Peter Broün, who lived in Alabama. She would be bedeviled by these legal issues for the next 20 years, well into the 1870's. (From the private collection of Lynn Landreth.)

21. Just how convoluted were the legal issues involved with Colonel Singleton's estate and debts? In the 1921 obituary of Richard Singleton, Mattie's and Matthew's son, it was noted that one of the things he was most proud of was that he had finally settled all the business affairs of his

grandfather, Colonel Richard Singleton. *The State*, Columbia, July 1, 1921.

22. The old McCord's Ferry road lay 1/3 of a mile from the Mansion. Part of that road still exists on the property. The present day McCord's Ferry Rd, Highway 261, was re-routed in the 1930's and lies about 2/3 of a mile from the Mansion.

-Old road to Mansion -2160 feet (1/3 mile)

-New road to Mansion-3570 feet (2/3 mile)

-Mansion to Acton Station RR Depot-2482 feet (1/2 mile)

-Mansion to Acton House (Cleland Singleton's residence)-2000 feet (4/10 mile)

(The Mansion is 85'6" x 72'1" with 11 of its 29 rooms upstairs. It was surrounded by 50 landscaped acres.)

23. Macaulay, *Kensington*, 6.

24. Ralph Boyd, Union Camp's director for the Kensington restoration in the 1980's, mentioned in an interview that he was struck by some similarities in design features between the Kensington Palace in London and the Kensington Mansion. Mr. Boyd had visited the Palace on several occasions and observed that the dining room ceiling was painted to look like it was vaulted and designs around the parlor doors were also similar to the Kensington mansion. Since Matthew Richard Singleton had been attached to the American Embassy in London and would have visited the Kensington Palace (the royal residence at that time), Mr. Boyd speculated that Matthew may have been influenced by what he saw and incorporated those features into the Kensington Mansion. Ralph Boyd interview and letter, October 29, 2012.

25. Triad, *he Kensington House*, 6-7.

26. Ibid., 4.

27. Kensington Plantation (Main house), Historic American Building Survey, HABS # SC—129 , Data files, 8, *Library of Congress*. http://www.loc.gov;

According to a later family descendent, Eliza Barron Macaulay, Matthew used the house like his father did at Home Place, as the center pivot of a wheel design with the spokes being trees (water oak, magnolia, cedar and holly) emanating from the house. An English gardener, which he shared with his father, designed and maintained the boxwood bordered, formal gardens behind the house. A vegetable garden was planted close behind the house, hidden behind ornamental shrubbery. Haw trees (crabapple) were also planted as an experiment to produce fence posts for the pastures, for the blooded horses. Macaulay, *Kensington*, 7.

28. Triad, *The Kensington House*, 11-12.

29. Aerial photographs taken in 1939 and 1941 reveal a greenway with two double rows of trees, beginning about ½ to ¾ mile back from the house, providing an open viewing corridor down to the riverbank.

30. An 1857 plat shows a road running past "the street" to the river. An 1878 Plat shows a ferry, docks and barns by the riverside and a pond located approximately 300 yards southeast of the Mansion.

31. George Egleston Woodruff, *Boyhood Sketches* (Charlotte, NC: Privately printed, 1914), 2.

32. Stroyer, *My Life in the South* (1898 edition), 30-34.

33. U.S. Bureau of the Census, Original Agricultural Schedules for 1850 and 1860, Microfilm editions, for Richland District, South Carolina; (Return of Crops and Other Statistics for Richland County), South Carolina Department of Archives and History.

34. Crawford, "Martha Singleton", 33.

35. Ibid., 34-35; Stroyer, *My Life in the South* (1898 edition), 13.

36. William Glaze to Wade Hampton III, May 1860, Kenneth Stampp, ed., *Records of Ante-bellum Southern Plantations from the Revolution through the Civil War, Series J*, Bethesda, Maryland: University Publications of America,1990, Microfilm of the Singleton Family Papers, UNC.

37. Letter, Angelica Van Buren to Martha Singleton, 31 March 1856, Singleton Family Papers, UNC.

PART TWELVE-THE CIVIL WAR

1. Walter Edgar, *South Carolina: A History* (Columbia: University of South Carolina Press, 1998), 287.

2 1860 wealth calculations made from data in Eighth Census of the United States, Statistics of the United States, 1860 (Washington, D.C. 1866), pp. 294–319, 339; Edgar, *South Carolina: A History*, 275,285-286.

3 Martin and Avary, *Diary From Dixie*, 184.

4. Ibid., 194-195, 203.

5. Louise Haskell Daly, *Alexander Cheves Haskell: Portrait of a Man* (Norwood, Massachusetts: Plimpton Press [Privately printed], 1935), 151.

6. Dwight, My Long Life, 8.

7. Daly, *Haskell*, 159.

8. Martin and Avary, *Diary from Dixie*, 1905 ed., 208.

9. Ibid., 238.

10. Broadwell, *Sketches of Planters, Plantations, and Living Along the Great Road*,47.

11. Dwight, *My Long Life,*2.

12. *Charleston Courier*, August 30,1862 .

13. Martin and Avary, *Diary From Dixie*, 240-241.

14. Singleton, *Genealogy of the Singletons,* 29.

15. Confederate Army war records, South Carolina Department of Archives and History, researched by Tim Bradshaw, local historian; In the Signal Corp, signals were sent using flags, torches, flares and rockets from a natural high point of land or man made structure so they could be clearly seen by the recipient, but it also made the operators subject to sniper and artillery fire. It is estimated that 1 in 12 operators was killed, wounded or captured.

16. Macaulay, *Kensington*, 7.

17. Stroyer, *My Life in the South* (1898 edition), 82,86-87,94; A receipt written to Martha Singleton details the sending of fifteen slaves to work on the Columbia fortifications in preparation for the impending threat of Sherman. Receipt to Mrs. M.R. Singleton, 25 January 1865, Singleton Family Papers, SCL.

18. Stroyer, *My Life in the South* (1898 edition), 95-97.

19. Receipt from the Confederate Quartermaster's office, received of Mrs. Martha R. Singleton, [2?] November 1863, Singleton Family Papers, SCL.

20. U.S. War Department, *The War of the Rebellion: A Compilation of the Official Records of the Union and Confederate Armies* (Washington D.C: Government Printing Office, 1895) ser.1, vol. 44, O.R., 799. (Henceforth O.R.)

21. Ibid., 743.

22. Bradley T. Johnson, ed., *A Memoir of the Life and Public Service of Joseph E Johnston, Once the Quartermaster General of the Army of the United States and a General in the Army of the Confederate States of America* (Baltimore: R. H. Woodward and Company. 1891),142.

23. Luis F. Emilio, *A Brave Black Regiment: History of the 54th Regiment of Massachusetts Volunteer Infantry, 1863-1865*. (Boston :The Boston Book Company, 1891), 272.

24. Walter Brian Cisco, *War Crimes Against Southern Civilians* (Gretna, Louisiana: Pelican Publishing Company, 2007), 145-146.

25. Weekly News and Courier, *Our Women in the War, The Lives They Lived; The Deaths They Died* (Charleston: The News and Courier Book Presses,

1885), 328.

Virginia Taylor Green under nom de plum, "Old Dominion", wrote a chapter (pgs.326-331) in *Our Women in the War*. She was the mother of Allen Jones Green, the sick son in the story, who married Helen Coles Singleton in 1868.

26. David P. Conyngham, *Sherman's March through the South, with Sketches and Incidents of the Campaign* (New York: Sheldon and Company, 1865), 344.

27. Oscar L. Jackson, *The Colonel's Diary* (Sharon, Pa: published privately, 1922), 191.

28. Ibid., 192.

29. (Letter of Union private)___to my dear uncle, 28 March 1865, Sherman Papers, Clinton Haskell Collection, William L. Clements Library, University of Michigan.

30. George Ward Nichols, *The Story of the Great March from the Diary of a Staff Officer* (New York: Harper and Brothers, 1865),131 , 140.

31. Ibid.,150.

32. Ibid.,170-171.

33. Kenneth Lyftogt, *Left For Dixie: the Civil War Diary of John Rath* (Iowa City, IA: Press of the Camp Pope Bookshop,1991, New materials copyright 2004),75.

34. The pillared ruins of the Hampton plantation house, Millwood, once a showplace of the South, is located at 6100 Garner's Ferry Road (US 76), *Columbia*, *South Carolina*, directly across from Shoppes at Woodhill /Target. The property is privately owned.

35. The Albemarle tract was sold in 1862 by Mary (Bonnie) L. Singleton to George A. Trenholm. In 1862 Mary L Singleton bought a house in town located at 1603 Senate St. It is now located at 1816 Henderson. She kept 40 acres and a dwelling on the Albemarle tract. In 1870, she sold the property to the Haskell family. The location of the house on the once 40 acre tract is 1116 Belmont. After selling her property, she along with her adopted granddaughter, Rebecca Mary Haskell, daughter of Decca Singleton Haskell, moved back to her home county, Albemarle Virginia. Anonymous source

36. Hyer, "Relics From Home Place," *International Studio*, November 1924, 44.

37. Earl Schenck Miers, ed., *When The World Ended: The Diary of Emma LeConte*, (New York: Oxford University Press, 1957), xii.

38. Deposition of Sherman, in Barklay vs. United States, Dec.11, 1872.

39. Miers, *When The World Ended* , 56.

40. Deposition given by William Tecumseh Sherman in J. J. Browne vs. The United States Federal case on December 11,1872, James G. Gibbes, *Who Burnt Columbia ?* (Newberry , SC : Elbert H. Aull Company,1902),105-106.

41. Letter, William Sherman to SHM Byers, February 10, 1888, *20 years in Europe: A Counsul General's Memories of Noted People, With letters from General W.T. Sherman* , by S. H. M. Byers (Chicago and New York: Rand McNally and Company, 1900), 293.

42. The Kensington was saved, but other area plantation homes were not so lucky. The Cabin Branch (Oldfield) plantation home and the Mill plantation house, fifteen miles away from Kensington, both owned by Keziah Goodwyn Hopkins Brevard, were burned down by Sherman's men. The James Uriah Adams house in Gadsden, ten miles from the Kensington as well as a Weston family home in the area suffered the same fate.

43. Various versions of this story have been handed down for generations.

44. *O.R.*, Vol. 47, Part 2, chapter 49, Correspondence, 857.

45. Ibid., Vol. 47, Part 2, 176.

46. Hyer, "Relics from Home Place," *International Studio*, 44.

47. Emilio, *Brave Black Regiment*, 306.

PART THIRTEEN-POSTWAR

1. Edgar, *South Carolina: A History,* 374-375.

2. Ibid.

3. Macaulay, *Kensington*, 8.

4. Letter, Mr.[Keley?] to Mrs. M. R. Singleton, 25 May 1867, Singleton Family Papers, SCL.

5. Martha R. Singleton family legal papers, 1836-1878. (431.02 (S) 18) South Carolina Historical Society.

6. U.S. Bureau of the Census, Original Agricultural Schedules-1860, Microfilm editions, for Richland District, South Carolina; State of South Carolina Agricultural Census Schedule, 1868, Richland District, (Return of Crops and Other Statistics for Richland County), South Carolina Department of Archives and History.

7. Freedman's Contract between C. K. Singleton and 32 Freedmen, 22 January 1867, Singleton Family Papers, SCL.

8. Martha R. Singleton family legal papers, 1836-1878. (431.02 (S) 18)

South Carolina Historical Society.

9. J S G Richardson, (*The State* reporter) ed., *Reports of Cases Heard and Determined by the Supreme Court of South Carolina*, (Columbia: R.L. Brian,1879), Vol. 9, November 1876 to November 1877 inclusive, 465-492; Alexander Cheves Haskell had been appointed to the South Carolina Supreme Court in 1877 by Wade Hampton III. Haskell had been the husband of Martha's niece, Decca Singleton Haskell, who had died during the Civil War. Did he recuse himself from the Martha Singleton vs. Charles T. Lowndes case?

10. Dwight, *My Long Life* , 64.

11. Ibid., 6.

12. The background of the Home Place stoneware is robin's egg blue, with figures of deeper blue and gilt. In 1806 the Prince of Wales, later George IV, visited the factory, placing several orders. From that time a crown was added to the maker's mark. The Singleton China does not have that. It must predate 1806. The china and glass and some of the furniture stayed in Singleton family hands until at least 1924. In the article "Relics of Home Place", published that year, Mrs. Leroy Halsey (nee Decca Coles Singleton), great granddaughter of Richard Singleton and daughter of Richard Richardson Singleton, still owned six of the maple chairs, two armchairs and one baby high chair. She reported that the china had remained in constant use by the family for over a hundred years, except for the interruption of the war. She said it was never relegated to an exhibition shelf in a corner cupboard and except for the cover of the vegetable dish, had remained unharmed. Hyer, "Relics from Home Place," *International Studio*, 143-144.

13. Dwight, *My Long Life*, 5-6,10-11.

14. Ibid., 2.

15. For an in-depth look at Singleton family lawsuits, See *The Singleton Family of South Carolina: A Story of Divorce, Mayhem, Greed, Destruction (The Real Story of the Singleton Lawsuits),* by Charles Broadwell, available through the Sumter County Genealogical Society.

16. Halsey, *Sketches of Singleton Family*, 9.

17. Letter, Martha Singleton to Cleland Singleton, 24 January 1874, Singleton Family Papers, SCL.

18. Dwight, *My Long Life*, 64.

19. Obituary, Angelica Singleton Van Buren, January 1878, Singleton Family Papers, SCL.

20. Macaulay, *Kensington* , 8.

21. Letter, A. Burnett Rhett to Cleland Singleton, 22 June 1875, Singleton Family Papers, SCL.

22. She weighed herself and wrote "I weighed the other day at Hendersonville-128 quite enough!" She tells Cleland that her uncle, Mr. Aiken, who arrived 2 days earlier with his wife, told her about his journey by rail and stage from New York to Flat Rock. "They left New York at 3 PM on Thursday and reached Greenville [S.C] at 2 AM on Saturday. So by taking the stage which left by 7, they could have reached Flat Rock that afternoon, being 48 hours from New York. Is it not marvelous ." Letter, Martha Singleton to Cleland Singleton, 1 September 1875, Singleton Family Papers, SCL.

23. Letter, Richard Singleton to Cleland Singleton, 8 September 1876, Singleton Family Papers, South Caroliniana Library, University of South Carolina.

24. Letter, Louis LeConte to Cleland Singleton, 24 July 1878, from the private collection of Sara Moore.

25. Richland County Register of Deeds Office, Deeds recorded on 6 January 1879, Deed Book L, pgs.593,596.

26. Sumter County Register of Deeds Office, Deeds recorded on 6 January 1879, Deed Book WW, pgs. 260,263,264,267.

27. Title to Real Estate, Martha Singleton to Helen S. Green, 23 June 1879, Singleton Family Papers, SCL.

28. Woodruff, *Boyhood Sketches*, 44.

29. Letter, Martha Singleton to Cleland Singleton, 26 September 1873, Singleton Family Papers, SCL.

30. Letter, Richard Singleton to Cleland Singleton, 8 September 1876, Singleton Family Papers, SCL.

31. *The Columbia Daily Register* , December 28, 1880.

32. United States Censuses of 1880, 1900, 1920, Richland County, South Carolina.

33. Gazetteer of Richland County, Villages in the County, from Columbia City Directory, 1879-1880.

34. *The State*, Columbia, SC, July 1, 1921.

35. Macaulay, *Kensington*, 9-10.

36. Dwight, *My Long Life,*63; The station at Acton was a 1/2 mile south of the house and was called a flag station. The train could be flagged down to stop as needed. The train delivered the mail to that stop every day. As noted earlier,

it is thought that locating a station there was the result of Col. Richard Singleton's prominence in the South Carolina Railroad company. It is also said that immediate family members had life-time passes to the railroad. The railroad played an important part in the life of the Kensington commercially and socially.

37. Ibid., 3.

38. One account says they moved in 1878.The 1880 United States Census says that the Greens still lived in Lower Richland County.

39. As a young woman of twenty, Mary Carter Singleton Dwight, was visiting Kensington when Martha Singleton was stricken with typhoid fever at her daughter's home in Columbia. Richard Singleton and Eliza (Green) Singleton went to stay with Martha during her illness. Mary Dwight wound up babysitting for the Singleton children along with the governess, Miss S, as Miss Sallie Gillespie was known. Dwight, *My Long Life*, 14.

40. Letter, Eliza and Richard Singleton to Cleland Singleton, 17 May 1892, Singleton Family Papers, SCL.

41. *The State*, Columbia, June 14 1892.

42. Martha R. Singleton estate, Richland District Probate Court Estate Papers, Box 144,Package 3671, Microfilm reel E0367, South Carolina Department of Archives and History.

43. Dwight, *My Long Life,* 63.

44 A full account of the Cantey Rebellion is in *The South Carolina Historical Magazine*, January 2002, Volume 103, #1. The article is entitled "Discipline and Rebellion: The Citadel Rebellion of 1898", by Alexander S. Macaulay, Jr., pgs.30-47.

PART FOURTEEN-THE SINGLETON ERA ENDS

1. Eliza Singleton Macaulay Carney and Eliza Singleton Carney Hamrick, with assistance from Eliza Singleton Barron Macaulay and Eliza Singleton Hamrick, compilers, *The Book of Elizas* (Unpublished, July 1998), 7.

2. *The State*, Columbia, April 23, 1907. A detailed account of the wedding was published in *The State* and is in the Appendix. It is thought to have been written by Mary Carter Singleton Dwight, Daisy's cousin.

3. *The State* , January 15,1910.

4. *The State*, March 27, 1910.

5. Richland County Deed Office Records, Richland County Probate Court, Box 108 package.

6. Dwight, *My Long Life,* 63.

7. Ibid.,63, 3-4; Eliza (Green) Singleton compiled *The Genealogy of the Singletons After Their Emigration to America.* It was printed in 1914. Its thirty-five pages remain the single best resource for a snapshot of the Singleton family and an invaluable family history of mini biographies and genealogy.

8. Carney, et al., Book of Elizas, 4.

9. Dwight, My Long Life, 3-4.

10. *The State*, February 14, 1918.

11. *The State*, May 20, 1920.

12. *The State*, May 20, 1920.

13. *The State*, June 23, 1920.

14. *The State*, July 1, 1921.

15. *The State,* November 15,1922.

16. Carney, *The Book of Elizas*, 7.

PART FIFTEEN-NEW OWNERS

1. *The State*, September 10,1912; "He was the largest individual landowner in the state,..." and the largest cotton planter in South Carolina, the largest in the South, planting over 5000 acres, according to his daughter, to the best of her knowledge,. Flora Janie Hamer Hooker, *A Sketch of Robert Pickett Hamer, Jr. Of Hamer South Carolina* (Unknown publisher, 1944), 21, 23.

2. *The State*, September 10,1912. Mr. Robert Lee Scarborough, grandson of Robert Pickett Hamer Jr., believed that his grandfather died of heatstroke repairing the roof on his vacation home. A granddaughter said that he died of a heart attack. According to his daughter Flora Janie Hamer Hooker, he died of kidney trouble. Hooker, A Sketch of Robert Pickett Hamer, Jr., 22. (Heat prostration can cause kidney damage or increase your chances of succumbing to a heart attack.)

3. Untitled typescript-Hamer family time at Kensington, unpublished typescript,1-3.

4. Alfred Scarborough, father of Robert Lee Scarborough, actually made the purchase and assigned the deed to Robert C. Hamer. Richland County Deed Office, Deed Book C.E. Pg.594, 1925.

5. Cleland's home was known as Acton. James Christie Lanham, Jr. and later his brother, Butler, last private owners of the Kensington, each lived at Acton. While Butler lived there, the house caught fire and burnt to the ground.

6. Untitled typescript-Hamer family time at Kensington, unpublished typescript,3-4.

7. Robert Pickett Hamer - Lydie Holland Leake Hamer (RPH-LHL),6-19-37—6-19-87. (50th Anniversary Sketches), unpublished typescript, 11.

8. A 1912 survey of the Hamer plat shows that land was worked by tenants, possibly a hold over from the way that Richard Singleton had the land worked; According to the U.S. Department of Agriculture, Bureau of Agricultural Engineering report for the R.C. Hamer owned Kensington Plantation in 1931, tenants, share croppers and wage earners were working the land. This was another indication that different methods were tried to make farming profitable. According to Robert Lee Scarborough, there were forty or fifty families who share cropped. Families received ration tickets to purchase their basic staples and at the commissary, RPH – LHL, 12.

9. Untitled Hamer family time at Kensington, unpublished typescript, 7

10. Ibid.,6-7.

11. Go to http://www.lancingtournament.com/index.html for more information about lancing

12. General Warranty Deed, recorded in the office of the clerk of court for Richland County in deed book FA page 158 on June 2, 1941; A total of 56, 595 acres in South Carolina were purchased by the Farm Security Administration, an agency of the federal government, set up in 1937, as part of the New Deal. Under its auspices, a number of projects were put in motion in South Carolina as relief measures. The only exception was the Palmetto Farms Inc. project which was designated for relocations, primarily families displaced by war camps and war plants. The Kensington and surrounding acres comprised a part of the Palmetto Farms, Inc, project which totaled 15,793 acres. Palmetto farms Inc. -- Purpose: to meet the social problem arising from the displacement of low income farm families within the area of the Santee - Cooper project and Camp Jackson enlargement Project, etc. To buy and sell real estate, etc. To be operated on a nonprofit basis. Dissolved: June 15, 1953." By January of 1946, 42,207 acres, of the original 56,595 had been sold off.

13. One source said the Lanham's herd consisted of 800 head of dairy cattle and 1,000 head of beef cattle. Melvin Lanham, youngest son of J.C. Lanham, said that they had 1,000 Herefords (beef cattle). And still another source said the Lanhams had 2,000 head of Herefords.

PART SIXTEEN-PRESERVATION AND RESTORATION

1. Dwight, *My Long Life,* 63-64.

2. Russell Maxey, "Kensington: The Plantation Escaped Sherman, But Is Losing Its Battle Against Time," *Sandlapper Magazine*, April 1971.

3. Ann Jennings, "Kensington: An Uncovered Treasure," *The State,* 1977.

4. Bunny Richardson, "New Life," *Columbia Record*, October 15, 1981.

5. John Califf interview, August 2011.

6. Ibid.,

7. The purchase was made from the three surviving sons of James Christie Lanham, Sr. and Edith Gloria Hill Lanham: J.C. Lanham Jr., C. Butler Lanham and Melvin E. Lanham. Another son, Edward Lee Lanham, had died in a farm accident earlier at the age of 25.

8. Russell Maxey, "New Hope For An Historic Old Friend...Kensington," *The State Magazine*, June 7 1981.

9. Kensington Plantation (Main house), Historic American Building Survey, HABS # SC – 129, Data files, 1-2,8-9,*Library of Congress*. http://www.loc.gov.

10. Ralph Boyd interview and letter, October 29, 2012.

11. Taken from a Scarborough-Hamer foundation statement of purpose, by Rickie Good, Director of the Scarborough-Hamer Foundation.

12. Ibid.

Appendix

1 Robert W. Andrews, *The Life and Adventures of Capt. Robert W. Andrews, of Sumter, South Carolina* (Boston: Printed by E.P. Whitcomb, 1887) , 11-12.

2 Selby, *Reminiscences of Columbia*, 15.

3 For more on William Ellison and family, See *Black Masters A Free Family of Color in the Old South*, Michael P. Johnson and James L. Roark, Copyright 1984, Published by W.W. Norton and Company, NY and London.

4 Sarah Harvey Porter, *The Life and Times of Anne Royall* (Cedar Rapids, Iowa: The Torch Press Book Shop,1909). 229.

5 *Boston Herald*, June 3, 1901.

6 *Boston Herald*, February 10, 1908.

7 *Salem Evening News*, February 10, 1908.

8 #79 Washington Race Course, 1792-1900, accessed 24 September 2015, www.halseymap.com/Flash/window.asp?HMID=29, Preservation Society of Charleston.

9 John Califf interview, August 2011.

10 *The State*, April 23, 1907.

11   David Crockett, *The Life of Martin Van Buren, Heir-Apparent to the "Government" and the Appointed Successor of Gen. Andrew Jackson* (Philadelphia: Robert Wright, 1835), 80-81.

12   *Southern Chronicle and Camden Literary and Political Register*, June 4, 1825.

13 Andrews, *Capt. Andrews*, 29-30.

14 Moore, *Columbia and Richland County* ,150.

15   Samuel Leland Journal, 7 October 1854, Samuel Wells Leland Papers, 1845-1876, SCL.

16 Williams, *Diary From Dixie*, 247.

17   Tyrone Power, Esq., *Impressions of America During the Years 1833, 1834 and 1835*, Volume 2,(Philadelphia: Carey, Lea and Blanchard,1836), 56-57.

18 Irving, *South Carolina Jockey Club*, 44-45.

19 *Charleston Courier*, August 28, 1854.

20 *The State*, June 14, 1892.

Selected Bibliography

Manuscripts used for this book came primarily from the South Caroliniana Library at the University of South Carolina and from the Southern Historical Collection at the Louis Round Wilson Special Collections Library at The University of North Carolina. Both institutions have large collections of Singleton family documents.

The South Carolina Department of Archives and History and The David M. Rubenstein Rare Book & Manuscript Library at Duke University, also made key contributions. I also utilized material from the Library of Congress, The South Carolina Historical Society and The Sumter County Genealogical Society.

The works listed below were key resources in the writing of this book. They represent only a small portion of the works I consulted.

Diaries and Memoirs

Dwight, Mary Carter Singleton. *A History of My Long Life to Leave My Children and Other Descendants.* Privately printed, circa 1960.

Stroyer, Jacob. *My Life in the South*. Salem, MA: Newcomb and Gauss, 1898. (There were five editions. This is the fourth. Jacob Stroyer's account is a must-read for a first-hand account of plantation life at the Kensington.)

Woodward, C. Vann, ed. *Mary Chesnut's Civil War* . New Haven and London :Yale University Press, 1981. (Of the three editions of Mary Chesnut's diary, this is considered the most accurate and scholarly.)

Family Histories, Genealogies and Sketches, including unpublished works

Carney, Eliza Singleton Macaulay and Eliza Singleton Carney Hamrick, with assistance from Eliza Singleton Barron Macaulay and Eliza Singleton Hamrick, compilers. *The Book of Elizas*. July 1998, unpublished.

Halsey, Mrs. LeRoy, nee Decca Coles., compiler. *Sketches of the Singleton Family*. Sumter County Genealogical Society, Sumter, South Carolina.

Macaulay, Eliza Barron. *Kensington*, unpublished typescript.

Singleton, Virginia Eliza (Green). *Genealogy of the Singletons After Their Emigration to America*. Columbia SC, 1914. (Privately printed. It is an account of the Singleton family, containing genealogies, thumbnail biographies, and stories.)

Untitled account of Hamer family time at the Kensington, unpublished typescript.

Histories

Broadwell, Charles. *Sketches of Planters, Plantations, and Living Along the Great Road Saint Marks Parish 1700-2000*. Charles Broadwell, 2010. Available at Sumter County Genealogical Society.

Broadwell, Charles. *The Singleton Family of South Carolina: A Story of Divorce, Mayhem, Greed, Destruction (The Real Story of the Singleton Lawsuits)*. Charles Broadwell, 2013. Available at Sumter County Genealogical Society.

Crawford, Lindsay Berit. "Martha Rutledge Kinloch Singleton of Kensington Plantation: Portrait of a South Carolina Widow." Master's Thesis, University of South Carolina, 2007.

Edgar, Walter. *South Carolina: A History*. Columbia: University of South Carolina Press, 1998.

Gregorie, Anne King. *History of Sumter County South Carolina* . Sumter : Library Board of Sumter County, 1954.

Irving. John Beaufrain. *The South Carolina Jockey Club* (also known as *History of the Turf in South Carolina*). Charleston: Russell and Jones,1857.

Johnson, Michael P. and James L. Roark . *Black Masters A Free Family of Color in the Old South*. NY and London: W.W. Norton and Company, 1984.

Moore, John Hammond. *Columbia and Richland County: A South Carolina Community, 1740-1990*. Columbia: University of South Carolina Press, 1993.

Nicholes, Cassie. *Historical Sketches of Sumter County: Its Birth and Growth*. Sumter, SC ; Sumter County Historical Commission,1975.

Reniers, Perceval. *The Springs of Virginia: Life, Love and Death at the Waters 1775-1900.* Chapel Hill: University of North Carolina Press, 1941.

Wood, Kirsten E. *Masterful Women: Slaveholding Women from the American Revolution Through the Civil War.* Chapel Hill and London: University of North Carolina Press, 2004.

Survey

Triad Architectural Associates, *The Kensington House: An Architectural and Historical Survey*, Columbia, South Carolina, 1980.

Tools and Sources

"Internet Archive" is a non-profit library of millions of free books, movies, software, music, and more. Visit https://www.archive.org. It is an invaluable resource for public domain (pre-1923) books.

An invaluable tool for comparing worth from the past to present day values is found at   www.measuringworth.com/uscompare/ on a website created by the Economic History Association.

Image Credits

Cover: Photograph in the Carol M. Highsmith Archive, Library of Congress, Prints and Photographs Division, LC-HS503- 3337

Page 34: Courtesy of Lynn Landreth

Page 35: Courtesy of Mary Singleton Clement Porcher

Page 40: Courtesy of Mary Singleton Clement Porcher

Page 80: Library of Congress, Prints and Photographs Division, HABS WVA,13-WHISP,1D--1

Page 81: Library of Congress, Prints and Photographs Division, HABS WVA,13-WHISP,1J--1

Page 144: Courtesy of Carl Dubose

Page 173: Library of Congress, Prints and Photographs Division, HABS SC,40-COLUM.V,1--2

Page 177: Courtesy of Mrs. Jeanie Clay Curry. Photograph by Tim Bradshaw

Page 191: Courtesy of Mrs. Jeanie Clay Curry

Page 193: Courtesy of Bill Hamer

Page 197: Courtesy of Joel A. Smith & Daisy Barron Leland

Page 200: Courtesy of Joel A. Smith

Page 201: Courtesy of Eliza Singleton Macaulay Carney

Page 211: Courtesy of Bill Hamer

Page 213: Courtesy of Robert Hamer Peery

Page 216: Courtesy of Robert Hamer Peery

Page 219: Courtesy of Luke Lanham

Page 228: Library of Congress, Prints and Photographs Division, HABS SC, 40-EAST.V,1—2

Page 231: Photograph in the Carol M. Highsmith Archive, Library of Congress, Prints and Photographs Division, LC-HS503- 5399

Page 232: Photograph in the Carol M. Highsmith Archive, Library of Congress, Prints and Photographs Division, LC-HS503- 3382

Page 236: Courtesy of Carl DuBose

Page 251: Courtesy of Robert Buckley

Page 258: Courtesy of Bob Coglianese

Page 263: Courtesy of Harriet Dwight Travers Yarbrough

www.ingramcontent.com/pod-product-compliance
Lightning Source LLC
Chambersburg PA
CBHW062149080426
42734CB00010B/1617